2ND EDITION

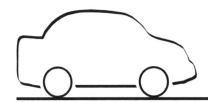

AUTO UPKEEP

BASIC CAR CARE, MAINTENANCE, AND REPAIR

MICHAEL E. GRAY
AND
LINDA E. GRAY

Rolling Hills Publishing

www.rollinghillspublishing.com

New Windsor, Maryland

Rolling Hills Publishing
www.rollinghillspublishing.com

Auto Upkeep: Basic Car Care, Maintenance, and Repair
2nd Edition
Michael E. Gray and Linda E. Gray

Executive Editor, Illustrator, Production Director: Linda E. Gray
Editorial Assistant: Kyle A. Johnson
Young Adult Usability Proofreader: Zach D. Johnson

Printed in the United States of America
11 10 09 08 07   10 9 8 7 6 5 4 3 2

Publisher's Cataloging-in-Publication

    Gray, Michael E.
      Auto upkeep : basic car care, maintenance, and repair
    / Michael E. Gray and Linda E. Gray. -- 2nd ed.
      p. cm.
      Includes index.
      LCCN 2007920997
      ISBN-13: 978-0-9740792-1-9
      ISBN-10: 0-9740792-1-9

      1. Automobiles--Maintenance and repair--Popular
    works.   I. Gray, Linda E. II. Title.

    TL152.G73 2007   629.28'72

For more information contact: Rolling Hills Publishing, New Windsor, Maryland
Phone and Fax: 1-800-918-READ
Email: info@autoupkeep.com
Website: www.autoupkeep.com

NOTICE TO THE READER

The publisher, authors, www.rollinghillspublishing.com, www.autoupkeep.com, and those associated with the text do not warrant or guarantee any procedure, process, products, or websites presented in the text. Extensive effort has been made to ensure accuracy in the text and illustrations throughout the book. However, due to the vast number of automotive manufacturers and related products, the reader should follow all procedures provided with the vehicle or by the product manufacturer. The book is sold with the understanding that the publisher, authors, www.rollinghillspublishing.com, www.autoupkeep.com, and those associated with the text are not engaged in rendering any specific mechanical, safety, diagnostic, legal, accounting, or any other professional advice. The reader assumes all risks while following activity procedures, is warned to follow all safety guidelines, and should avoid all potentially hazardous situations. The publisher, authors, www.rollinghillspublishing.com, www.autoupkeep.com, and associates shall not be liable for damages to vehicles, their components, or injuries to individuals using or relying on this material.

PRODUCT DISCLAIMER

The publisher, authors, www.rollinghillspublishing.com, www.autoupkeep.com, and associates do not endorse any company, product, service, or website mentioned or pictured in the book. The company names, products, services, and websites were noted and pictured because they are readily available, easily recognizable, and may help the reader understand the content. It is acknowledged that other company names, products, services, and websites could work as substitutes for those given throughout the text.

PREFACE

INTRODUCTION

Auto Upkeep: Basic Car Care, Maintenance, and Repair is an introductory book that is intended to provide individuals with the knowledge to make economical decisions and take preventative measures to enhance the overall satisfaction of being an automotive consumer. *Auto Upkeep* text and activities provide the fundamental knowledge and experience in owning and maintaining an automobile.

FEATURES OF THE TEXT

Each chapter includes an introduction, essential questions, objectives, chapter content, and summary. Chapters also include helpful guides regarding servicing, tech tips, troubleshooting, average prices of replacement parts, frequently asked questions, web links, and career paths.

ON THE INTERNET

Auto Upkeep can also be experienced online at www.autoupkeep.com. This website provides answers to commonly asked questions, links to industries, educational institutions, and individuals teaching basic automotive programs. It serves as an additional resource for you to communicate to people within the automotive field or purchase automotive supplies. The website is continually updated with new links, so keep checking it for additional automotive resources and new publications. Activities that correlate with the book's content are available for free download or in the *Auto Upkeep* workbook. Online/workbook activity information is on page 178.

WEB LINKS

Due to the nature of the Internet, web links listed throughout the book may become inactive or be redirected to unanticipated content. If this text is used in an educational institution it is recommended that the instructor review websites before sending students to them.

REVIEWERS

Thanks to all of the instructors who gave valuable input during the review process. Their suggestions, technical expertise, and feedback were greatly appreciated.

Rick Andruchuk
CTS (Career and Technology Studies) Teacher
James Fowler H.S., Calgary, AB, Canada

Adam Burlett
Automotive Instructor
Turner USD 202, Kansas City, KS

David Farrell
Technology Education Instructor
Carmel H.S., Carmel, NY

Michael Farren
Technology Education Instructor
Valley Forge H.S., Parma Heights, OH

Melvin Higgs
Automotive Instructor
J.M. Tawes Tech. & Career Center, Westover, MD

Tim Isaac
Automotive Instructor
Foothills Composite H.S., Okotoks, AB, Canada

Justin Miller
Automotive Instructor
Brigham Young University, Rexburg, ID

J. Bruce Osburn
Associate Professor Automotive Technology
Chaffey College, Rancho Cucamonga, CA

Ray Quon
Dept. Chair and Coord. Automotive Technology
San Diego - Miramar College, San Diego, CA

Jim Sainsbury
Automotive Instructor
Madison Memorial H.S., Madison, WI

John Stokes
Automotive Instructor
Cuesta College, San Luis Obispo, CA

John Sweet
Automotive Department Chair
Victor Valley College, Victorville, CA

Eric Zebe
Automotive Instructor
Cuesta College, San Luis Obispo, CA

ABOUT MIKE

Mike has roots in the automotive service industry. He began diagnosing and fixing cars at a young age in his family's service station. He has worked in automotive parts supply stores, towing companies, and service facilities. After graduating from St. Cloud State University (MN) with a Bachelor's degree, he implemented and taught a basic car care program at the high school level. During work on his Master's degree at Illinois State University (IL), he was a curriculum specialist on a National Science Foundation project where he co-authored ten integrated mathematics, science, and technology books designed for team teaching. Currently he supervises over 60 teachers in Career and Technology Education. "Working in the towing industry I remember driving over 60 miles on a rural Minnesota road to put on a spare tire for a driver. The driver had the physical capability, tools, and a spare tire, but admittedly did not know how to change it. The cost to change the tire was well over $100. These encounters and my student teaching experience made it clear to me that basic car care education should be a focus for anyone who drives a car. *Auto Upkeep* was born."

ABOUT LINDA

Linda was motivated to learn about cars early on by her desire to be self-reliant and save money. As basic maintenance and repairs were needed on her car she figured out how to do them. She could often be found working on her Pontiac Fiero and reupholstering automotive interiors at her family's upholstery shop. She found guidance from automotive manuals, her family, friends, and husband Mike. During her studies at the University of Redlands (CA), she worked with classmates to design, build, and test a hybrid electric vehicle. After graduating with a Bachelor's degree in Engineering, Linda worked as a Project Engineer for a bicycle component company. Linda's other interests include alternative energies, home renovation, graphic design, and writing. "I will never forget my first incident as an inexperienced car owner. My brakes were squealing, so a friend helped me take the tire off to inspect them. He explained that the little tab was making the noise and all I needed to do was bend it back a bit. It worked - no more squeal. Then a few weeks later I started to hear a grinding noise. I did not realize that the little tab was a wear indicator and the squeal was telling me that I needed new brake pads right away. I ended up having to replace the brake pads and rotors. If I had replaced the pads when I heard the first squeal I would have saved a ton of money and work. I have learned the value of knowing the basics and want to share that knowledge to help others be safe and well-informed automotive consumers."

ACKNOWLEDGMENTS

The idea for this text came from Mike's student teaching experience. During that experience Mike worked under a talented and enthusiastic veteran teacher, Tim Goodner. Tim taught a class called *Car Upkeep*. Immediately Mike was impressed with the course. This wasn't another course just for future auto technicians, but a course for the average automotive consumer. This student teaching experience inspired Mike to implement a similar program. In the first year that the course was offered, it became one of the most popular elective courses at the school.

We would like to thank all of our former teachers in giving us the classroom experiences and instilling positive work ethics that made us successful in our lives. A special thanks to all of our family, friends, and colleagues for inspiring us.

TABLE OF CONTENTS

CHAPTER 1

INTRODUCTION AND HOW CARS WORK

FUEL FOR THOUGHT

- How do cars work?
- How are vehicles classified?
- Why is it a good idea to know the size of your vehicle's engine?

Introduction

For hundreds of years people have been compelled to find a better way to travel. It would be impossible to credit just one person for the development of the automobile. The word "automobile" literally means self-moving. People wanted a vehicle that could take them to new places. For many years people worked and lived within miles of where they were born and where they eventually died. Before the automobile, most people traveled on land from one place to another by foot, train, bicycle, or horse and carriage. Within a few years of the turn of the 20th century, the automobile would change society forever. Today, there are millions of vehicles on the roadways.

Objectives

Upon completion of this chapter and activities, you will be able to:

- Identify people that have impacted the development of the automobile.
- Differentiate between vehicle manufacturers, makes, models, and types.
- Describe how cars work.

Major Automotive Contributors

One of the earliest recorded major milestones in the development of the automobile was the Cugnot steam traction engine in 1769-1770. Even though this self-powered road vehicle was rather impractical, it was a starting point for the automobile. The development of the internal combustion engine in 1860 made road vehicles more promising. Then in 1886 Carl Benz was credited with building the world's first practical motorcar. At the turn of the century, blacksmith shops around the country were hand-building cars. Henry Ford, who introduced the Model T in 1908, put an end to many of the small hand-building automotive shops. The Model T was mass-produced, cutting the production time for a car down to minutes. Ford even selected black paint because it dried faster than any other color. By 1920, half the cars in the world were Model T Fords. In 1923 alone, Ford produced over 1.8 million Model T's (*Figure 1.1*). The last Ford Model T rolled off of the assembly line in 1927. Ford produced over 15 million Model T's, but that was not enough for it to remain the best selling car in history. Dr. Ferdinand Porsche invented the highly popular "people's car" the Volkswagen Beetle in the

1930s, eventually selling over 20 million. The Toyota Corolla has the record for the best selling car ever, with over 30 million sold. Over the last hundred years, automobile production has grown substantially. In 1900 about 9500 motor vehicles were produced in the world. That number grew to over 50 million per year just a century later.

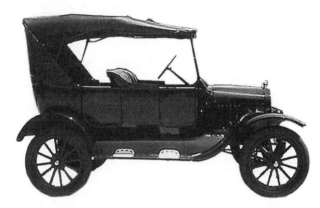

Figure 1.1   **Model T**
Courtesy of Taylor Virdell, Llano, TX

Automotive Milestones

Automobiles have gone through a large number of changes since Carl Benz's 1886 Motorcar. Numerous milestones and significant automotive events (*Figure 1.2*) have made vehicles more efficient, comfortable, and reliable.

 Web Links

Automotive Museums
Antique Automobile Club of America Museum
↳   www.aacamuseum.org
Gilmore Car Museum
↳   www.gilmorecarmuseum.org
Henry Ford Museum
↳   www.thehenryford.org
Manitoba Antique Auto Museum
↳   www.mbautomuseum.com
National Automobile Museum
↳   www.automuseum.org
Petersen Automotive Museum
↳   www.petersen.org
Smithsonian National Museum
↳   www.americanhistory.si.edu/onthemove

1769-1770	Nicholas Cugnot built and demonstrated the Cugnot steam traction engine.
1876	Nikolaus Otto developed four-stroke engine.
1886	Carl Benz patented world's first practical motorcar. Daimler-Benz Company formed.
1892	Rudolf Diesel patented diesel engine.
1895	The word "automobile" coined.
1897	Automotive insurance introduced. Olds Motor Vehicle Company is organized.
1900	Steam and electric more popular than gasoline powered vehicles.
1901	Speedometers introduced on Oldsmobiles.
1902	American Automobile Association (AAA) formed. Stanley Motor Carriage Company formed. Cadillac Automobile Company organized.
1903	Ford Motor Company formed. Buick Motor Company founded. Windshield wiper invented by Mary Anderson.
1908	Model T introduced and sold for $850. General Motors Company organized.
1911	Chevrolet Motor Company organized. Self starter invented.
1914	Cleveland, Ohio the first city with traffic lights. Henry Ford raised the minimum daily wage from $2.30 to $5.00.
1916	Brake lights installed.
1917	The all-steel wheel developed.
1918	Chevrolet joined General Motors.
1928	Chrysler took over Dodge.
1937	Toyota Motor Company, Ltd. established.
1938	Volkswagen Beetle produced.
1939	Nash Motor Company offered air conditioning. Hydra-matic (automatic) transmission introduced.
1942-1945	U.S. automotive manufacturers supported Allied Powers by producing airplanes, tanks, etc.
1948	Honda Motor Co. formed with $3,300.
1951	Power steering installed in cars.
1953	Michelin marketed the first radial ply tire.
1954	Fuel injection used on Mercedes-Benz 300SL.
1965	Motor Vehicle Air Pollution Control Act passed, the first federal emissions standards.
1973	Arab oil producers imposed export ban of oil to U.S.
1986	Centennial of the automobile.
1996	OnStar introduced by GM.
1997	Toyota Prius introduced and sold in Japan.
1998	DaimlerChrysler formed.
1999	Honda Insight Hybrid introduced in U.S.
2004	First Hybrid SUV (Ford Escape) sold.
2006	Ford Motor Company planned to cut North American workforce by 25%.
2007	Tire pressure monitoring system required.

Figure 1.2   **Significant Automotive Events**

How Cars Work

Currently the most common propulsion system in an automobile is the internal combustion engine (ICE). ICEs burn fuel in a combustion chamber inside the engine. Examples include the four-stroke, two-stroke, rotary, and gas turbine engines. The four-stroke internal combustion engine (also known as the Otto cycle, named after Nikolaus Otto) is the most common type used in automobiles. In a four-stroke engine the piston makes reciprocating (back and forth or up and down) movements to convert the chemical energy of fuel into mechanical energy of motion (kinetic energy). Spark ignition engines are fueled by gasoline, propane, natural gas, or gasoline/alcohol blend. Compression ignition engines are fueled by diesel. This section focuses on:

- Engine Components
- Power Transfer
- Four-Stroke Engines

Engine Components

The basic parts in a four-stroke engine include intake valves, exhaust valves, pistons, connecting rods, engine block, cylinder head(s), crankshaft, camshaft(s), and oil pan (*Figure 1.3*).

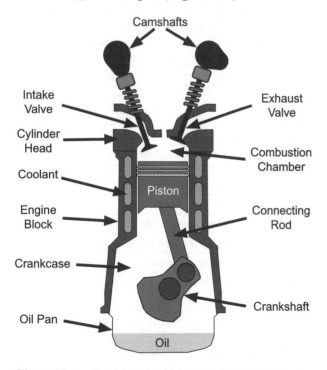

Figure 1.3   Dual Overhead Camshaft (DOHC) Engine

Power Transfer

Several processes have to happen in order for a vehicle to move. The following are the basic power transfer steps (*Figure 1.4*) in a common gasoline powered (non-hybrid) automobile.

Power Transfer Steps in a Gasoline Powered Vehicle	
1	Fuel is stored as chemical energy in the gas tank.
2	Fuel is transported to the engine by a fuel pump.
3	Air-fuel mixture enters the engine.
4	Electrical energy is used to create a spark at the spark plug.
5	Combustion occurs, converting the chemical energy to kinetic energy. The piston moves linearly, reciprocating up and down or back and forth.
6	The reciprocating motion of the pistons is converted to rotary (circular) motion of the crankshaft.
7	The crankshaft's rotary motion turns the transmission.
8	On FWD vehicles, rotary motion is transferred through a transaxle. A transaxle combines the transmission and differential. From the transaxle, rotary power is moved through constant velocity (CV) shafts. On RWD vehicles, rotary power is transferred from the transmission through the drive shaft then to a differential and final drive assembly. In this situation, the differential changes the power flow 90° and allows the drive wheels to turn at different speeds when cornering. Power is transferred from the differential to axle shafts.
9	The axle shafts or constant velocity (CV) shafts turn the wheels.
10	The rotary motion of the wheels converts to linear motion on the roadway.

Figure 1.4   How Power is Transferred

Four-Stroke Engines

The four-strokes of the spark ignition engine (*Figure 1.5*) and the compression ignition engine (*Figure 1.6*) are intake, compression, power (combustion), and exhaust. To complete the four strokes, the crankshaft makes two revolutions. The four-strokes of the compression ignition engine are similar to the spark ignition engine, except fuel is not mixed with air in the intake system. Instead diesel is injected directly into the combustion chamber or indirectly into a swirl (precombustion) chamber. Once in the combustion chamber, the diesel combusts spontaneously from the high pressure and heat. Compression ignition engines do not use spark plugs like spark ignition engines.

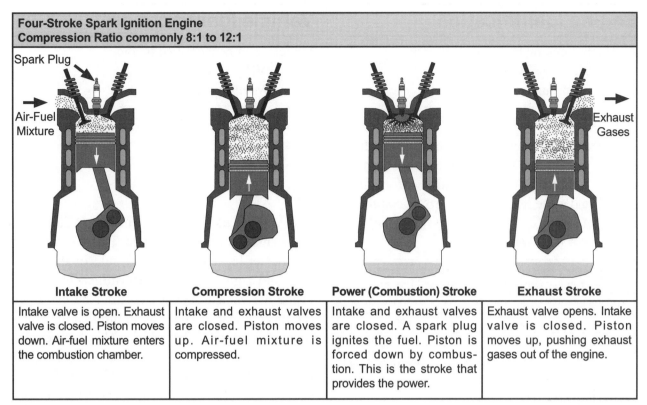

Four-Stroke Spark Ignition Engine
Compression Ratio commonly 8:1 to 12:1

Spark Plug

Air-Fuel Mixture

Exhaust Gases

Intake Stroke	Compression Stroke	Power (Combustion) Stroke	Exhaust Stroke
Intake valve is open. Exhaust valve is closed. Piston moves down. Air-fuel mixture enters the combustion chamber.	Intake and exhaust valves are closed. Piston moves up. Air-fuel mixture is compressed.	Intake and exhaust valves are closed. A spark plug ignites the fuel. Piston is forced down by combustion. This is the stroke that provides the power.	Exhaust valve opens. Intake valve is closed. Piston moves up, pushing exhaust gases out of the engine.

Figure 1.5   *Four-Stroke Spark Ignition Engine*

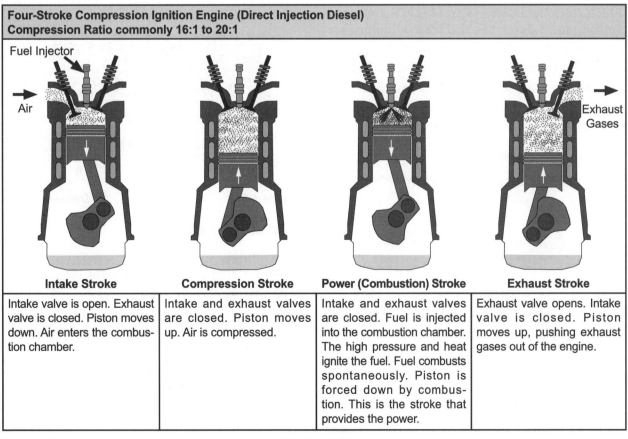

Four-Stroke Compression Ignition Engine (Direct Injection Diesel)
Compression Ratio commonly 16:1 to 20:1

Fuel Injector

Air

Exhaust Gases

Intake Stroke	Compression Stroke	Power (Combustion) Stroke	Exhaust Stroke
Intake valve is open. Exhaust valve is closed. Piston moves down. Air enters the combustion chamber.	Intake and exhaust valves are closed. Piston moves up. Air is compressed.	Intake and exhaust valves are closed. Fuel is injected into the combustion chamber. The high pressure and heat ignite the fuel. Fuel combusts spontaneously. Piston is forced down by combustion. This is the stroke that provides the power.	Exhaust valve opens. Intake valve is closed. Piston moves up, pushing exhaust gases out of the engine.

Figure 1.6   *Four-Stroke Compression Ignition Engine (Direct Injection Diesel)*

Engine Identification

A vehicle's engine is classified by its:
- Size/Displacement
- Configuration

Size/Displacement

The size of the engine is the combined volume of the cylinders. Engine size can be found on the vehicle emission control information sticker under the hood. Engine size is commonly listed in liters or cubic inches (*Figure 1.7*). *Note: 1 L = 61.02 cu. in.*

International System of Units (Metric System) and U.S. Customary Units (English System) Equivalent	
1.8 L = 110 cu. in.	5.0 L = 305 cu. in.
2.4 L = 147 cu. in.	5.3 L = 323 cu. in.
4.6 L = 281 cu. in.	6.8 L = 415 cu. in.

Figure 1.7   *Common Engine Sizes*

Configuration

Engine configuration is the design of the engine block. Common engine configurations include inline, opposed, slant, or V (*Figure 1.8*). The configuration describes the way cylinders are arranged in the block. The number of cylinders within the engine block is also used to identify the type of engine design. Engines have 3, 4, 5, 6, 8, 10, or 12 cylinders. The most common engine configurations are inline 4s, V6s, and V8s.

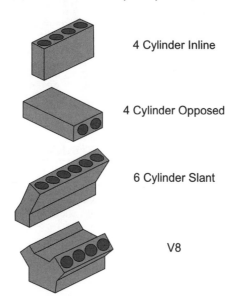

4 Cylinder Inline

4 Cylinder Opposed

6 Cylinder Slant

V8

Figure 1.8   *Engine Configurations*

Vehicle Identification

Vehicles can be identified by the:
- VIN
- Manufacturer
- Make
- Model
- Year
- Type

VIN

The Vehicle Identification Number (VIN) is an important number on a vehicle. This 17-character number is located on the left side of the dash. Left and right sides are determined by sitting inside the vehicle facing forward. You can often see this number as you look in through the windshield from outside the vehicle. This number also appears on the vehicle certification label on the inside of the driver's doorjamb (*Figure 1.9*) and also on the vehicle's title card. The VIN contains information specific to that vehicle. Automotive parts stores may need this number to find the correct replacement parts for a vehicle.

```
MFD. BY HONDA OF AMERICA MFG., INC.  11/'05
GVWR 3737LBS  GAWR F 1973LBS  R 1764LBS
GVWR 1695KG   GAWR F  895KG   R  800KG
THIS VEHICLE CONFORMS TO ALL APPLICABLE
FEDERAL MOTOR VEHICLE SAFETY, BUMPER,
AND THEFT PREVENTION STANDARDS IN EFFECT
ON THE DATE OF MANUFACTURE SHOWN ABOVE.
V.I.N.:1HGFA16876L026954  TYPE:PASSENGER CAR

SNE 6  AG9  -R525P        -H    -L
```

Figure 1.9   *Doorjamb VIN*

Manufacturer

An automotive manufacturer is a company that produces vehicles. Through the years some manufacturers have taken over others, joined forces, or completely gone out of business. The following figure shows recognized manufacturers (*Figure 1.10*).

Figure 1.10   *Automotive Manufacturer Logos*

Make

Automotive manufacturers identify the various vehicles they produce by their "make". The following table lists manufacturers and their makes (*Figure 1.11*).

Manufacturer	Make
GM	GMC, Pontiac, Saturn, Buick, Cadillac, Hummer, Saab, and Chevrolet
DaimlerChrysler	Chrysler, Dodge, Mercedes-Benz, Maybach, and Jeep
Ford	Ford, Lincoln, Mercury, Jaguar, Land Rover, Volvo, and Aston Martin
Toyota	Toyota, Lexus, and Scion
Volkswagen	Volkswagen, Audi, and Lamborghini
Honda	Honda and Acura
Hyundai	Hyundai and Kia
Nissan	Nissan and Infiniti
Fiat	Fiat, Ferrari, and Maserati
Mitsubishi	Mitsubishi
BMW	BMW, MINI, and Rolls-Royce
Mazda	Mazda

Figure 1.11   ***Examples of Makes***

Model

The model (*Figure 1.12*) of a vehicle refers to the specific name of each vehicle within a make. The model names often change over time.

Make	Model
Chevrolet	Cobalt, Malibu, Impala, Camaro, Corvette, Tahoe, Suburban, Silverado, and Avalanche

Figure 1.12   ***Examples of Models***

Year

The model year of the vehicle is not necessarily the year in which it was built. A vehicle built in October 2007 most likely would be considered a 2008 model year vehicle. To find the actual model year of the vehicle look at the vehicle emission control information (VECI) sticker under the hood. This sticker indicates the year of pollution standards conformance, which is also the model year. The date of manufacture is listed inside the driver's door on the vehicle certification label. This is the actual month and year that the vehicle rolled off the assembly line.

✓ Tech Tip
Date of Manufacture

The date of manufacture and the model year of a vehicle may differ. Manufacturers produce millions of vehicles each year by continuous manufacturing. Vehicle assembly lines rarely shut down. Next year's models often appear on showroom floors in late summer or early fall.

Type

Automotive manufacturers design many different types (*Figure 1.13*) of vehicles to meet consumer demands. The following table lists the main types with example models.

Type	Model
Microcar	Smart Fortwo and GEM e2
Subcompact Car	Echo, Yaris, Rio, Aveo, and Accent
Compact Car	Focus, Civic, Corolla, and Golf
Mid-size Car	Malibu, Camry, Stratus, and Accord
Full-size Car	Impala, Avalon, and Maxima
Sports Car	Corvette, Viper, and Porsche 911
Mini SUV	Suzuki SX4, EcoSport, and Wrangler
Crossover SUV	Freestyle, Murano, and Pacifica
SUV	Suburban, Nitro, and Expedition
SUT	Avalanche, Hummer H2 SUT, EXT, and Ridgeline
Compact Pickup	Colorado, Ranger, and Tacoma
Mid-size Pickup	Dakota
Full-size Pickup	Silverado, Sierra, Ram, Titan, F-Series, and Tundra
Minivan	Caravan, Sienna, and Sedona
Van	E-Series, Express, and Savana

Figure 1.13   ***Examples of Types and Models***

✓ Tech Tip
Identifying Vehicle Parts

To purchase the correct maintenance items (e.g., filters) or replacement parts (e.g., alternators and starters), it is important to know the vehicle's VIN, make, model, engine size/configuration, and model year.

Common Fuels and Designs

Most of the 225 million vehicles registered in the United States today burn either gasoline or diesel in an internal combustion engine. This section focuses on:

- Gasoline Powered Vehicles
- Diesel Powered Vehicles

Gasoline Powered Vehicles

Passenger cars and light trucks powered solely by burning gasoline in an internal combustion engine are the most popular. Gasoline engines use spark plugs to ignite the air-fuel mixture in the engine. There are several reasons for the popularity of gasoline powered vehicles. They are currently affordable (this depends on the price (*Figure 1.14*) of gas), easy to refuel (gas stations in just about every town), they meet performance expectations (range, acceleration, and speed), and we are most familiar with the technology. One of the major disadvantages of gasoline is that once the fuel is burned, it is gone forever. In addition, gasoline engines emit hydrocarbons, nitrogen oxides, carbon monoxide, and carbon dioxide. Hydrocarbons and nitrogen oxides contribute to smog formation. Carbon monoxide can enter the bloodstream, reducing the flow of oxygen throughout the body. Carbon dioxide is considered a greenhouse gas which impacts global climate change (global warming).

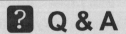

Figure 1.14 **U.S. Gasoline Prices in 2006**

❓ Q & A

More Alternative Fueled Vehicles

Q: Why do automotive manufacturers not produce more alternative fueled vehicles?
A: It is expensive to develop new technologies that meet our high performance expectations. Many customers are not willing to buy newer technologies, especially when gas and diesel fueled vehicles are meeting their expectations.

Diesel Powered Vehicles

Diesel as a fuel source (*Figure 1.15*) has gained attention in the past couple of years in passenger cars. When thinking of diesel, a medium or heavy-duty truck might first come to mind. Diesel powered specialty vehicles (e.g., garbage trucks, school buses, fuel delivery trucks, and fire engines) and semi trucks pulling trailers are very common. Diesel engines have also become popular in light trucks (e.g., F-250s, 2500s, F-350s, and 3500s). Diesel engines are compression ignition engines; they do not have spark plugs.

Figure 1.15 **Auto Diesel Fuel Dispenser**

Diesel engines have been used by manufacturers for a number of years in some select passenger cars. Recently, there has been a resurgence of diesel powered passenger cars. In Europe, diesel powered passenger cars are fairly common, making up about one-half of new passenger cars. Diesel fuel has more energy per gallon as compared to gasoline, making it more efficient for every gallon of fuel burned. In addition to greenhouse gas pollutants, diesels emit nitrogen oxides, sulfur dioxide, and particulate matter. Sulfur dioxide contributes to acid rain. Particulate matter can be in small dust forms, soot, or smoke. The fine particles in particulate matter can penetrate into the lungs and cause a variety of health problems. Newer engine designs with particulate traps and ultra-low sulfur diesel have greatly decreased the amount of particulate matter released into the air.

The Future

Automobiles of the future will be faster, sleeker, have more features, and be more energy efficient. Future automobiles may be powered by alternative fuel sources. When U.S. gas prices at the pump exceeded $3.00 a gallon in 2006 many consumers began seriously considering more energy efficient automobiles. Near the turn of the millennium, Toyota (*Figure 1.16*) and Honda started mass-producing hybrid (i.e., gas and electric) vehicles that reached approximately 50+ miles per gallon (mpg). *Note: Miles per gallon is predominately used in the United States. Other countries commonly use liters per 100 kilometers, abbreviated L/100 km.* The depletion of fossil fuels will have a great impact on future vehicle design.

Figure 1.16   *Toyota Prius Hybrid*

Summary

Since the beginning of the modern era, people have been eager to explore new and exciting places. The automobile has made personal land transportation easy. Automobiles allow people to work great distances from where they live, sometimes commuting hours each way. Cugnot, Benz, Ford, and Porsche, among others, changed the development of the automobile forever. In a little over one hundred years, automobiles have become extremely popular. With an ever-growing number of vehicles on the road and demand for oil increasing, fossil fuel prices will certainly rise. Today, manufacturers are producing hybrid electric vehicles and other alternatives to eventually diminish our reliance on fossil fuels.

 ## Web Links

Automotive Manufacturers

BMW of North America
↳   www.bmwusa.com
DaimlerChrysler
↳   www.daimlerchrysler.com
Fiat
↳   www.fiat.com
Ford Motor Company
↳   www.ford.com
General Motors
↳   www.gm.com
Honda Motor Company
↳   www.honda.com
Hyundai Motor Company
↳   www.hyundai-motor.com
Mitsubishi Motors
↳   www.mitsubishicars.com
Nissan Motor Company
↳   www.nissanusa.com
Toyota Motor Corporation
↳   www.toyota.com
Volkswagen of America
↳   www.vw.com

 ## Activities

Introduction and How Cars Work

- Car Identification Activity
- Chapter 1 Study Questions

Activities can be accessed in the Auto Upkeep workbook or online at www.autoupkeep.com.

Career Paths

Automotive Teacher

Education: Bachelor's Degree and/or ASE Cert.
Median Income: $45,000
Job Market: High Growth
Abilities: Good with students in a technical hands-on environment.

CHAPTER 2

BUYING AN AUTOMOBILE

Introduction

Second to a home, the purchase of an automobile will probably be your next largest financial investment. The car buying process is amazing; you can walk into a car dealership (*Figure 2.1*) and often within an hour drive away in an automobile. Take your time when buying an automobile. Remember, the new pretty red car that you just have to have will be there next week (or dealers can often get another just like it). Since many people will buy a used car the first time, this chapter will present the process of buying a used as well as a new automobile.

Objectives

Upon completion of this chapter and activities, you will be able to:
- Differentiate between your needs and wants in relation to good transportation.
- Determine an automobile budget.
- Identify the steps in purchasing an automobile.
- Identify the places to buy an automobile.

Figure 2.1   *Car Dealership*

Purpose of Buying

Why do you need an automobile? This is an easy question to answer, right? You need to be able to get from place to place. Now think again. Do you need this vehicle to get to work? Do you need it for cruising on Saturday night? Automobiles are extremely expensive to own and operate. Do you need a car or do you want one? Either way, you may own one someday. If you do decide to use mass transit (e.g., bus or train) you will be saving money and natural resources (using mass transit is much more environmentally friendly). The reality is that most families in the United States and Canada travel by car. Maybe once gasoline becomes extremely expensive more people will start to use mass transit.

Buying Steps

Several steps are involved in buying a car. Buying a car is a large financial decision, so visit your local library or surf the Internet to read more about the process. This section will briefly describe some of the common steps such as:

- Determining Your Budget
- Identifying Your Wants and Needs
- Financing the Purchase
- Identifying Places to Purchase
- Understanding Car Dealerships
- Safety Feature Considerations
- Completing Comparables

Determining Your Budget

The first thing you should do before buying a car is determine your budget. Can you really afford to buy a car? Your budget will ultimately determine the car that you can afford. Your choices may be limited if you have $500 in the bank and work earning minimum wage. For example, working 20 hours a week making $8.00 an hour will yield a gross income (before taxes and social security withholdings) of $160 a week or about $8,000 a year. Do you want to work one year of your life just to own a car? In the previous scenario if you bought an $8,000 car and spread the cost out over 3 years (36 months) at an interest rate of 9.9%, your monthly payment would be $258. This means you would actually end up paying $9,288 for that car after interest charges (and that doesn't include taxes, licenses, insurance, maintenance, unexpected repairs, or fuel). The first thing you should do is determine your budget. This is restated because it is extremely important to know what you can afford. Chapter 3, *Automotive Expenses*, will detail the total financial cost of owning and maintaining a car.

Price Guide

CARFAX Report (Vehicle History)
↳ $19.99
Technician Inspection
↳ $40.00 - $100.00

✓ Tech Tip

Do Not Get in Over Your Head

Know your financial ability and security. If you cannot put down at least 20% of the total cost, you probably cannot afford the car. Figure out all of the expenses of owning: maintenance, insurance, licenses, fuel, etc.

Identifying Your Wants and Needs

Confusing wants and needs is easy. Why else would people be driving Corvettes, Ferraris (*Figure 2.2*), and Hummers? Sure, they provide reliable transportation, but at what cost? No offense to anyone…most of us would have a difficult time turning down driving an exotic sports car or the ultimate SUV. Different types of vehicles provide for different needs and wants. You might find that with all of the models available it is a challenge to compare the options.

Figure 2.2   *Ferrari*

✓ Tech Tip

Take a Road Test

Go on a test drive if you are buying a used or new car. Drive your normal travel routes, including city streets and highways. Listen for any noises that may seem suspicious. Test all accessories, power windows, power seats, and door locks. Inspect all the vital systems. If you know a reputable technician or have friends that know about cars, take the vehicle to them and let them look at it. Inspect and drive a car before you buy, not after.

Financing the Purchase

If you cannot afford a vehicle outright, you may have to make monthly payments (*Figure 2.3*). If this is the case, you should go to several financial institutions to obtain financing information and loan qualifications. If you do not have any credit or are under 18, you may need to have someone co-sign the loan with you (that means they are responsible for the loan if you default). If you have had a loan, you should request a personal credit report. A credit report will show your credit history. A bank will check your credit report to quote you an interest rate. Check current interest rates at several banks on automobile loans. Depending on the economy, financial institution, and your credit history, interest rates commonly range from 3.9 to 15.9%. However, automotive manufacturers may offer interest free (0.0%) or low (0.9 to 2.9%) interest loans to qualified buyers. The interest rate that you ultimately pay makes a big difference on the overall price you pay for your vehicle. For example, on a 36-month $6,000 loan at 3.9% you will pay $6,372 for your vehicle with a monthly payment of $177.

However, changing to a 36-month $6,000 loan at 15.9% you will end up paying $7,596 for the same purchase with a monthly payment of $211. Understanding interest rates is a necessity if you plan to borrow money. Once you have researched and mastered this, you will better understand what you will really be able to afford.

Figure 2.3   Monthly Auto Loan Payment Booklet

🖩 Calculations

Interest Rate Calculations

The following calculations are based on a vehicle loan of $6,000 for 36 months with interest rates from 3.9% up to 15.9%.

Interest Rate	Monthly Payment	Total Cost
3.9%	$177	$6,372
7.9%	$188	$6,768
11.9%	$199	$7,164
15.9%	$211	$7,596

If you have to take out a loan, finding the lowest rate can save you hundreds or even thousands of dollars over the term of the loan.

❓ Q & A

Buy or Lease

Q: Should I buy or lease a new car?
A: Leasing will generally get you into a new car for a lower monthly payment than if you were buying it with a loan. However, at the end of the lease term (commonly 36 months) you do not own anything. If you always like driving a new car with the assurances of a factory warranty, then leasing may be for you. If you like the idea of driving a car without payments for a couple of years, then getting a loan may be for you. Purchasing makes more sense if you drive more than 15,000 miles (≈24,000 km) a year, drive the vehicle for 5+ years, or personalize the vehicle's appearance or accessories. If you use your car for business, check with your tax advisor for any tax benefits that may apply when buying or leasing.

❓ Q & A

Free Credit Report

Q: How do I get my credit report?
A: The consumer reporting companies (TransUnion, Equifax, and Experian) are each required under the Fair Credit Reporting Act to supply you with a free credit report once every 12 months. If you would like your report three times a year, alternate requests between these three companies every four months. To request your credit report go to www.annualcreditreport.com. Be careful to only use this site. Imposter sites on the internet also advertise free credit reports.

Identifying Places to Purchase

Several places exist for you to buy a vehicle. The most common are private-party sellers, used car lots, new car lots, and on the Internet. People that try to sell their used car themselves are called private-party sellers. People sell their car mainly for three reasons: they cannot afford their current car; they decide to upgrade to a newer car; or, their car is a "lemon" and they do not want to deal with it anymore. Try to determine why someone is selling their "good" used car. This may save you thousands in future repairs. Private-parties will sell their cars using newspapers, automotive publications, signs in the car's windows (*Figure 2.4*), or the Internet.

Figure 2.4   *Private-Party Seller Sign*

A used car lot (*Figure 2.5*) is another place to find a car. When purchasing a vehicle from a used car lot make sure you have done your homework. Research the car's historical service records and thoroughly check the car over. When in the market for a new car, people will commonly go to a car dealership. New cars offer the satisfaction of a warranty. Another place to buy new or used

cars is on the Internet. Hundreds of websites offer cars to consumers. If you do not know about a particular business, check the company's record with the Better Business Bureau (BBB).

Figure 2.5   *Used Car Lot*

⌖ Q & A

Lemon Law

Q: What is a lemon law?

A: Lemon laws vary depending on where you live. In general a new car is a lemon if it has been in a shop four times for the same problem or for an extended period of time (usually 30 days) in the first 12 to 24 months of ownership. Go to www.autosafety.org to read the specific lemon law in your area. Always keep detailed records to support a claim.

🖱 Web Links

Auto Buying Related Sites

Automobile
↳   www.automobilemag.com

AutoTrader.com
↳   www.autotrader.com

AutoWeek
↳   www.autoweek.com

Car and Driver
↳   www.caranddriver.com

CARFAX
↳   www.carfax.com

CarMax
↳   www.carmax.com

Edmunds
↳   www.edmunds.com

Green Car Journal
↳   www.greencar.com

Insurance Institute for Highway Safety
↳   www.iihs.org

Kelley Blue Book
↳   www.kbb.com

MotorWeek
↳   www.motorweek.com

Motor Trend
↳   www.motortrend.com

NADA Guide
↳   www.nada.com

Road & Track
↳   www.roadandtrack.com

SaferCar.gov
↳   www.safercar.gov

Understanding Car Dealerships

Manufacturers makes thousands of each model every year. The one on the lot is not the only one out there. When buying a new car, check out the model's history. Does the car have records of reliability and safety? Does it receive good consumer remarks? Sometimes buying a new car with substantial model changes is not a good idea. The "bugs" may not have been worked out. The window sticker (*Figure 2.6*) lists the standard and optional equipment installed by the manufacturer and the Manufacturer's Suggested Retail Price (MSRP). Remember that the manufacturer's sticker does not include dealer installed items. The dealer may add an additional sticker that highlights the options they have installed.

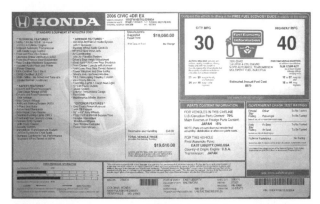

Figure 2.6   *Window Sticker with MSRP*

There are several terms you need to know when purchasing a vehicle (*Figure 2.7*). You should end up paying from $250 below dealer invoice to $500 above dealer invoice depending upon the model. Being educated about the dealer's cost will give you an edge in negotiating a deal. Negotiate up from the dealer cost, not down from the MSRP. If you are making a fair offer, a reasonable dealership will take it.

Dealer Terms	
MSRP	The Manufacturer's Suggested Retail Price (MSRP) is commonly called the sticker price. Few automotive models sell at MSRP.
Dealer Invoice	In the past, this was the price car dealerships paid for their vehicles. The dealer invoice price is helpful and is available in magazines, books, and Internet sites.
Factory Holdbacks	An average factory holdback is commonly 2-3% and can be estimated off the dealer invoice.
Factory to Dealer Incentives	Dealers may receive a cash incentive to sell end-of-year or slow moving models. An incentive may range from a few hundred dollars to several thousand dollars.
Dealer Cost	This is the amount that the dealer will actually pay for the vehicle after holdbacks and incentives. If you can determine the actual dealer cost (Dealer Cost = Dealer Invoice – Factory Holdback – Factory Incentives) it is reasonable and fair to offer 4% more than dealer cost.

Figure 2.7   *Dealer Terms*

✓ Tech Tip

Be Aware of the Add-ons

When buying from a dealership, salespeople will try to add on things such as rustproofing, extended warranties, fabric protector, paint sealant, or pin striping. These are high dollar profit items for the dealer. If you want these extras, get several price quotes from local reputable businesses. Learn the facts about your standard warranty and determine if you really need any add-ons. You should also determine what accessories (e.g., bug deflectors or running boards) you want. If you are handy, buy the accessories and install them yourself.

🖩 Calculations

Calculating a Reasonable Offer

For example, a car may have an MSRP of $34,000 and a dealer invoice of $30,000.

Dealer Invoice	EXAMPLE	$30,000
- Factory Holdback		-$900
- Factory to Dealer Incentives		-$400
= Dealer Cost		**$28,700**
Dealer Cost	EXAMPLE	$28,700
x 1.04		x 1.04
= Your Reasonable Offer		**$29,848**

Your reasonable offer for this vehicle would be $29,848. This is $4,152 off MSRP.

Don't forget to include other cost factors (*Figure 2.8*) when determining your out the door expense.

Vehicle Purchase Factors	Cost or Credit
Sales Tax	Additional Cost
Vehicle License, Title, and Registration	Additional Cost
Dealer Installed Items	Additional Cost
Dealer Documentation and Prep Fees	Additional Cost
Destination Charge	Additional Cost
Extended Warranty	Additional Cost
Customer Rebates (From Factory)	Credit
Trade-In	Credit

Figure 2.8   *Common Purchase Cost Factors*

Safety Feature Considerations

Safety features are constantly improving. It is smart to figure out which vehicles have the highest governmental and unbiased test safety ratings. Plan to factor safety information into your buying decision. Some of the features to look for include seatbelt design, airbag design (cutoff switch and force sensors), head restraint design and position, ABS and braking ability, stability control, traction control, visibility, and tire quality. Take some time to learn more about the vehicle by using online resources. It could save your life.

Completing Comparables

You should complete comparables whether you are trying to sell your car on your own or trying to figure out if the car you are looking at is a good deal. Many publications are available in book form or on the Internet. Some examples include *Kelley Blue Book*, *NADA*, and *Edmunds*. You can also look at other individuals selling a car similar to yours. However, you do need to be reasonable. Just because your neighbor sold her car for $1,000 more than you are asking does not mean your car is worth that much. The actual value may be due to several factors such as paint quality, interior condition, or mileage on the vehicle.

Summary

Automobiles are becoming more and more expensive to own each year. Knowing your budget, identifying your wants and needs, identifying ways to finance the deal, and identifying the abundant places to purchase a car will give you a step up. Remember that this is a large financial purchase – take your time, complete research, and be educated about the car buying process.

? Q & A

Exchange a New Car

Q: Is there a three day exchange or cancellation policy mandated by law when buying a new automobile?
A: The three day cancellation policy (sometimes called the three day cooling off rule) generally applies to door-to-door sales or sales made away from normal business locations. When buying a new vehicle, unless it is written into the contract or mandated by local law, you cannot return it after you have signed the paperwork and taken possession of it. When purchasing a pre-owned or used vehicle, some dealers do have exchange policies. It is important to read the fine print before making your final decision. Check with your local consumer protection agency to find out what is applicable in your area. For more information, go to www.consumeraction.gov.

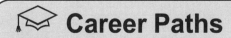

Activities

Buying an Automobile

- Buying an Automobile Activity
- Chapter 2 Study Questions

Activities can be accessed in the Auto Upkeep workbook or online at www.autoupkeep.com.

🎓 Career Paths

Automobile Salesperson

Education: No Formal Education
Median Income: Commission System
Job Market: Average Growth
Abilities: Strong communication skills, experience in sales, patience, and positive attitude.

CHAPTER 3

AUTOMOTIVE EXPENSES

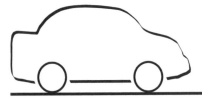

FUEL FOR THOUGHT

- What are some financial disadvantages of owning an automobile?
- Why is liability insurance commonly required?
- How can routine maintenance save you money?

Introduction

Before purchasing an automobile it is important to estimate all of the expenses that go along with ownership. Just because you can afford the monthly payment doesn't mean you can afford the vehicle. Sometimes the monthly payment is only half of your total monthly expenses. Many automotive expenses start after the vehicle purchase. When determining if you can afford a specific car, take into consideration car payments, insurance, fuel expenses, annual license and registration, routine maintenance, and unexpected repairs (*Figure 3.1*). This chapter will identify and describe the most common expense areas of owning and operating a vehicle.

Figure 3.1   *Unexpected Repair*

Objectives

Upon completion of this chapter and activities, you will be able to:

- Identify automotive expenses.
- Identify ways to save money.
- Describe insurance coverage levels.
- Calculate specific automotive expenses.

? Q & A

Auto Club Membership

Q: Is it cost effective to enroll in an auto club?
A: Auto clubs, such as AAA, can provide added assurance if you drive an older car or do lots of traveling. Most clubs cover tows (up to a certain distance), jump starts, lockout services, and recoveries (e.g., winched from a ditch). Memberships commonly cost between $50-100 a year depending on the extent of services. Some auto clubs also provide free maps and discounts on travel related services (e.g., hotels and rental cars). An alternative is to check with your auto insurance company. You can often add emergency roadside service to your policy for minimal cost.

Car Payments

Often people take out a three-, four-, or five-year loan to pay for their vehicle. Remember that this is a long-term commitment between you and the bank. If you lose your job or other family income sources, a monthly car payment could negatively impact your remaining financial commitments. Your monthly payment is dependent on the amount you financed, duration of the loan, and interest rate (*Figure 3.2*). Use a free online loan calculator to simplify the calculation.

Monthly Loan Payment Calculation Factors	
$	Amount Financed (Vehicle Cost – Down Payment)
#	Duration of the Loan (Number of Months)
%	Interest Rate (Annual Percentage)

Figure 3.2   *Loan Calculation Factors*

⌐ Web Links

Insurance Companies

Allstate Insurance Company
  ↳   www.allstate.com
American Automobile Association (AAA)
  ↳   www.aaa.com
American Family Insurance
  ↳   www.amfam.com
Country Companies Insurance
  ↳   www.countrycompanies.com
Farmers Insurance Group
  ↳   www.farmers.com
Geico Direct
  ↳   www.geico.com
Liberty Mutual
  ↳   www.libertymutual.com
Nationwide Insurance
  ↳   www.nationwide.com
Progressive Insurance
  ↳   www.progressive.com
State Farm Insurance
  ↳   www.statefarm.com

Insurance

Insurance premiums can be a major factor in your automotive decision. Most states/provinces require that automobiles be insured. If you have a loan on the vehicle, insurance is mandated by the bank to assure loan payment if the vehicle is wrecked. Auto insurance can protect against damage and theft, property damage, and personal bodily injury expenses. Many insurance coverage levels can be purchased. The contract that you decide on is called your insurance policy. Insurance costs depend on your age, driving record, gender, marital status, grades, vehicle model, where you live, and normal driving routes. For beginning drivers, auto insurance can be expensive. Speeding, moving violations, and accidents can substantially increase your insurance premiums. Insurance premiums are usually set up on a monthly, 3-month, 6-month, or yearly billing cycle. Be sure to have your insurance card (*Figure 3.3*) in your car at all times. Auto insurance coverage levels include:

- Deductible
- Liability
- Collision and Comprehensive
- Medical Payment, Personal Injury, and No-Fault
- Uninsured and Underinsured Motorist
- Umbrella
- Rental, Towing, and Total Replacement

Figure 3.3   *Vehicle Insurance Card*

Deductible

An insurance deductible is the amount you must pay when you make a claim before your insurance kicks in. For example, if you have a claim for $1,000 and your deductible is $250, your insurance will pay $750. One way to decrease insurance premiums is to increase your deductible.

Liability Insurance

The minimum policy commonly required is liability insurance. Liability insurance covers third party bodily injury or property damage claims that you cause. For instance, if you were in an accident and it was determined to be your fault, your insurance would pay the victim's claims (up to a certain dollar amount minus your deductible). Liability insurance policies are stated in numerical terms such as 20/40/10 (*Figure 3.4*). The first number indicates that this policy would have $20,000 bodily injury coverage per person. The second number indicates that this policy would have a limit of $40,000 bodily injury coverage per accident. The third number sets the property damage limit at $10,000. Minimum insurance requirements vary. A 20/40/10 policy, a minimum required by law in some areas, is usually inadequate considering the cost of medical and legal issues. For instance, if you did not have enough insurance coverage and you caused a serious accident, a person could sue you and put a lien on your assets. Many insurance companies suggest that people should have 100/300/50 coverage.

Liability Insurance Numbers	Bodily Injury per Person	Bodily Injury per Accident	Property Damage Limit
20/40/10	$20,000	$40,000	$10,000
100/300/50	$100,000	$300,000	$50,000

Figure 3.4   *Liability Insurance Numbers*

Collision and Comprehensive Insurance

In addition to liability coverage, if you have a loan you will be required to add collision and comprehensive insurance on your policy. Collision insurance covers the cost to repair your vehicle if you were at fault in an auto accident (*Figure 3.5*).

Figure 3.5   *Collision Insurance*

Comprehensive insurance covers the costs to repair your vehicle for damage that might occur from things such as natural disasters, vandalism, theft, fire, or hitting an animal on the road (*Figure 3.6*).

Figure 3.6   *Comprehensive Damage Examples*

Medical Payment, Personal Injury, and No-Fault Insurance

Another protection that can be added to a policy is medical payment, personal injury protection, and no-fault insurance. Medical payment insurance covers you and your passengers if you were at fault in an accident. Personal injury protection covers such things as incurred lost wages if you could not work because of an accident. No-fault protection allows policyholders to submit a claim to their insurance company for reimbursement instead of waiting to see whom the insurance company tries to hold liable for the accident.

? Q & A

Reducing Insurance Expense

Q: What types of cars are the most expensive to insure and what can be done to lower rates?
A: In general, sports cars and sport-utility vehicles are the most expensive to insure. Look for cars that have antilock brakes, airbags, and anti-theft devices. To find safety ratings on specific cars, go to the Insurance Institute for Highway Safety's website at www.iihs.org. Keep your driving record free of tickets and accidents. Discounts may be available for accredited driver education safety courses. Students on the honor roll can often get a 10 to 25% good grade discount. Contacting several insurance companies for price quotes may save you hundreds of dollars per year.

Uninsured and Underinsured Motorist Insurance

Another insurance required in many areas is uninsured motorist coverage. This covers you if someone without insurance injures you or damages your car in an automobile accident. Underinsured motorist coverage will pay for damages or injuries that occur to you by someone else, if the damages exceed the other party's policy limits.

Umbrella Insurance

Umbrella insurance (*Figure 3.7*) is an additional form of liability protection. The insurance company would pay when damages exceed your other insurance limits if you are at fault in an accident and someone sues you for bodily injury, property damage, or lost wages. Without this coverage your personal assets are at risk in a lawsuit. Depending on your insurance company, umbrella insurance may add an additional 1 to 10 million dollars worth of coverage. It covers the cost of a legal defense, false arrest, slander, and provides you with personal liability coverage wherever you travel around the world. For so much additional protection you might be surprised to know that the cost is minimal to add umbrella insurance to an existing eligible policy. Keep in mind that it will not cover any business related claims, even if it is a home based business.

Rental, Towing, and Total Replacement Insurance

Other features that can be added to insurance policies are rental coverage, towing (*Figure 3.8*), and total replacement coverage. Rental coverage will pay your car rental fees while your vehicle is being repaired. Towing coverage will pay for vehicle towing up to a certain limit. Total replacement coverage will pay the replacement cost of your vehicle if it is totaled (beyond fixing) instead of its depreciated value.

Figure 3.8   *Tow Truck*

? Q & A

Car Rental Insurance

Q: Should I pay for the insurance add-on when I rent a car?

A: If you have an automotive insurance policy that includes third party liability, collision, and comprehensive it may cover the insurance on rental cars. It is best to contact your insurance agent to clarify whether or not you need to purchase additional coverage when renting a car. Call your credit card company too. Some credit card companies offer car insurance if you charge the rental car on your card. Also check your insurance policy to see if it covers the cost of the rental car. If your vehicle is being repaired and is covered by your collision or comprehensive insurance, you may have a car rental endorsement that pays that expense. If you do not hold a car insurance policy, you should pay the extra money for the rental insurance to cover you from lawsuits and property damage if you get in an accident during the rental period.

Figure 3.7   **Umbrella Insurance Protection**

Fuel Expenses

Fuel costs have been on the rise in the United States. In 2005 and 2006 gas reached a high of over $3.00 per gallon, with some areas exceeding $4.00 per gallon. Rising prices have made mass transit a more economical and practical means of transportation. Fuel economy varies greatly depending on the vehicle. Pickups and sport utility vehicles commonly get 12-20 mpg, compact cars can get 30-40 mpg, and hybrids can get 50-70 mpg (*Figure 3.9*). *Note: In other countries fuel economy is calculated in L/100 km.*

MPG	Price per Gallon	1,000 Miles Monthly	12,000 Miles Yearly
20	$3.00	$150.00	$1,800.00
40	$3.00	$75.00	$900.00
60	$3.00	$50.00	$600.00

Figure 3.9   ***Effect of MPG on Fuel Cost***

Gasoline prices are set by crude oil prices (priced by the barrel), supply and demand, refinery production, octane rating, and specific regional formulation. Crude oil goes through a distillation process at a refinery to make gasoline and other products. There are 42 gallons (159 L) of crude oil in one barrel. According to the American Petroleum Institute, one barrel of crude oil can make about 19.4 gallons (73.44 L) of gasoline, 9.7 gallons (36.72 L) of fuel oil, and smaller quantities of other products. The price per gallon of gasoline also includes taxes. *Note: 1 gallon = 3.785 L*

License and Registration

You will be required by law to license and register your vehicle with your motor vehicle department. When buying a vehicle you also have to pay sales tax and title fees (*Figure 3.10*). If you have a loan on your vehicle the title will identify the lien holder.

Figure 3.10   ***Vehicle Title***

License plate tags (*Figure 3.11*) need to be periodically renewed. Convenient online tag renewal services are becoming more popular.

Figure 3.11   ***License Plate with Tags***

🖩 Calculations

Monthly Fuel Expense

Miles Driven Between Fill-ups		EXAMPLE	300
÷ Gallons of Fuel Used			÷ 12
= MPG			**25**

(Miles Per Month ÷ MPG)		EXAMPLE	(1,000 ÷ 25)
x Fuel Cost Per Gallon			x $2.58
= Fuel Cost Per Month			**$103.20**

Driving a vehicle with high fuel mileage will lower your monthly expenses.

🖱 Web Links

Fuel Cost Related Sites

AAA Fuel Cost Calculator
  ↳   www.fuelcostcalculator.com
Edmunds.com
  ↳   www.edmunds.com/fueleconomy
FuelEconomy.gov
  ↳   www.fueleconomy.gov
GasBuddy.com
  ↳   www.gasbuddy.com
How Stuff Works
  ↳   www.howstuffworks.com/gas-price

Maintenance and Repairs

Car manufacturers are producing more reliable vehicles than ever before. However, even reliable vehicles have:

- Routine Maintenance
- Unexpected Repairs

Routine Maintenance

Routine maintenance expenses include oil changes, tune-ups, brake service, and replacing the tires, battery, windshield wipers, timing belt, and drive belts. These services vary in cost depending on the owner's ability and vehicle. If you are able to perform many of these tasks yourself, you can save hundreds of dollars each year. Routine maintenance expenses should be included in your budget. Your vehicle owner's manual should have a maintenance section that identifies when to perform routine maintenance (*Figure 3.12*). If routine maintenance is ignored, it usually costs more money to fix as an unexpected repair and possible tow.

Example Maintenance Schedule 3,000 miles (5,000 km) or 3 Months	
☐	Change Engine Oil and Filter
☐	Check Transmission/Transaxle Fluid
☐	Check All Fluid Levels and Conditions
☐	Inspect Exhaust System
☐	Inspect Brakes for Wear (Front and Back)
☐	Inspect CV Boots (FWD)
☐	Inspect Drive Belt

Figure 3.12   *Example Maintenance Schedule*

✓ Tech Tip

Do Maintenance When Required

It is easy to ignore vehicle maintenance if there is no apparent problem. Skipping oil changes can cause costly engine damage. Not replacing worn or damaged tires can lead to a safety hazard. Brake maintenance is also very important. Don't ignore a new sound or vibration, it probably means it's time for service.

Unexpected Repairs

Unexpected repair expenses include diagnosing engine problems, drivetrain damage, and repairing suspension and steering components. Other problems include replacing the alternator, starter, or the worst – internal engine or transmission repairs. New cars commonly come with a standard 3-year/36,000 mile (60,000 km) bumper-to-bumper warranty. Some manufacturers have a much longer powertrain (e.g., engine, transmission, and drivetrain) warranty. Warranties apply as long as scheduled maintenance has been performed. After the manufacturer warranty expires, repairs will be your responsibility. If your car's warranty has expired, it is always good to have money in reserve to take care of unexpected repairs.

Summary

Automobiles are expensive to own. The financial obligations to own and operate a vehicle range from monthly car payments to insurance premiums to unexpected repairs. Knowing your budget and planning for routine maintenance and unexpected expenses will prepare you for the financial responsibility of vehicle ownership.

🚗 Activities

Automotive Expenses

- Automotive Expenses Activity
- Chapter 3 Study Questions

Activities can be accessed in the Auto Upkeep workbook or online at www.autoupkeep.com.

🎓 Career Paths

Insurance Claims Adjuster

Education: Collision Repair Training
Median Income: $46,000
Job Market: Average Growth
Abilities: Estimating, communication, and computer skills.

CHAPTER 4

REPAIR FACILITIES

FUEL FOR THOUGHT
- What makes a quality auto repair facility?
- What are the different types of auto repair facilities?
- What types of auto repair warranties are available?

Introduction

Even do-it-yourselfers may periodically need to visit a repair facility. Being an educated consumer can save you time, money, and headaches. Repair facilities come in a variety of sizes. Some facilities are one person operations, while others may have many employees. Remember to check the warranty (*Figure 4.1*) on your vehicle first to see if a repair is covered by the manufacturer.

Figure 4.1   *Warranty Booklet*

Objectives

Upon completion of this chapter and activities, you will be able to:
- Identify a quality repair facility.
- Communicate effectively with a technician or service writer.
- Interpret a repair invoice.
- Locate a car care education program.

Key Characteristics of a Quality Repair Facility

Quality repair facilities take pride in their work and keep a clean and organized workspace. They provide written estimates, charge a reasonable rate, hire certified technicians, and are honest with the customer. This section focuses on:
- ASE Certified Technicians
- AAA Approved Auto Repair
- Business Ethics
- Reasonable Costs
- Better Business Bureau

ASE Certified Technicians

Repair facility quality depends on the quality of the technicians, support staff, tools, and equipment. Troubleshooting automotive problems takes expert training and often high dollar diagnostic equipment. In the past automotive technicians were called mechanics. Today's technicians require extensive training that needs to be updated frequently because the technology on vehicles continuously changes. The National Institute for Automotive Service Excellence, an independent non-profit organization, certifies technicians through national certification tests. Exams are grouped by specific content area to test technician competence in diagnosing and repairing automobiles. In addition to passing an exam, a technician is also required to have two years of related experience to become certified. One thing to look for is an Automotive Service Excellence (ASE) sign (*Figure 4.2*). Technicians can become certified in a variety of areas, such as: automatic transmissions, brakes, electrical/electronic systems, engine repair, engine performance, heating and air conditioning, manual drive train and axles, and suspension and steering. Currently, there are over 400,000 ASE certified technicians, with about 113,000 being Master Technicians. Technicians that become certified in several areas can become a Master Technician. To stay current, ASE requires technicians to retest every five years. Look for a shop with certified technicians with several years of experience in the area in which your vehicle needs servicing. *Note: In Canada look for Journeyperson Automotive Service Technicians.*

Figure 4.2   **ASE Repair Facility Sign**
Courtesy of National Institute for Automotive Service Excellence

AAA Approved Auto Repair

The American Automobile Association (AAA) approves auto repair facilities that meet strict standards in repair, service, and facility cleanliness. AAA Approved Auto Repair facilities also have to provide a 1 year/12,000 mile (20,000 km) repair warranty. Look for a facility that proudly displays the AAA Approved Auto Repair sign (*Figure 4.3*).

Figure 4.3   **AAA Approved Auto Repair**
Courtesy of AAA

Business Ethics

It is critical to find a service facility that is honest and reliable. Just as these characteristics are important in everyday life, they are also important in business. Unfortunately a few service facilities take advantage of customers because the automobile is an extremely complex machine. Look for service writers and technicians that are courteous and willing to explain the diagnosis. Reliable facilities have few customer complaints and get the job done right the first time. ASE technicians pledge a Code of Ethics (*Figure 4.4*).

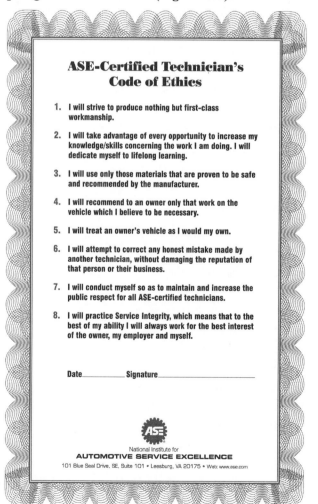

ASE-Certified Technician's Code of Ethics

1. I will strive to produce nothing but first-class workmanship.

2. I will take advantage of every opportunity to increase my knowledge/skills concerning the work I am doing. I will dedicate myself to lifelong learning.

3. I will use only those materials that are proven to be safe and recommended by the manufacturer.

4. I will recommend to an owner only that work on the vehicle which I believe to be necessary.

5. I will treat an owner's vehicle as I would my own.

6. I will attempt to correct any honest mistake made by another technician, without damaging the reputation of that person or their business.

7. I will conduct myself so as to maintain and increase the public respect for all ASE-certified technicians.

8. I will practice Service Integrity, which means that to the best of my ability I will always work for the best interest of the owner, my employer and myself.

Date_____ Signature_____

National Institute for
AUTOMOTIVE SERVICE EXCELLENCE
101 Blue Seal Drive, SE, Suite 101 • Leesburg, VA 20175 • Web: www.ase.com

Figure 4.4   **ASE Technician's Code of Ethics**
Courtesy of National Institute for Automotive Service Excellence

Reasonable Costs

Repairing a vehicle can be costly. That is why it is extremely important to follow the manufacturer's service interval recommendations. If your car is in need of a repair be cautious when shopping around, the lowest price may not be your best choice. Most facilities charge labor rates in two ways: flat rate (also known as book time) or actual time. Flat rate uses a manual to look up the time it should take to complete that repair. If it takes more or less time than the flat rate, you are still charged the same. Facilities that charge actual time bill out the actual time that it takes to repair your vehicle. Some services may have an advertised set cost (e.g., oil change for $24.99).

Better Business Bureau

The Better Business Bureau is a neutral non-profit organization between companies and consumers to promote ethical practices. The Better Business Bureau works to prevent consumer and business fraud. It is the go-between connecting the consumer to the business to help resolve issues. The Better Business Bureau reports on public complaints, scams, and a company's reliability.

Facility Types

Repair facilities can be small, medium, and large. Some are corporate owned, while others are independently owned. The key is to find a quality facility with competent technicians. Communicating your vehicle's problem clearly with the service writer or technician is critical and can save valuable time during diagnosis. This section focuses on:

- Dealership Repair Facilities
- Independent Repair Facilities
- Specialized Repair Facilities

Dealership Repair Facilities

Automotive dealerships sell and service specific makes and models of vehicles. Dealerships are known for having up-to-date repair information on cars that they sell. Technicians are frequently factory trained for new vehicles being released. New car warranties are handled through dealerships. Some dealerships service all makes of vehicles, but it is best to use a dealership specific to your vehicle for major repairs.

🖱 Web Links

Consumer Groups

American Automobile Association
   ↳   www.aaa.com
Better Business Bureau
   ↳   www.bbb.org
Car Care Council
   ↳   www.carcare.org
Clean Car Campaign
   ↳   www.cleancarcampaign.org
Consumer Action Website
   ↳   www.consumeraction.gov/carman.shtml
Motorists Assurance Program
   ↳   www.motorist.org
National Inst. for Automotive Service Excellence
   ↳   www.ase.com
Public Citizen
   ↳   www.citizen.org/autosafety

❓ Q & A

Choosing an Auto Repair Facility

Q: How do I choose an auto repair facility?
A: Look for shops that display its employees' ASE certifications. Ask your co-workers and friends for recommendations. Find a shop that specializes in the service you need. For example, some facilities specialize in suspension repair, tires, and alignments. Others may specialize in transmission repair and service. If you don't know what your vehicle needs your best bet may be to go to the dealership. Generally dealerships will be able to fix any problem. Once you find a shop you trust, build a rapport with the service writers and technicians. This relationship will help you if you ever get in a bind and need emergency service.

Independent Repair Facilities

Sometimes known as "ma and pa" shops, independent repair facilities are usually started by a technician that wants to run his or her own business. Some of these are quite large and have highly skilled technicians. Others may resemble a garage in a residential setting with little resources. An independent shop may have several family members contributing in various roles. Independent shops can offer a personal touch. At these establishments you can build long-lasting relationships, especially if the owner is dedicated to providing high quality service at a reasonable cost.

Specialized Repair Facilities

Repair facilities that specialize in one area of service are gaining popularity. Common areas of specialty include brakes, mufflers, tires, oil changes, alignments, or electrical problems. Specialized repair facilities can sometimes save you money due to the volume of business that they complete in one specific area. For example, facilities that specialize in tire replacement may purchase such large quantities of tires that they can pass the savings on to the customer. Technicians employed by specialty shops can become extremely skilled in one area of the automobile. They also only have to buy and maintain the tools that relate directly to their specialty.

 $ Price Guide

Oil Change
  ↪ $20.00 to $30.00 (parts and labor)
Engine Rebuild/Replacement
  ↪ $2,000.00 to $4,000.00 (parts and labor)
Headlight Bulb Replacement
  ↪ $20.00 to $40.00 (parts and labor)
Serpentine Belt Replacement
  ↪ $50.00 to $75.00 (parts and labor)
Transmission Rebuild
  ↪ $1500.00 to $2500.00 (parts and labor)
Wheel Alignment
  ↪ $50.00 to $150.00 (parts and labor)

Estimates and Repair Orders

This section focuses on:
- Estimates
- Repair Orders

Estimates

Estimates are prepared before a repair is performed. An estimate should include the description of the repair, the labor rate, estimated time to complete the repair, and a list of parts. Ask the repair facility to review your customer rights and get it in writing for your records (*Figure 4.5*). Identifying your preferences will let the facility know what you want them to do if they run into unforeseen problems that would put the repair over the original estimated cost.

Customer Rights (Repair Estimate/Order)	
Do you want your parts returned?	Yes ☐ No ☐
Do you want a written estimate?	Yes ☐ No ☐
If the job exceeds the estimate by 10% or more, do you authorize us in proceeding?	Yes ☐ No ☐
If additional repairs are found necessary, do you authorize us in proceeding?	Yes ☐ No ☐
Do you request a written estimate for repairs with cost in excess of $50.00?	Yes ☐ No ☐

Figure 4.5   *Customer Rights Questions*

Repair Orders

A repair order (also known as a repair ticket, invoice, or work order) summarizes work completed. The repair order should list the labor, parts, shop supplies used, environmental fees, and taxes. The VIN, odometer reading, and warranty information (if applicable) should also be listed.

✓ Tech Tip

Part Replacement

Depending on the repair and faulty component, a part may be new, rebuilt, remanufactured, or from a salvage yard. Before having work completed, ask the service writer what type of parts will be used. Some replacement parts like starters, alternators, and water pumps are commonly remanufactured.

Warranty Considerations

It is important to know whether or not your vehicle is covered under warranty. It would be unfortunate if you spent your money at an independent repair facility to find out afterwards that the service would have been covered by the factory warranty at no charge by the dealership. This section focuses on:

- Factory Warranties
- Certified Used Car Warranties
- Extended Warranties
- Chain Warranties
- Independent Warranties
- Battery and Tire Warranties

Factory Warranties

New cars often come with several different types of factory warranties: bumper-to-bumper, powertrain, corrosion perforation, emission, safety restraint, and hybrid related components. You should understand each of the warranties that your vehicle manufacturer provides. Each type of warranty may have different time periods.

Certified Used Car Warranties

Certified used car warranties (*Figure 4.6*) have become popular in recent years. These are different than used cars sold with extended warranties. Certified used cars have met strict inspections by the dealership and are backed by extended warranties by the manufacturer. Sometimes the word "certified" gets thrown around to mean less than it was intended. Be sure if you are looking at a certified used car that it is backed by the manufacturer, not just the dealer. Then when you need warranty repair work while traveling, any dealership should be able to assist you.

Figure 4.6   *Certified Used Car Warranty*

Extended Warranties

If you purchased an extended warranty on your new vehicle it is important for you to read the warranty on reimbursement procedures so you are not denied a claim. Identify what is and what is not covered. A used vehicle may also come with an extended warranty. Look for a warranty sign in the window (*Figure 4.7*) to learn the details of what the seller will cover.

Figure 4.7   *Used Car Extended Warranty Sign*

Chain Warranties

If you have your car repaired at a chain service center a warranty may be included. The benefit of a chain warranty is that it is guaranteed by any repair facility within the chain.

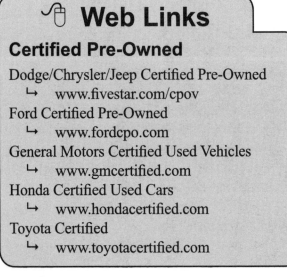

Web Links

Certified Pre-Owned

Dodge/Chrysler/Jeep Certified Pre-Owned
↳ www.fivestar.com/cpov
Ford Certified Pre-Owned
↳ www.fordcpo.com
General Motors Certified Used Vehicles
↳ www.gmcertified.com
Honda Certified Used Cars
↳ www.hondacertified.com
Toyota Certified
↳ www.toyotacertified.com

Independent Warranties

Independent repair facilities may have their own warranties to stand behind their work. Like any warranty, be sure it is in writing. The disadvantage here is that you will most likely have to bring it back to the shop where it was fixed. This may be an impractical task if you are traveling on a trip or if you move from the area.

Battery and Tire Warranties

Automotive batteries and tires have their own warranties. For example, if you have trouble with a specific brand of tire you should be able to have any tire dealer that sells that brand warranty it. Most tires and batteries have pro-rated warranties. Pro-rated means you will have to pay for part of the replacement cost, depending on how old or worn the component is that you are trying to get covered. Some tire and battery manufacturers have a full replacement period that lasts for a designated time.

Web Links

Chain Repair Centers

AAMCO Transmissions, Inc.
↳   www.aamco.com
American Car Care Centers
↳   www.accconline.com
Car-X Auto Service
↳   www.carx.com
Firestone Complete Auto Care
↳   www.firestonecompleteautocare.com
Jiffy Lube International, Inc.
↳   www.jiffylube.com
Maaco Collision Repair and Auto Painting
↳   www.maaco.com
Meineke Car Care Center
↳   www.meineke.com
Midas International Corporation
↳   www.midas.com
NAPA Auto Care Center
↳   www.napaautocare.com
Valvoline Instant Oil Change
↳   www.vioc.com

✓ Tech Tip
Community Education Programs

Contact local service centers to see if they have community education programs for car care. Dealerships, specialized repair centers, and independent repair facilities will often hold "Saturday Car Clinics" or something similar to educate consumers. These education programs help them build a positive relationship with their clients and better serve the public.

Summary

Whether you need an oil change or transmission overhaul, you have a wide variety of repair centers to choose from to have your vehicle fixed. When choosing a facility, check its quality, service, price, reputation, and warranties. It is important to have a clear understanding what service work is being completed and how you are being charged for that service with a written estimate. Maintain an open communication with the technician and service writer. Keep good records of all work completed on your vehicle.

Activities
Repair Facilities

• Repair Facilities Activity
• Chapter 4 Study Questions

Activities can be accessed in the Auto Upkeep workbook or online at www.autoupkeep.com.

Career Paths
Automotive Technician

Education: Technical Experience or ASE Cert.
Median Income: $40,000
Job Market: Average Growth
Abilities: Diagnostic, communication, problem solving, and hands-on technical skills.

CHAPTER 5

SAFETY AROUND THE AUTOMOBILE

FUEL FOR THOUGHT
- What safety equipment is required when working on vehicles?
- How can you safely lift and support a vehicle?
- How are fire extinguishers classified?

Introduction

If the correct precautions are not taken, working on automobiles can be dangerous. In a school lab, in your garage, or at an automotive repair facility you need to be aware of people and your surroundings at all times. People are needlessly hurt each year through carelessness. This chapter provides the information necessary to safely work on the automobile. When safety precautions are followed, working on the automobile can be a rewarding experience. Safety glasses, eyewash stations, first aid kits, fire extinguishers, and Material Safety Data Sheets (MSDS) are some of the items that should be available in an automotive work area.

Objectives

Upon completion of this chapter and activities, you will be able to:
- Safely work on and around a vehicle.
- Safely jack and support a vehicle.
- Identify basic types of vehicle lifts.
- Safely raise and lower a vehicle on an automotive lift.
- Identify types of fire extinguishers.

 ## Web Links

Safety Related Sites

AAA Foundation for Traffic Safety
↳ www.aaafoundation.org

American National Standards Institute
↳ www.ansi.org

Canadian Center for Occ. Health and Safety
↳ www.ccohs.ca

Dangerous Decibels
↳ www.dangerousdecibels.org

FireExtinguisher.com
↳ www.fireextinguisher.com

National Highway Traffic Safety Administration
↳ www.nhtsa.dot.gov

National Safety Council
↳ www.nsc.org

Occupational Safety and Health Administration
↳ www.osha.gov

PureSafety
↳ www.puresafety.com

Safety and Pollution Prevention
↳ www.sp2.org

The Center for Auto Safety
↳ www.autosafety.org

Laboratory Safety

In a laboratory setting it is important to think safety. Moving engine parts, explosive fuels, and hot components can make working on vehicles dangerous. The following is a list of safety precautions (*Figure 5.1*) for the general vehicle lab. If you are in an educational institution, your instructor may personalize this list to fit your specific situation. If you are working in your own garage, modify the personal protection, shop/lab procedures, and equipment safety precautions as you see fit. Always follow the safety instructions that accompany any tool or piece of equipment.

Personal Protection
• Safety glasses are not optional. Wear them at all times when working on a vehicle. ***Warning: Ordinary prescription glasses are not safety glasses. You can purchase approved prescription safety glasses with sideshields.***
• Do not have bare feet or wear open-toed sandals. Wear shoes that protect your feet.
• Loud noises can damage your hearing, so wear ear protection (e.g., earplugs).
• Keep your tools and hands free of grease and oil. Wearing mechanic gloves is smart, but do not wear gloves when moving parts are present. Keep your hands away from moving parts. Never use your hands to stop components that are moving.
• Remove your rings, watch, and other jewelry.
• If you have long hair, tie it back. It could get caught in moving parts.
• Do not wear loose or baggy clothing that could get caught in moving parts.
• Do not work on a hot engine.
• Do not touch spark plug wires while the engine is running. Tens of thousands of volts are present.
• Never put your hands on or near the cooling fan. Many fans are electric and can start at anytime, even if the ignition is off.

Figure 5.1a   ***Electric Fan Caution Label***

• Never open a hot radiator cap.
• Use proper lifting procedures to avoid injury. Use your legs, not your back.

Shop/Lab Procedures
• Know the location and operational procedures of fire extinguishers, first-aid kits, eyewash stations, and a telephone. Dial 911 for emergencies.

Figure 5.1b   ***Eyewash Station***
Courtesy of Guardian Equipment Company

• Someone must be sitting in the driver's seat whenever a car is started and/or running.
• The exhaust system of a running engine must be connected to a ventilation system if the vehicle is in an enclosed location such as a garage. ***Warning: Carbon monoxide is a colorless, odorless, and poisonous gas. Proper ventilation is required.***
• Always engage the parking brake to prevent the vehicle from moving.
• Put oily rags in an approved can for combustible materials.
• Always clean up spilled oil and grease off the floor. Sawdust, kitty litter, and oil dry work well for this.
• Never pour chemicals, solvents, antifreeze, or oil down the sanitary drain. Put them in their proper containers to be recycled.
• Use an approved safety cabinet for flammable materials.

Figure 5.1c   ***Materials Safety Cabinet***
Courtesy of Justrite Manufacturing Company

Equipment Safety
• Stand creepers up when not in use.
• Place floor jack handles in the up position when not being used.
• If a car is off the ground (except when on an automotive lift) it must be supported by jack stands.
• Use the proper tool for each job.
• Do not put tools on top of a vehicle's battery. Accidentally touching both terminals will cause a spark, which could lead to an explosion.

Figure 5.1   ***Safety Precautions***

OSHA

The Occupational Safety and Health Administration (OSHA) was created in 1971 in the United States to prevent work related deaths, illnesses, and injuries. OSHA sets and enforces health and safety standards (*Figure 5.2*) for the workplace. Even though OSHA only regulates safety in the workplace, it is still a good idea when working at home to follow these safe work practices. Go to www.osha.gov to learn more about this organization. *Note: In Canada, the federal agency is the Canadian Center for Occupational Health and Safety (www.ccohs.ca).*

Title	Regulation
Eye and Face Protection 1910.133(a)(1)	The employer shall ensure that each affected employee uses appropriate eye or face protection when exposed to eye or face hazards from flying particles, molten metal, liquid chemicals, acids or caustic liquids, chemical gases or vapors, or potentially injurious light radiation.
Jacks 1910.244(a)(1)(i)	The operator shall make sure that the jack used has a rating sufficient to lift and sustain the load.
Hand and Body Protection 1915.157(a)	The employer shall ensure that each affected employee uses appropriate hand protection and other protective clothing where there is exposure to hazards such as skin absorption of harmful substances, severe cuts or lacerations, severe abrasions, punctures, chemical burns, thermal burns, harmful temperature extremes, and sharp objects.

Figure 5.2   ***OSHA Regulation Examples***
Obtained from www.osha.gov

✓ Tech Tip

Learn Safety Online

CareerSafe (www.careersafeonline.com) offers online occupation safety and health training for young workers. After successfully completing the program students receive an approved OSHA wallet card. This card is evidence that the individual has fundamental knowledge in regards to being safe in the workplace.

Safety Equipment

When working on vehicles, think safety first. You should use the proper tools and clothing to protect yourself. This section focuses on:
*   Eye and Face Protection
*   Hand Protection
*   Ear Protection
*   First Aid

Eye and Face Protection

Eye protection is a must when working on cars. Eyes are very fragile. Safety glasses and goggles (*Figure 5.3*) will help prevent foreign materials from entering your eyes. These are especially important when inspecting the underbody of a vehicle and working around chemicals. Goggles can be used over prescription glasses. Eyewash stations are used to flush foreign bodies from eyes. Face shields, used in conjunction with safety goggles, provide maximum protection when working with chemicals or grinding.

Figure 5.3   ***Safety Glasses and Goggles***

💰 $ Price Guide

A-B-C Fire Extinguisher
↳ $25.00 to $50.00 each
Automotive Lift
↳ $2,000.00 to $10,000.00
Disposable Gloves
↳ $5.00 box of 100
Earmuffs
↳ $10.00 to $20.00 each
Earplugs
↳ $1.00 pair
Mechanic Gloves
↳ $15.00 to $30.00
Safety Glasses
↳ $5.00 to $15.00 each

Hand Protection

To protect your hands from cuts, scratches, burns, bruises, and chemicals use mechanic or work gloves (*Figure 5.4*). Form fitting mechanic gloves can also help you grip tools. Work gloves provide good protection and are great for performing work on tires and exhaust. Extremely worn tires can have sharp steel belts poking out from the tread. Exhaust systems can be hot and have rusty holes that can cut your hands. Do not wear gloves around moving machinery or parts.

Figure 5.4   *Mechanic and Work Gloves*

Use disposable gloves (*Figure 5.5*) when you are working with oils, greases, and chemicals.

Figure 5.5   *Disposable Gloves*

Ear Protection

Use earmuffs or earplugs (*Figure 5.6*) when the work area is excessively loud. Noise levels that exceed 85 decibels (dB) can damage your hearing.

Figure 5.6   *Earmuffs and Earplugs*

First Aid

A first aid kit (*Figure 5.7*) should contain supplies and equipment appropriate for injuries that may occur while working on an automobile such as cuts, burns, and slivers. Be aware and protect yourself from bloodborne pathogens.

Figure 5.7   *First Aid Kit*

❓ Q & A

Used Oil Precaution

Q: Why should I wear disposable gloves when changing the oil in my car?
A: Prolonged exposure to used oil on your skin can increase your chances of developing skin and health problems. Used oil has been shown to cause cancer in laboratory animals. Your body will absorb chemicals that come in contact with your skin. If you do get any chemicals on your skin, thoroughly wash them off with soap and water.

❓ Q & A

Material Safety Data Sheet (MSDS)

Q: What is a MSDS?
A: A MSDS provides detailed information on the possible hazards of working with a chemical product. It explains emergency procedures, physical properties, and how to handle, store, and dispose of the specific material.

Fire Extinguishers

Flammable and combustible materials are present in automotive shops. It is important to know where the fire extinguishers (*Figure 5.8*) are, how to use them, and what type of fires they put out. For a fire to exist it needs oxygen, heat, and fuel. A fire extinguisher must remove at least one of these components to put a fire out. Fire extinguishers are designed to put out specific types of fires. Most automotive shops will have a combination A-B-C fire extinguisher. Fires are classified by the following:

- A-Type
- B-Type
- C-Type
- D-Type

Figure 5.8 **Fire Extinguisher and Gauge**

🖰 Web Links

Safety Equipment Related Sites

Conney Safety Products
↳ www.conney.com
Fisco-Elvin
↳ www.fisco-elvin.com
Lab Safety Supply
↳ www.labsafety.com
Leonard Safety
↳ www.leonardsafety.com
Rx Safety Wear
↳ www.rx-safety.com
Uvex
↳ www.uvex.com

A-Type

A-type extinguishers put out wood, paper, cloth, rubber, plastic, and upholstery fires (*Figure 5.9*). They do this by coating or lowering the temperature of the burning materials.

Figure 5.9 **A-Type: Trash - Wood - Paper**

B-Type

B-type extinguishers put out gasoline, oil, grease, and paint fires (*Figure 5.10*). They do this by smothering the fire. Never put water on a B-type fire. Water will spread the fire.

Figure 5.10 **B-Type: Gasoline - Oil - Grease**

C-Type

C-type extinguishers put out electrical fires (*Figure 5.11*). They do this by using a nonconducting agent.

Figure 5.11 **C-Type: Electrical**

D-Type

D-type extinguishers put out combustible metal fires (*Figure 5.12*). They smother and coat the metal with a special agent to put the fire out.

Figure 5.12 **D-Type: Combustible Metal**

Automotive Lifts

Most repair shops and educational automotive labs have automotive lifts. Automotive lifts are more convenient than using a jack and jack stands. The greatest advantage is that they allow the technician to access the whole underside of the vehicle. Types of lifts include surface-mounted and inground (**Figure 5.13**). Inground lifts generally take up less space. Their configuration varies depending on design and age of lift.

Figure 5.13   **Inground Vehicle Lift**
Courtesy of Rotary Lift

A surface-mounted lift, powered by an electric motor, is bolted to the garage floor. A hydraulic pump pushes fluid in hydraulic cylinders to lift the vehicle. This section focuses on surface-mounted lifts:

- Two-Column
- Four-Column

Two-Column

The two-column drive through frame engaging lift is often called a two-post lift (**Figure 5.14**). Two-post lifts have lift arms that ride up each column. The arms are synchronized so they go up evenly.

> ✓ **Tech Tip**
>
> **Buying a Lift**
>
> Surface mounted lifts have become extremely popular. With the advent of the "extreme" garage, more and more automotive enthusiasts are installing lifts at home. If you buy a lift make sure it is certified through the Automotive Lift Institute. For a list of complying manufacturers and the latest lift safety information go to www.autolift.org.

This type of lift is commonly used for doing any kind of under-the-car service work. Since the lift contacts the frame, and not the wheels, it is an ideal setup for completing tire rotations, brake inspections, and suspension work. In addition, it is also commonly used for doing undercarriage work on exhaust systems and performing oil changes. By far, the two-post lift is the most popular type of surface mounted automotive lift.

Mobile
Wheel Lift

Figure 5.14   **Two-Post Vehicle Lift**
Courtesy of Rotary Lift

Four-Column

The four-column drive on lift is often called a four-post lift (**Figure 5.15**). Four-post lifts have runways. Once the vehicle is driven onto the runways, it is raised by its tires exposing the underside. This type of lift is most common in muffler and oil change shops. It is relatively safe and easy to use. The main disadvantage of this lift is the inability to perform services that require the removal of the tires without adding special adapters. Special adapters, called rolling lift jacks (**Figure 5.15**), are available from many manufacturers that can be added to this type of lift to allow the vehicle to be lifted off the runways. These lift jacks allow the removal of the wheels while the vehicle is still on the four-post lift.

Rolling Lift Jacks

Figure 5.15 Four-Post Lift with Rolling Lift Jacks
Courtesy of Rotary Lift

Lifting a Vehicle Safely

It is imperative to read and review lift safety procedures. If an accident occurs, it could easily be fatal. A person is no match for a vehicle. Safely lifting a vehicle requires reading and understanding the following:

- Safety, Warning, and Caution Labels
- Lift Constraints
- Two-Post Lift Operating Procedure
- Four-Post Lift Operating Procedure

Safety, Warning, and Caution Labels

Automotive lifts should have safety, caution, and warning labels (*Figure 5.16*) attached to the column that houses the controls for the lift. Frequently review these labels for safety.

Lift Constraints

Vehicle lifts are designed to only lift vehicles. Never use a lift to remove an engine or other heavy component from a vehicle. Also, never overload the lift. The load capacity of the lift is located on the manufacturer's nameplate.

✓ Tech Tip

Falling Vehicle

If a vehicle appears to be falling from a lift, clear the area immediately. Warn others in the shop. Do not position yourself between a wall and the lift. If the vehicle falls in that direction, you may be severely injured.

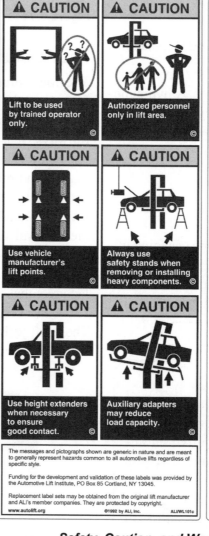

Figure 5.16   ***Safety, Caution, and Warning Labels for Automotive Lifts***
Courtesy of Automotive Lift Institute, Inc. - www.autolift.org

Two-Post Lift Operating Procedure

When using a lift have a partner direct you into the lifting area. *Warning: Stand to one side, not in front of the vehicle.* Line the center of gravity of the vehicle with the posts or as required by the lift manufacturer. On rear-wheel drive vehicles the center of gravity is usually directly below the driver's seat. However, on front-wheel drive vehicles, it is usually slightly in front of the driver's seat. Make sure the lift arms are contacting the vehicle's lift points. When vehicles still had full frames, the lifting points were easy – the frame. Today many automobiles do not have full frames, but unibodies. The frames on unibody vehicles are integrated with the body. When lifting a vehicle, use a manual to identify the correct lift points. Lift the vehicle about a foot off the ground. Then gently push on the front and rear bumper to make sure the vehicle is stable. Visually recheck the lift point connections. Raise the vehicle to the desired height and inspect the lift points again. *Warning: Some two-post lifts have overhead devices.* Do not lift the vehicle so that the roof of the vehicle comes in contact with overhead devices. Once at the desired height lower the lift onto the load holding device (safety locks). After work is completed remove everything from under the vehicle. First raise the vehicle off the load holding device to disengage the latches, then lower it to the ground. Always refer to the lift manufacturer instructions for specific lifting procedures.

Four-Post Lift Operating Procedure

Drive the vehicle on the runways, centering the weight of the vehicle on the lift. Chock both sides of at least one wheel and apply the parking brake. Raise the vehicle to the desired height. Once at the desired height lower the lift onto the load holding device (safety locks). After work is completed remove everything from under the vehicle. First raise the vehicle off the load holding device to disengage the latches, then lower it to the ground. Always refer to the lift manufacturer instructions for specific lifting procedures. The Automotive Lift Institute has up-to-date manuals, videos, CD-Roms, DVDs, and other materials to safely operate automotive lifts (*Figure 5.17*).

🖱 Web Links

Automotive Lift Sites

Automotive Lift Institute
↳   www.autolift.org
Bend-Pak Inc.
↳   www.bendpak.com
Challenger Lifts
↳   www.challengerlifts.com
Forward Lift
↳   www.forwardmfg.com
Hennessy Industries, Inc. (Ammco Lifts)
↳   www.hennessy-ind.com
Hunter Engineering Company
↳   www.hunter.com
Mohawk Lifts
↳   www.mohawklifts.com
Rotary Lift
↳   www.rotary-lift.com
Snap-on Equipment
↳   www.snaponequipment.com
Western Hoist, Inc.
↳   www.westernhoist.com

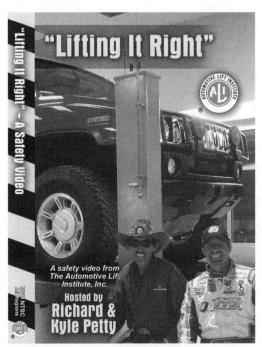

Figure 5.17   *Lifting It Right Safety DVD*
Courtesy of Automotive Lift Institute, Inc. - www.autolift.org

Using Jacks and Jack Stands

You should never go under a jacked-up vehicle unless it is supported by jack stands. Safety jack stands are inexpensive and a must when completing repairs or service procedures under a vehicle. The following are the steps for jacking up a vehicle (*Figure 5.18*). *Warning: Never use concrete blocks or other inadequate devices for supporting a vehicle.*

Jacking a Vehicle Procedure	
STEP 1	Position the floor jack so that it comes in contact with the frame or another solid chassis component. Do not use the oil pan, body, or other fragile component as lifting points when jacking up the vehicle. Serious damage could result. Check your owner's manual for specific lift points.
STEP 2	Chock the wheels still on the ground. Wheel chocks are used to minimize the risk of the vehicle rolling and falling off the jack.

Wheel Chock   Wheel Chock

Figure 5.18a   *Chocked Wheel*

STEP 3	Slowly pump the jack and lift the vehicle.
STEP 4	Once at the desired height, position the jack stands under the frame or specified jacking points. Ratchet the jack stands to the desired height.
STEP 5	Slowly lower the vehicle onto the jack stands and remove the floor jack.

Jack Stands

Figure 5.18b   *Jack Stands in Position*

STEP 6	Reposition the floor jack, lift the vehicle off the jack stands, remove the jack stands from under the vehicle, lower the jack, and remove chocks.

Figure 5.18   *Jacking a Vehicle*

Safety Around Airbags

Since 1998, dual frontal airbags for the driver and front passenger have been standard equipment for all passenger cars sold in the United States. Since 1999, all light trucks, vans, and SUVs were also required to have dual airbags. Over the years, airbag improvements have been made. Advanced frontal airbags are required in all new vehicles manufactured since September 1st, 2006 (2007 model year vehicles). Advanced systems use various sensors to minimize the risk of being injured by an airbag deployment during an accident, especially for children and small adults. These sensors commonly detect the size of the person sitting in the seat, the severity of the crash, the position of the seat, and whether or not the occupant is wearing a seatbelt. The advanced systems inflate according to the sensor input. This section focuses on:

- Working on Airbag Systems
- Working Near Airbag Components

Working on Airbag Systems

Do not attempt to work on airbags, part of the Supplemental Restraint System (SRS), without professional training. Do not disturb, hit, or tamper with airbag system components when working on a vehicle (*Figure 5.19*). *Warning: Airbags may deploy rapidly without warning causing serious injury or death.*

SUPPLEMENTAL RESTRAINT SYSTEM (SRS) A9

This vehicle is equipped with front airbags, side airbags in the front seats, front seatbelt tensioners, and side curtain airbags.
All SRS electrical wiring and connectors are colored yellow.
Tampering with, disconnecting or using test equipment on the SRS wiring can make the system inoperative or cause accidental deployment.

⚠WARNING

Accidental deployment can seriously hurt or kill you.
Follow Service Manual instructions carefully.

Figure 5.19   *SRS Warning Label*

Figure 5.21   *Airbag Indicator Light Example*

Summary

Safety in an automotive lab or shop is essential. Fires are classified by the type of material burning. The best type of fire extinguisher to have when working on an automobile is a combination A-B-C. Proper jack procedures enable you to lift a vehicle safely and without damage. Three types of lifts are common in automotive shops: inground, two-post, and four-post. The four-post is easier to use than the two-post, but it is not as versatile without special adapters. The four-post lift is generally used for oil changes and undercarriage inspections, while the two-post is commonly used for tire, brake, or suspension work. Be extremely careful when working around airbag system components. They can be dangerous if accidentally deployed.

...take your ... do inad-... the airbag ...ash airbag

...g injured ...ident? ...nt is not ...National ...stration ...dvanced ...: (a) use ...0 inches (25 cm) from the airbag cover, (c) remember that children 12 and under should sit in the back seat, and (d) never use a rear facing infant seat in the front seat of an airbag equipped vehicle. The back seat is the safest location during a crash. Some vehicles, especially those without rear seats (e.g., two seat sports cars and pickup trucks) have a manual override to turn the airbag off if it is necessary to transport a child. Follow the manufacturer's instructions in the owner's manual. For more information about airbag safety, go to www.safercar.gov.

 Activities

Safety Around The Automobile

- Automotive Safety Activity
- Chapter 5 Study Questions

Activities can be accessed in the Auto Upkeep workbook or online at www.autoupkeep.com.

Career Paths

Health and Safety Specialist

Education: Cert. and/or Bachelor's Degree
Median Income: $52,000
Job Market: Average Growth
Abilities: Good at data collection, analysis, and at identifying hazardous conditions.

CHAPTER 6

BASIC TOOLS

FUEL FOR THOUGHT

- What hand tools are commonly used while working on the automobile?
- Why is it important to use the correct tool?
- Where can you find information to help you with an automotive repair?

Introduction

Using the right tools when working on your car will make the job easier and safer. An ASE (Automotive Service Excellence) certified technician typically has hundreds of common and specialty tools to work on a variety of vehicles. However, every auto owner should have some basic hand tools to perform periodic maintenance and minor repairs.

Objectives

Upon completion of this chapter and activities, you will be able to:
- Recognize basic hand tools.
- Identify the correct tool for the job.
- Use tools properly.
- Identify types of service manuals.

Common Hand Tools

Common hand tools are necessary when performing basic vehicle maintenance and repair work. You may find that you already own many of these tools.

This section focuses on:
- Wrenches
- Ratchets
- Sockets
- Pliers
- Screwdrivers
- Hammers
- Pry Bars

Wrenches

Wrenches come in various sizes and designs. Adjustable, open-end, box-end, combination, and specialty wrenches are important tools to have for basic maintenance and repair. Both standard and metric fixed sized wrenches should be included in a basic tool kit. Metric sizes commonly increase by 1 millimeter (mm), so a metric wrench set may have the following sizes: 7mm, 8mm, 9mm, 10mm, 11mm, 12mm, 13mm, 14mm, 15mm, etc. Standard wrenches commonly increase by 1/16″ for each wrench size increase. *Note: The double prime sign (″) is a symbol for inch units.* For example, a standard wrench set may have these sizes: 1/4″, 5/16″, 3/8″, 7/16″, 1/2″, 9/16″, 5/8″, 11/16″, 3/4″, etc.

The two most common types of wrench ends are box and open. A combination wrench (*Figure 6.1*) has a box-end on one end and an open-end on the other. Use the box-end whenever possible.

Open-end   Box-end

Figure 6.1   ***Combination Wrench***

The size corresponds to the distance between the two jaws in an open-end wrench (*Figure 6.2*).

Size

Figure 6.2   ***Open-End Wrench Size***

The box-end usually has 6-points or 12-points (*Figure 6.3*). Use the box-end 6-point when a great amount of torque is required to reduce the chance of stripping the fastener (i.e., a nut or bolt). An open-end is handy when the fastener position will not allow access with the box-end. If you need more leverage, use a longer wrench.

6-Point End   12-Point End

Figure 6.3   ***6-Point and 12-Point Box-Ends***

✓ Tech Tip

Wrench and Socket Selection

You should only use a wrench or socket that fits the fastener snugly. If it is even a little loose it may round the fastener corners. If the head of a nut or bolt is slightly rounded, use a 6-point socket or box-end wrench. The 6-points lessens the likelihood of stripping the fastener head. In contrast, use the 12-points if you have a limited amount of space for movement. The 12-points allow for twice the number of placements on the fastener.

✓ Tech Tip

Flip the Wrench

To loosen a fastener with an open-end wrench in a tight location remember that you can flip the wrench. Open-end wrench ends are offset, so you can flip the wrench over and then grip the fastener in a different location. You may need to flip the wrench after each turn if you are in an extremely tight situation.

An adjustable wrench (*Figure 6.4*) is a versatile second choice if a fixed sized jaw wrench is not available. The jaw can be adjusted to fit metric or standard nuts and bolts. However, it does not fit as snugly on the fastener as a fixed sized jaw wrench. In addition, the head of an adjustable wrench may not fit in all locations and is not as strong. An adjustable wrench is sometime called a Crescent® wrench (an industry brand name). If you are going to have only one wrench in your tool box, choose an adjustable wrench.

Figure 6.4   ***Adjustable Wrench***

Ratchets

Ratchets in combination with sockets are used to quickly turn nuts and bolts. A ratchet is basically a lever with a pivoting mechanism, which allows the user to tighten or loosen a fastener without removing the tool. Ratchets are sized according to the square driver head (*Figure 6.5*). For example, 1/4″ drive ratchets have driver heads that are 1/4″ x 1/4″. Common ratchet sizes are 1/4″, 3/8″, and 1/2″. A 3/8″ ratchet is the most common size found in a basic tool kit.

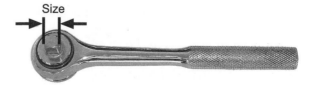

Size

Figure 6.5   ***Ratchet***

Sockets

Sockets can be directly connected to the ratchet or first connected to a universal joint or driver extension (*Figure 6.6*). Sockets are classified as regular or deep well. Deep well sockets can fit over the threads of a long bolt. Sockets, like wrenches, have points inside that fit over the fastener and come in both metric and standard sizes. Common sockets will have either 6-points or 12-points.

Figure 6.6   *Socket Set*

Some sockets are specially designed. Do not use them on common nuts and bolts. For example, a spark plug socket (*Figure 6.7*) has a rubber boot insert to hold and protect the plug from cracking.

Figure 6.7   *Spark Plug Socket*

Impact sockets (*Figure 6.8*) are used in situations where high torque and speed are needed, especially when using an electric or pneumatic (air powered) impact wrench. ***Warning: Never use a non-impact socket on a power tool and always wear safety glasses.*** Impact sockets have thicker sides than standard sockets and are often black.

Figure 6.8   *Impact Sockets*

Pliers

Pliers are handy adjustable tools that can be used in a variety of situations. Pliers are used to grab, turn, cut, or bend. Types include slip joint, locking, groove joint, needle nose, and diagonal cutters. Pliers consist of two levers that pivot at one point. This pivoting point is called a fulcrum. Slip joint pliers (*Figure 6.9*) are one of the most basic and versatile hand tools. However, do not use slip joint pliers in situations where a wrench would be better (e.g., turning a nut or bolt). Trying to loosen a stubborn nut with slip joint pliers can strip the head. Also if the pliers slip your knuckles could get bruised or cut.

Figure 6.9   *Slip Joint Pliers*

Locking pliers (*Figure 6.10*) are sometimes called Vise-Grips® (an industry brand name). Locking pliers are used to tightly grip and then lock on the fastener. These pliers come in handy when a bolt or nut is already stripped beyond the point where a wrench will work. Grabbing onto flat pieces of metal or oddly shaped items are additional functions of locking pliers.

Figure 6.10   *Locking Pliers*

Also called adjustable pliers or Channellocks® (an industry brand name), groove joint pliers (*Figure 6.11*) adjust to a wide range of sizes. These are especially useful for gripping cylindrical objects, like pipes.

Figure 6.11   *Groove Joint Pliers*

Needle nose pliers (*Figure 6.12*) have long pointed jaws. These can be used to grip or pull objects that are in hard-to-reach areas. Sometimes there is also a cutting mechanism next to the fulcrum.

Figure 6.12   *Needle Nose Pliers*

Also called side cutters, diagonal pliers (*Figure 6.13*) have sharp edges instead of gripping jaws like most pliers. They are commonly used for cutting wires.

Figure 6.13   *Diagonal Pliers*

Screwdrivers

Just about everyone is familiar with screwdrivers (*Figure 6.14*). They turn screws or other fasteners. Some screwdrivers have magnetic tips to help with positioning fasteners in tight spaces. *Warning: Do not use screwdrivers as pry bars.*

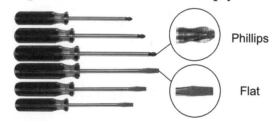

Phillips

Flat

Figure 6.14   *Screwdriver Set*

The head of a fastener determines the type and size of screwdriver tip that is needed. The proper tip will fit in a fastener head snugly. Damage or tool slippage may occur if an incorrect sized tip is used. Common types of screwdriver tips include Phillips, slotted, square, Allen, Torx, and hex (*Figure 6.15*). Screwdriver tips are also made as bits that can be placed in a socket to ratchet in tight places.

Phillips   Slotted   Square   Allen   Torx   Hex

Figure 6.15   *Fastener Head Types*

Hammers

Sometimes what you are working on needs a little more persuasion. Using the correct hammer will ensure that you don't damage components. A ball peen hammer (*Figure 6.16*) is commonly used to drive a chisel or a punch. *Warning: Always wear eye protection.*

Figure 6.16   *Ball Peen Hammer*

A rubber mallet (*Figure 6.17*), a hammer with a rubber head, comes in handy to drive on stubborn wheel covers and other parts without damaging them.

Figure 6.17   *Rubber Mallet*

Pry Bars

Pry bars (*Figure 6.18*) are long bars with handles that come in a variety of sizes and styles. They can be useful for gaining leverage on a component that is heavy or stuck.

Figure 6.18   *Pry Bar*

💰 Price Guide

Ball Peen Hammer
↳ $10.00 to $15.00
Combination Plier Set
↳ $15.00 to $30.00
Pry Bar
↳ $10.00 to $20.00
Ratchet and Socket Set
↳ $50.00 to $150.00
Screwdriver Set
↳ $15.00 to $50.00
Wrench Set
↳ $30.00 to $70.00

Lifting Tools

When performing work under a vehicle it is often necessary and convenient to raise the vehicle off the ground with a floor jack and jack stands or drive-on ramps. Work safely by using lifting equipment on a surface that is solid and chock the wheels still on the ground. ***Warning: The weight of the vehicle being lifted should not exceed the lift ratings on the equipment.*** This section focuses on:

- Floor Jack
- Drive-on Ramps
- Wheel Chocks
- Jack Stands

Floor Jack

A floor jack (***Figure 6.19***) is used to lift a vehicle. Be sure to place the jack's lifting pad under the frame or other solid chassis component. Lifting by the sheet metal underbody may cause damage to a vehicle and make it more likely to fall off the jack. ***Warning: To prevent serious injury or death, jack stands must be used. Do not go under a vehicle that is only supported by a jack.***

Figure 6.19   *Hydraulic Floor Jack*

Drive-on Ramps

Drive-on ramps (***Figure 6.20***) can make raising one end of your vehicle very easy. All you need to do is line the ramps up in front of your tires, drive onto them, set your parking brake, and chock the wheels remaining on the ground. Since the vehicle is still resting on its tires, don't plan on doing any wheel work. Ramps are convenient for oil changes and undercarriage inspections.

Figure 6.20   *Drive-on Ramps*

Wheel Chocks

To prevent a vehicle from moving forward or backward, wheel chocks (***Figure 6.21***) are used to block a wheel when jacking. Place the wheel chocks in front and in back of the wheels that are not being lifted.

Figure 6.21   *Wheel Chocks*

Jack Stands

Jack stands (***Figure 6.22***) are used to hold a vehicle up after a jack has raised it. ***Warning: Do not use concrete blocks or other non-approved stands to hold up a vehicle.***

Figure 6.22   *Jack Stands*

> ### 💰 Price Guide
>
> Air Pressure Gauge
> ↳ $1.00 to $15.00
> Drive-on Ramps
> ↳ $40.00 to $60.00
> Hydraulic Floor Jack
> ↳ $40.00 to $150.00
> Safety Jack Stands
> ↳ $20.00 to $50.00 pair
> Tread Depth Gauge
> ↳ $1.00 to $3.00
> Wheel Chocks
> ↳ $10.00 to $20.00
> 4-Way Tire Tool
> ↳ $10.00 to $20.00

Tire Tools

This section focuses on:
- 4-Way Tire Tool/Cross/Lug Wrench
- Bottle and Scissor Jacks
- Tread Depth Gauge
- Tire Pressure Gauges

4-Way Tire Tool/Cross/Lug Wrench

A 4-way tire tool (*Figure 6.23*) is more versatile for removing lug nuts than the basic manufacturer lug wrench (i.e., tire iron) supplied with your vehicle. A 4-way has a different size on each end and allows for more leverage.

Figure 6.23   *4-Way Tire Tool*

Bottle and Scissor Jacks

Many vehicles have a bottle jack (*Figure 6.24*) or scissor jack stored in the trunk for emergency tire changes. These manufacturer supplied jacks are not as easy or as safe to use as a hydraulic floor jack. Save them for roadside emergencies and invest in a hydraulic floor jack for your garage.

Figure 6.24   *Bottle Jack with Lug Wench*

Tread Depth Gauge

A tread depth gauge (*Figure 6.25*) is a simple measuring device to help determine the actual amount of tread remaining on your tires. It provides a depth reading from the top of the tread surface to the bottom of the tread groove.

Figure 6.25   *Tread Depth Gauge*

Tire Pressure Gauges

Tire pressure is measured with a tire pressure gauge (*Figure 6.26*) in pounds per square inch (psi) or kilopascals (kPa) and should be checked at least once a month (*Figure 6.27*). Recommended tire pressure is calculated according to the tire type, vehicle weight, and the desired ride. Maintaining the recommended tire pressure is critical to minimizing tire wear and optimizing handling stability. For every 10 degrees (F) the temperature drops, tire pressure drops by 1 psi (6.9 kPa). The inverse also occurs as temperature rises.

Figure 6.26   *Dial and Stick Pressure Gauges*

Tire Pressure Check	
STEP 1	Look in your driver's side door or other location as identified by the manufacturer for a tire placard that lists the correct pressure for each tire.
STEP 2	Check tire pressure when the tires are cold and you have access to an air compressor. Remove the valve stem cap.
STEP 3	Push the tire gauge firmly onto the valve stem. You should hear air rush into the gauge. Note the reading.

Figure 6.27a   *Tire Gauge on Valve Stem*

STEP 4	Add air if the reading is below the recommended pressure and repeat Step 3 and Step 4 as necessary. Do not overinflate.
STEP 5	If you added too much air, bleed some air from the tire. Many air gauges have a special tip for pressing in the valve to release air pressure. Repeat Step 3.
STEP 6	Once the tire is at the correct pressure, replace the valve stem cap and check the other tires.

Figure 6.27   *Checking Tire Pressure*

Measuring Tools

Measuring accurately requires the use of measuring tools like rulers, gauges, and micrometers. This section focuses on:

- Systems of Measurement
- Rulers
- Torque Wrench
- Coolant Tester
- Spark Plug Gauge
- Precision Measuring Tools

Systems of Measurement

Two systems of measurement (*Figure 6.28*) are used: International System of Units (metric system) and U.S. customary units (English system).

	Metric System	English System
Length	meter	inch, foot, mile
Mass	gram	ounce, pound, ton
Volume	liter	cubic inches, pint, quart, gallon
Power	watt	horsepower
Torque	Newton-meter	pound-foot
Temperature	degree Celsius	degree Fahrenheit

Figure 6.28 **Common Metric and English Units**

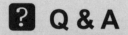

❓ Q & A

Breaker Bar or 4-Way

Q: I can't loosen my wheel lug nuts with my L shaped lug wrench. What can I do?

A: You need a tool with a longer handle. With a longer handle you can exert more torque using the same force (Torque = Force x Length). A 4-way lug wrench is designed so you have two handles - one to push down on and one to pull up on. A breaker bar, a long handled tool used in conjunction with a socket, is another method to gain leverage. Nearly all vehicles have right-hand lug nut threads, meaning you turn them counterclockwise to loosen. Make sure the threads on your wheel studs are not left-hand threads that require clockwise rotation to loosen.

Rulers

Rulers are used to measure linear distances. Measuring tapes are used to measure large distances whereas small rigid rulers are used to measure short linear distances.

Torque Wrench

A torque wrench, either beam or clicker style (*Figure 6.29*), can be used to tighten a fastener to a specific amount of force. For example, wheel lug nuts should be tightened to the manufacturer's specifications. Lug nuts that are not tight enough could loosen over time. Lug nuts that are too tight are hard to remove, can warp brake rotors, and can damage the stud's threads. A torque wrench is also critically important when completing internal engine repairs.

Figure 6.29 **Clicker Style Torque Wrench**

Coolant Tester

A coolant tester (*Figure 6.30*) measures specific gravity to determine if the cooling system contains the correct mixture of antifreeze to water. To draw coolant up into the tester, squeeze the bulb while the tube end is inserted in the radiator or expansion tank, then release the bulb. An indicator inside the tester floats to give a reading based on the percentage of antifreeze in the coolant.

Figure 6.30 **Coolant Tester**

💰 Price Guide

Coolant Tester
↳ $3.00 to $8.00
Spark Plug Gauge
↳ $4.00 to $8.00
Torque Wrench
↳ $75.00 to $200.00

Spark Plug Gauge

A spark plug gauge tool (*Figure 6.31*) has various diameter wires for checking the electrode gap and benders to adjust the gap. The gap is the distance between the center and side electrodes on the spark plug. A spark must arc across the gap in order to ignite the air-fuel mixture in a cylinder. The correct gap may be located on the vehicle emission control information sticker in the engine compartment.

Figure 6.31   ***Spark Plug Gauge***

Precision Measuring Tools

Feeler gauges, calipers, micrometers, and dial indicators are used to obtain very precise measurements. These tools can provide measurements to the nearest thousandths (0.001) of an inch or to the nearest hundredths (0.01) of a millimeter. Feeler gauges (*Figure 6.32*) consist of flat metal blades that are a specific thickness. You can put several feeler blades together to obtain a desired thickness.

Figure 6.32   ***Feeler Gauge Set***

A caliper (*Figure 6.33*) is an especially versatile measuring tool able to measure inside, outside, and depth dimensions. However, when extremely precise measurements are required consider using a micrometer.

Figure 6.33   ***Digital Caliper***

Micrometers (*Figure 6.34*) are particularly good for measuring the diameter of objects.

Figure 6.34   ***Outside Micrometer***

Electric Related Tools

If you plan to maintain a vehicle's electrical system some electrical tools will be necessary. At the very least every vehicle should carry a set of jumper cables. This section focuses on:

- Fuse Puller
- Multimeter
- Wire Stripper
- Battery Load Tester
- Battery Brush
- Battery Terminal Puller
- Battery Hydrometer
- Battery Terminal Spreader
- Jumper Cables

Fuse Puller

Fuses are fairly small, very close to one another in a fuse junction block, and often tightly held, making it difficult to pull them out. A fuse puller (*Figure 6.35*) is a small plastic device designed to grasp a fuse so it can be pulled out easily.

Figure 6.35 **Fuse Puller**

💰 Price Guide

Battery Brush
↳ $4.00 to $8.00
Battery Load Tester
↳ $40.00 to $300.00
Battery Terminal Puller
↳ $10.00 to $20.00
Battery Terminal Spreader
↳ $5.00 to $10.00
Fuse Puller
↳ $1.00 to $2.00
Jumper Cables
↳ $15.00 to $50.00
Multimeter
↳ $25.00 to $200.00
Wire Stripper
↳ $10.00 to $15.00

Multimeter

A multimeter (*Figure 6.36*) makes a great addition to any toolbox. Multimeters can be used to measure voltage, resistance, and amperage.

Figure 6.36 **Multimeter**
Courtesy of Snap-on Tools Corp and TPI

Wire Stripper

A wire stripper (*Figure 6.37*) can be used to remove wire insulation, cut wires, and to crimp solderless connectors and terminals.

Figure 6.37 **Wire Stripper**

Battery Load Tester

A battery load tester (*Figure 6.38*) is a specialty tool used to evaluate a battery's condition. The tester should be set to the battery's temperature and cold cranking amperage (CCA) rating to receive accurate results. *Note: Some automotive parts stores will test your battery for free.*

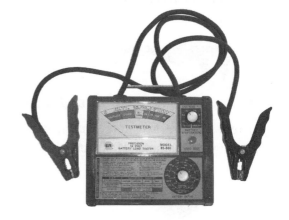

Figure 6.38 **Battery Load Tester**

Battery Brush

Once the battery terminal clamps have been disconnected from the battery posts, use battery brushes (*Figure 6.39*) to scrape off any visible corrosion. Rotate the external wire battery brush inside each clamp and the internal wire battery brush over each post. See page 169 for more on cleaning a battery. *Warning: Always wear eye protection and gloves when cleaning a battery.*

Figure 6.39   ***Battery Brushes***

Battery Terminal Puller

The battery terminal puller (*Figure 6.40*) is designed to remove a stubborn or corroded battery terminal clamp after the battery terminal nut has been loosened. The lower jaws of the puller are placed under the battery terminal clamp and then the top lever is turned to lower the center screw onto the terminal post until it forces the clamp free. This type of puller is only used on top post batteries.

Figure 6.40   ***Battery Terminal Puller***

Battery Hydrometer

A battery hydrometer (*Figure 6.41*) measures the specific gravity of the battery's electrolyte (water and sulfuric acid) solution. Knowing the specific gravity of the solution will indicate the cell's state of charge. The specific gravity can be measured in each cell. A 12V DC battery has six cells. See the Battery Activity for specific steps. *Warning: Be sure to wear safety goggles and gloves.*

Figure 6.41   ***Battery Hydrometer***

Battery Terminal Spreader

A battery terminal spreader (*Figure 6.42*) is specially designed to spread battery terminal post clamps. It can also be used to scrape corrosion from the inside of terminal clamps.

Figure 6.42   ***Battery Terminal Spreader***

Jumper Cables

A battery can discharge simply by leaving your lights on, a door ajar, or be a sign of an electrical problem. You should know how to properly hook up jumper cables (*Figure 6.43*). For steps on safely hooking up jumper cables see your owner's manual and the procedure on page 174. *Warning: Incorrectly jump-starting a battery can be dangerous. If cables are hooked up incorrectly the battery could explode or electrical components could be damaged.*

Figure 6.43   ***Jumper Cables***

✓ Tech Tip

Choosing Jumper Cables

Make sure your jumper cables have a cable diameter of at least 6 gauge, insulation which stays flexible in cold weather, strong terminal clamps, and are at least 12 ft (3.7 m) long. If your cables are short, it may be necessary to line the booster vehicle up right next to the discharged vehicle, which can be dangerous on a busy road.

Oil Change and Lube Tools

To perform an oil change and lubrication you will need a socket or wrench to remove the drain plug, lifting equipment, an oil drain pan, an oil filter wrench, a funnel, and a grease gun. See page 88 for oil change steps. This section focuses on:

- Oil Drain Pan
- Oil Filter Wrenches
- Funnel
- Grease Gun

Oil Drain Pan

An oil drain pan (***Figure 6.44***) helps to keep used oil from spilling. It should have a wide collection area, a place for the oil filter to sit while draining, enough capacity to hold at least one oil change, and a cap to prevent spilling during transportation to an oil recycling facility. Used oil is considered a carcinogen (causes cancer) and a hazardous waste. ***Warning: Always wear disposable gloves to prevent skin contact with used oil.***

Figure 6.44   ***Oil Drain Pan***

Oil Filter Wrenches

Two styles of oil filter wrenches are the most common. The band filter wrench (***Figure 6.45***) is made to adjust to several different sized filters within a range. For hard to reach filters get a filter wrench with a swivel handle.

Figure 6.45   ***Band Oil Filter Wrench***

The cup oil filter wrench (***Figure 6.46***) is used with a ratchet for leverage. Select the cup size that fits snugly on your filter.

Figure 6.46   ***Cup Oil Filter Wrench***

✓ Tech Tip

Oil Filter Wrench Size

When unsure what oil filter wrench size you need, find a replacement filter first and use it as a guide when selecting a wrench.

Funnel

A funnel (***Figure 6.47***) helps prevent spills when adding oil to the engine. Always make sure the funnel is clean so you don't contaminate the engine with other fluids or dirt.

Figure 6.47   ***Funnel***

Grease Gun

A grease gun (***Figure 6.48***), containing a grease cartridge, is used to lubricate steering, suspension, and drivetrain components. A vehicle's service manual should identify the location of lubrication fittings (if there are any) and the type of grease recommended. As technology advances more automotive parts are being manufactured with a permanent seal, so grease can't be added.

Figure 6.48   ***Hand Operated Grease Gun***

💰 Price Guide

Funnel Set
    ↳ $1.00 to $5.00
Grease Gun
    ↳ $10.00 to $25.00
Oil Drain Pan
    ↳ $5.00 to $15.00
Oil Filter Wrench
    ↳ $5.00 to $15.00

Cutting and Grinding Tools

Sometimes it is necessary to remove a piece of metal such as an exhaust pipe or a rusted bolt. To do this, cutting and grinding tools come in handy. This section focuses on:

- Grinder
- File
- Cold Chisel
- Punch
- Hacksaw

Grinder

An electric grinder (*Figure 6.49*) can be used to remove metal much faster than a file. *Warning: Grinding metal can create sparks. Be sure that all flammable materials are away from the grinding area and do not grind so that sparks go near the vehicle's fuel tank. It is also important to wear the appropriate safety gear, including a full face shield.*

Figure 6.49   *Electric Grinder*

File

A file (*Figure 6.50*) can be used to smooth, shape, and de-burr surfaces by removing metal. Common machinist files come in square, flat, half-round, and round types.

Figure 6.50   *Machinist File*

Cold Chisel

To use a cold chisel (*Figure 6.51*), place the chiseled end on an object, such as a seized/rusted nut or rivet, and hit the blunt end with a hammer. *Warning: Always wear eye protection.*

Figure 6.51   *Cold Chisel*

Punch

Punches (*Figure 6.52*) can be used to drive parts during removal or installation, mark points, or align objects. To use a punch, place the driving end on the object you want to move, mark, or align and hit the blunt end with a hammer. *Warning: Always wear eye protection.*

Figure 6.52   *Punch*

Hacksaw

Hacksaws (*Figure 6.53*) cut metal using thin blades. Blades commonly have 18, 24, or 32 teeth per inch (25 mm). Blades with more teeth cut cleaner and slower. Point the teeth away from the handle to cut mainly on the forward stroke.

Figure 6.53   *Hacksaw*

✓ Tech Tip

Emergency Tool Kit

To better prepare for the unexpected, carry an emergency tool kit in your vehicle at all times. Some essential items are listed below.

- First Aid Kit
- Jumper Cables
- Flash Light
- Locking Pliers
- Adjustable Wrench
- Phillips and Slotted Screwdrivers
- Duct and Electrical Tape
- Jack, Chocks, and Lug Wrench
- Work Gloves and Safety Glasses
- Warning Triangle and Road Flare
- Ice Scraper (Cold Weather)
- Fire Extinguisher
- Tire Pressure Gauge

Inspection Tools

If you are going to diagnose, maintain, and repair a vehicle, consider owning the following:
- Creeper
- Fender Cover
- Work Light

Creeper

A creeper (*Figure 6.54*) allows easier access to the undercarriage of a vehicle. With your head and body supported, you can comfortably roll around on your back in a low clearance space.

Figure 6.54   **Creeper**

Fender Cover

A fender cover helps to protect a vehicle's finish from scratches and dings while inspecting or working in the engine compartment.

Work Light

Seeing things in a quality light can really help when doing inspections and completing service work. Features to look for in a portable work light (*Figure 6.55*) include: impact and chemical resistant, ample light, low glare, stay cool casing, and a hook or clip for positioning.

Figure 6.55   **Fluorescent Work Light**

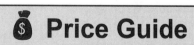

💰 Price Guide

Creeper
↳ $25.00 to $50.00
Service Manual
↳ $15.00 to $200.00
Work Light
↳ $10.00 to $50.00

Cleaning Supplies

This section focuses on:
- Shop Towels
- Floor Dry
- Hand Cleaner

Shop Towels

Shop towels and rags help you to keep your hands, tools, and vehicle components clean. If they have been used to wipe up combustible materials such as oil, fuel, or chemicals they should be stored in an approved container until they can be properly disposed or cleaned.

Floor Dry

To prevent accidents and to keep your work area safer, use floor dry to absorb oil and other spills. If you don't have floor dry, kitty litter also works.

Hand Cleaner

If you do not wear gloves you will probably want a good hand cleaner (*Figure 6.56*). Many automotive hand cleaners can be rubbed on and wiped off without water.

Figure 6.56   **Hand Cleaners**

Specialty Tools

Specialty tools encompass a wide range of hand tools and testing instruments. Some specialty tools are used for only one purpose. Technicians commonly have many specialty tools which include part pullers, hydraulic presses, tap and die sets, pneumatic tools, slide hammers, scan tools, and the list goes on. If you plan to become a professional technician you will need to learn more about the tools that will make your work possible.

Vehicle Service Manuals

You may find as you perform more complicated repair procedures that you need a reference guide with information specific to your vehicle. Vehicle specific service information is available in books, CDs, online, and at some public libraries. This section focuses on:

- Online Service Manuals
- Consumer Service Manuals
- Professional Service Manuals

Online Service Manuals

Many auto repair centers now subscribe to online service manuals. Online manuals have the benefit of taking up less space with everything accessible through a computer station. Another benefit is that these manuals are constantly updated.

Consumer Service Manuals

Most individuals who do some of their own mechanic work may eventually purchase a general service and repair manual for their vehicle. These independently published manuals cover a vehicle through a range of years, makes, and models in a condensed format. They are written for the average auto owner and often contain detailed photos (*Figure 6.57*) for a specific vehicle. Haynes and Chilton manuals are the most well known. They are sold online and at most automotive parts stores. If the information needed can't be found in this type of manual, then a professional service manual should be considered.

Figure 6.57   *Consumer Service Manual*

Professional Service Manuals

Each professional service manual, often containing several volumes, is specific to one year of a vehicle make and model (*Figure 6.58*). They cover almost every component and system with detailed illustrations, diagnostic checks, wiring diagrams, and step-by-step repair procedures.

Figure 6.58   *Professional Service Manuals*

Summary

Quality tools can be expensive, but having the right tool can make a difficult job easier. Use fixed sized wrenches and sockets instead of pliers to tightly grip nuts and bolts. When torque precision is necessary, use a torque wrench. A ratchet and socket will speed up the process of tightening or loosening a fastener. Start off with a basic tool set and then periodically add more specialized tools as you see a need and as your budget permits. Remember that caring for and cleaning your tools will help them last longer. Having the proper tools makes working on a vehicle easier, faster, and ultimately more enjoyable.

🚗 Activities

Basic Tools

- Basic Tools Activity
- Chapter 6 Study Questions

Activities can be accessed in the Auto Upkeep workbook or online at www.autoupkeep.com.

🎓 Career Paths

Tool Design Engineer

Education: Bachelor's Degree
Median Income: $52,000
Job Market: Average Growth
Abilities: Apply math, science, technology, and ingenuity to solve technical problems.

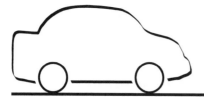

CHAPTER 7

AUTO CARE AND CLEANING

FUEL FOR THOUGHT
- What is the difference between a basecoat and a clearcoat finish?
- Why is it not recommended to wash a vehicle's finish with dish soap?
- Why is it so important to keep your windows clean?

Introduction

Some people say that when their vehicle is clean it actually runs better. With today's fast paced society, many people take their vehicle to a detail center or a car wash instead of doing the work themselves. If you do, look for facilities that recycle and filter their waste water. Detailing a car personally, however, can be very rewarding and can save money. The appearance of a vehicle does not actually change its performance, but it does improve its longevity. A vehicle that is kept clean inside and out will surely render a better value at trade-in time. Always conserve water by using a spray nozzle to control the flow and use cleaning products that are environmentally safe.

✓ Tech Tip

High Pressure Car Washes
Today the most popular automatic car washes are touchless, using high-pressure nozzles to clean a vehicle. This high pressure is hard on a vehicle's finish if the paint is already peeling or flaking. To be on the safe side, wash your vehicle by hand.

Objectives

Upon completion of this chapter and activities, you will be able to:
- Identify different automotive finishes.
- Explain the importance of washing, drying, and waxing a vehicle.
- Explain the importance of cleaning the inside of a vehicle.
- Correctly clean a vehicle inside and out.

Automotive Finishes

Up until the 1980s, most vehicles had a basecoat finish where the color was the topcoat. When waxing, the rag used would actually turn the color of the vehicle. The oxidized coat of paint would come off revealing a fresh layer. Automotive finishes have advanced significantly. The finish used on most vehicles today is a clearcoat finish. In this type of finish the color of the vehicle, the basecoat, is covered with a clearcoat that contains no color pigment. This extra layer adds protection and appearance to the basecoat. When waxing this type of finish, the rag does not turn the pigmented color because the oxidized layer is on the clearcoat.

Exterior Care and Cleaning

A vehicle's exterior has to withstand extreme conditions from the environment. Intense sun, road dirt, rain, dust, mud, snow, ice, and salt are all harsh elements. This section focuses on:

- Washing
- Removing Bugs and Tar
- Wheel Care
- Drying
- Polishing
- Waxing
- Trim Detailing

Washing

Keeping the finish clean is the first step in maintaining a vehicle's shine and endurance. If you brush up against a dirty vehicle you could scratch the finish. Do not wash a vehicle while it is hot. Park in the shade and hose off any loose dirt by rinsing the vehicle from the roof down. Don't neglect the wipers, wheel wells, and wheels. As you are washing keep your mitt clean to avoid scratching the finish. Use only approved car wash soap (*Figure 7.1*). Car wash soap is formulated to float away dirt and grime without harming the finish. Dish detergents are not chemically designed for vehicle finishes. They may strip the wax and dry out the finish, so don't use them. After washing an area rinse the soap off before it dries. To avoid water spots keep the vehicle's finish wet until you are ready to dry it.

Removing Bugs and Tar

Bug and road tar removers come in wipes, aerosol cans, gels, spray bottles, and pour bottles. Often you only have to apply the product, wait as directed, and wipe it off with a shop towel. Stubborn spots may require rubbing. Follow instructions on the product. Depending on the brand, bug and tar remover may strip the wax off the paint. After using bug and tar remover, wash the area with car wash soap, rinse, dry, and then apply a new coat of wax.

Wheel Care

Use a soft brush, cloth, or sponge to scrub the tire walls and rims. It is best to clean your wheels last to avoid contaminating the wash bucket with dirt that can scratch your vehicle's finish. Special tire and whitewall cleaners and conditioners (*Figure 7.2*) are available to protect your tires and can really make them shine.

Figure 7.2   *Tire Care Products*

Figure 7.1   *Car Wash Soap, Bucket, and Mitt*

❓ Q & A

Dirty Front Wheels

Q: Why do front wheels get dirty quicker?
A: When braking, a small amount of brake pad material wears off as dust and collects on your wheel or hubcap. The front brakes do more of the braking than the rear brakes, making them wear quicker. Also, if your car's rear brakes are drum style, the dust usually collects in the drum and then falls out on the backside of the wheel.

Drying

Water accelerates corrosion and hard water can leave damaging spots on a vehicle's finish. After washing, dry a vehicle with a clean microfiber detail towel or a super absorbent chamois (*Figure 7.3*). A chamois, usually made from sheepskin, will be hard and abrasive when dry, so wet it and ring it out first. Drag it across the finish to pull water off and then squeeze out the excess until the chamois is just damp. Make sure your chamois or detail towel remains clean to prevent scratches.

Figure 7.3   *Chamois*

It is also important to open the doors, trunk, and hood to wipe around them with a shop towel. Do not use a chamois or detail towel in these areas because you will pick up contaminants that were missed when you washed. Once the vehicle is dry you should evaluate the finish condition. Slide a clean, dry detail towel across your hood. If it does not glide effortlessly, then the finish should be waxed. Next move your finger along the paint, if it feels rough to the touch there are contaminants and oxidation on the surface. This roughness indicates that the finish also needs to be polished.

💰 Price Guide

Carnauba Wax
↳ $3.00 to $8.00 each bottle/can
Car Wash Soap
↳ $3.00 to $10.00 each bottle
Chamois
↳ $10.00 to $15.00 each
Synthetic Wax
↳ $5.00 to $15.00 each bottle
Touch Up Paint
↳ $3.00 to $15.00 each bottle

Polishing

Washing only removes surface dirt. To remove deeper oxidation, minor scratches, and old wax you many need to use a polish (*Figure 7.4*) or more aggressive rubbing compound before waxing. Polishes use abrasives and/or chemicals to rub off the very top layer of finish, so don't overuse them. On clearcoat finishes only use a polish that is specially formulated "clearcoat safe" and nonabrasive. If a polish rubbed between your fingers feels granular or gritty then it definitely contains abrasives and should not be used on a clearcoat finish. Always read the product label for specific recommendations.

Figure 7.4   *Polishing Compound*

🕐 Servicing

Care and Cleaning

*   Wash when dirty or every two weeks
*   Wax at least twice a year
*   Vacuum when dirty or every two weeks

❓ Q & A

Wax or Polish

Q: Is polish different from wax?
A: A polish removes minor scratches and oxidation by using special chemicals and abrasives. A wax is generally used after the car is polished to add a thin layer of protection over the vehicle's finish. Some cleaners combine a polish and wax into one product. However, a two step process using a polish first and then a wax generally produces a better overall finish.

Waxing

Waxing adds shine and enhances the look of a vehicle's finish, while also providing a final layer of protection from UV rays, pollution, and other damaging environmental conditions (*Figure 7.5*).

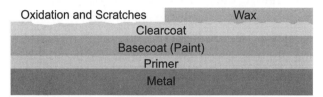

BEFORE WAX   **AFTER WAX**

Oxidation and Scratches	Wax
Clearcoat	
Basecoat (Paint)	
Primer	
Metal	

Figure 7.5   *Clearcoat Finish Layers with Wax*

Carnauba, a natural wax, tends to shed water by making the water bead and run off. Some synthetic waxes add an extra agent like silicone polymers to increase the slickness, shedding water even better. Water contacting waxed finishes slides right off, allowing a vehicle to dry much faster. The less time water and impurities sit on a vehicle's finish, the less chance they have to contribute to corrosion and oxidation. Some "cleaner waxes" (*Figure 7.6*) are also formulated to remove oxidation and minor scratches more gently than polish.

Figure 7.6   **Cleaner Wax**

Like washing, you should never apply wax on a hot vehicle or in direct sunlight. Remember to read the labels on the wax container for specific application information. Make sure the wax that you buy is suitable for your car's finish (*Figure 7.7*). Some waxes are safe for both basecoat and clearcoat finishes, others are not. Pure wax for a clearcoat finish should be nonabrasive.

Figure 7.7   **Automotive Waxes**

Trim Detailing

Once you are done waxing your vehicle's finish it is time to focus on detailing your mirrors, plastic accessories, and metal trim pieces. There are many different kinds of polishes (*Figure 7.8*) and dressings available, so find the ones appropriate for your vehicle.

Figure 7.8   **Metal Polish**

✓ Tech Tip

Wash Before You Wax

To avoid scratching the finish with dirt and trapping dust in fresh wax always wash your vehicle before you wax it, even if it looks clean.

❓ Q & A

Gasoline on Paint

Q: Will gas spilled on a car's finish damage it?
A: Gas may strip the wax, which could eventually lead to fading in that area. You should wash the area right away and wax it. Waxing will help to maintain the shine and protect the finish.

Interior Care and Cleaning

This section focuses on:
- Windows
- Vacuuming
- Upholstery Cleaning
- Stain Treatment
- Surface Protection

Windows

Dirty windows can lead to unsafe driving. At night, windows that have a film over them glare. Use an auto-approved glass cleaner that resists streaks. Old newspapers, lint free cloths, or microfiber cloths work well for wiping glass cleaner off windows. While you are cleaning, you should clean the rearview mirror too. If you have custom tinted windows where the tint is not part of the glass, do not use a window cleaner that contains ammonia. Using a windshield treatment product like Rain-X® (*Figure 7.9*) on the outside of the windshield can smooth the surface of the glass and repel water, providing protection similar to wax on a vehicle's finish. Wipers moving across a windshield that is smooth are less likely to skip.

Figure 7.9   ***Rain-X® Windshield Treatment***

Vacuuming

Vacuuming (*Figure 7.10*) cleans the inside of the vehicle. This includes vacuuming the carpet, floor mats, seats, headliner, door panels, and trunk. Dirty fabric will wear out quicker than clean fabric. Dirt accelerates wear by grinding away at the material's fibers.

Figure 7.10   ***Automotive Vacuum***

Upholstery Cleaning

Fabric, vinyl, leather, and carpet needs to be cleaned periodically with an interior or upholstery cleaner (*Figure 7.11*), even if there are no stains. Vacuuming will not remove all of the dirt that gets trapped in your upholstery and carpet fibers. Use fabric cleaners made for your vehicle's materials and follow the manufacturer's labels. Remember to use fresh rags frequently to help lift the dirt away. You might consider using a power carpet or steam cleaner.

Figure 7.11   ***Upholstery Cleaner***

Stain Treatment

Not all treatment products should be used on all stains and materials. Try to identify your vehicle's upholstery or carpet fabric and what caused the stain. Leather is especially unique. Find a product that best fits your stain and material. Follow the product instructions, which usually includes testing the product first in a hidden area to avoid potential discoloration problems. Without spreading the stain any further remove any loose material with a vacuum, brush, or clean rag. Blot the stain (*Figure 7.12*) with a white paper towel or clean white rag to draw the stain out. Apply the stain remover as directed. Repetition may be needed to lift the stain. Finally clean the whole area. If you only spot treat the stain the surrounding area may appear dirty afterward.

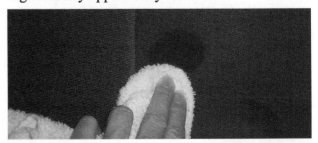

Figure 7.12   ***Blot the Stain***

Surface Protection

It is also important to wipe down and condition interior vinyl, plastic, and rubber components, because they have a tendency to dry out. Specially formulated interior protectants (*Figure 7.13*) are safe for most types of vinyl, plastic, and rubber, but always read the manufacturer's labels. Leather should also be conditioned with the appropriate product. Use cotton swabs to get into those hard to reach areas like vents. *Warning: To avoid hazardous driving conditions, do not use surface protectants on the driving controls (pedals, shifter, and steering wheel) or floor mats.*

Figure 7.13   **Interior Protectants**

Web Links

Automotive Care Sites

Armor All Products
↳   www.armorall.com
Dupli-Color Automotive Paints
↳   www.duplicolor.com
Radiator Specialty Company - Gunk
↳   www.gunk.com
Martin Senour Automotive Finishes
↳   www.martinsenour-autopaint.com
Mothers Polishes-Waxes-Cleaners
↳   www.mothers.com
Nu Finish
↳   www.nufinish.com
STP
↳   www.stp.com
Turtle Wax Inc.
↳   www.turtlewax.com

Engine Compartment Cleaning

Make sure the engine is cool before cleaning in the engine compartment. Spray an engine cleaner or an all purpose cleaner like Simple Green® (*Figure 7.14*) on a rag and then wipe down the surfaces. Do not spray the cleaner directly on engine components. Today's cars have lots of wires, connectors, and fuse blocks in the engine compartment. Moisture will cause damage to the electrical components. Again, spray the cleaner on a rag and then wipe. Take your time. After everything is clean, spray a product like Armor All® on a rag and wipe the rubber and plastic components. Don't use a hose or pressure washer to spray the engine. If your vehicle's engine compartment is dirty beyond wiping, it is best to take it to a professional engine cleaner.

Courtesy of www.gunk.com

Figure 7.14   **Cleaners for Engine Compartment**

❓ Q & A

Pressure Washing an Engine

Q: Why did my check engine light come on after I pressure washed my engine?

A: Pressure washing an engine without properly covering all electrical connectors, fuse blocks, and sensors can cause a variety of problems. The force from the pressure washer may have caused water to get into some of the wiring connectors or sensors. If water is in a connector it may be shorting out the electrical component or giving false voltage signals to the car's computer, which could trigger the check engine light.

Finish Repair

While cleaning the finish of your vehicle you may have noticed a scratch, chip, or dent. With a little bit of effort and know-how you can keep these imperfections from being so noticeable, while also preserving your vehicle's finish. This section focuses on:

- Paintless Dent Repair
- Paint Chips and Scratches

Paintless Dent Repair

Paintless dent repair is a process that removes dents, dings, creases, and even hail damage up to the size of a football without effecting the paint. A technician goes behind the panel using special tools to work out the dent. No sanding or body filler is used with this technique. Paintless dent repair methods can be used if the paint has not been scratched or cracked. However, not all dents can be repaired using this method. Since paintless dent repair requires special tools and training it is probably best to leave this to the professionals, especially if the damaged area is located near an airbag sensor.

Paint Chips and Scratches

Your vehicle's paint color code can be located in various places. It is often on the certification label in the driver's side doorjamb. You should be able to find a small bottle (***Figure 7.15***) or pen of touch up paint to match the color code, along with rust remover, sanding pen, touch up primer, and clearcoat at an auto parts store or dealer.

Figure 7.15   *Touch Up Paint*

The following is a general procedure for repairing a chip or scratch (***Figure 7.16***). Complete each step of the repair process carefully and check your owner's manual for any specific suggestions.

Chip and Scratch Repair Procedure	
STEP 1	Start by removing any rust or flakes. A rust remover can be used to dissolve larger rust areas.

Figure 7.16a   **Rust Remover**

STEP 2	If you only have a small chip with surface rust, consider using a sanding pen. The tip of a sanding pen is small to minimize disturbing surrounding painted areas.

Figure 7.16b   **Sanding Pen**

STEP 3	Clean the area with soap and water. Allow time for it to completely dry.
STEP 4	If rust was removed or metal is exposed you need to apply primer for the new paint to bond properly. Allow the primer time to dry. Read the label.
STEP 5	Stir the touch up paint and test for a color match.
STEP 6	Apply the paint with the cap applicator. Do not apply too much at once. Use several thin coats if necessary to fill the chip or scratch. Allow each coat to dry before applying another coat.

Figure 7.16c   **Paint Cap Applicator**

STEP 7	When the paint is dry, if the original finish has a clearcoat, apply the clearcoat over the repaired area.
STEP 8	Once the area has dried completely (wait at least a couple of days) use a polishing compound to blend in the repaired area.
STEP 9	As a final step, protect the repaired area and the rest of your vehicle's finish by waxing.

Figure 7.16   **Chip and Scratch Repair**

Forgotten Part Lubrication

If you hate the sound of annoying squeaks and creaks when you open your door (*Figure 7.17*) or move your seat, then it is probably time to lubricate some of your vehicle's most often forgotten, but important moving parts.

Figure 7.17   *Door Hinge*

Lubrication helps to reduce wear, rust, and corrosion, while keeping moving parts operating smoothly (*Figure 7.18*).

Area	Lubrication Part
Doors	Hinges, Latches, Locks, and Weather-striping
Trunk	Hinges, Latch, Lock, and Weather-striping
Seat	Rails
Hood	Hinges, Latch, and Weather-striping
Fuel Door	Hinges

Figure 7.18   *Lubrication Locations*

If you are having difficulty releasing the hood latch (*Figure 7.19*) clean and then lubricate the latch mechanism.

Hood Latch Handle

Hood Latch Mechanism

Figure 7.19   *Hood Latch*

There are various types of lubricant products such as motor oil, WD-40®, 3-In-One® oil, silicone spray, silicone paste, and lithium lubricants (*Figure 7.20*), so check your owner's manual to see what is recommended for your vehicle. Read product labels for exact procedures and applications. Before applying lubrication wipe off any dirt from the area. After application be sure to clean up any excess lubricant.

Figure 7.20   *Lubricants*

Summary

Keeping a vehicle clean is not difficult; it just takes a little time. Washing, waxing, and vacuuming will make your vehicle worth more and make it more appealing to drive and own. Finishes on vehicles have changed over time from basecoats to basecoat/clearcoats. Clearcoats add a deeper shine and a more durable finish. By spending a little extra time on paint repair and forgotten part lubrication you can keep your vehicle looking good and functioning properly. Most importantly control the environmental impact by selecting bio-degradable cleaners and learning local laws regarding washing cars at home.

ᗕᑐ **Activities**

Auto Care and Cleaning

- Interior Cleaning Activity
- Exterior Cleaning Activity
- Waxing Activity
- Chapter 7 Study Questions

Activities can be accessed in the Auto Upkeep workbook or online at www.autoupkeep.com.

🎓 **Career Paths**

Collision Repair Technician

Education: Technical Training or ASE Cert.
Median Income: $35,000
Job Market: Average Growth
Abilities: Detail oriented and fast learner. Math, reading, and computer literate.

CHAPTER 8

FLUID LEVEL CHECK

FUEL FOR THOUGHT

- Why is it best to check engine oil when the engine is cold?
- What fluids should be checked on an automobile?
- How can you use the color of a fluid to your advantage?

Introduction

Fluids provide cooling, cleaning, lubricating, and sealing to vehicle components. Components of various systems take different types of fluids. The do-it-yourselfer can maintain the different systems by simply checking fluid levels and conditions. When checking any fluid, it is important to park on a level surface. This chapter will guide you through checking and adding fluids to vehicle components.

Objectives

Upon completion of this chapter and activities, you will be able to:

- Identify different types of fluids used in the automobile.
- Analyze fluid conditions.
- Perform basic fluid level checks.

🕐 Servicing

All Fluid Level Checks

- Check all fluids at oil change intervals
- Check oil level every gas fill up

Types of Fluids

It is critical that you check the owner's manual for the correct type of fluid that is recommended for your specific vehicle. The most common fluids (*Figure 8.1*) that automobile owners need to check are:

- Windshield Washer Fluid
- Engine Oil
- Transmission Fluid
- Coolant
- Brake Fluid
- Clutch Fluid (Manual transmissions only)
- Differential Fluid
- Power Steering Fluid
- Battery Electrolyte (Maintenance style batteries only)

✓ Tech Tip

Leaking Fluids

Most fluids have distinct colors. Use this to your advantage. If you see your vehicle leaving a leak on the ground, note its color, texture, and position under the vehicle. This may lead you to the component that is failing.

Windshield
Washer Fluid

Power Steering
Fluid

Coolant Recovery
Tank

Brake
Fluid

Engine Oil
Fill Cap

Automatic
Transmission
Fluid
Dipstick

Radiator
Pressure Cap

Engine Oil
Dipstick

Battery Electrolyte
Cell Caps

Figure 8.1   ***Engine Compartment Common Fluid Locations***

Windshield Washer Fluid

Windshield washer fluid (***Figure 8.2***), usually blue in color, is an easy fluid to check. It is specially formulated to clean road grime from the windshield and to not freeze. Do not use only water. If the temperature drops below 32ºF (0ºC) and the water freezes, you will risk cracking the windshield washer fluid reservoir and pump. It could also freeze on your windshield.

Figure 8.2   ***Windshield Washer Fluid***

Do not confuse this reservoir with the coolant recovery tank – they often look similar. Never use cooling system antifreeze as it is not made for window cleaning and can damage a vehicle's

finish. The cap on a windshield washer fluid reservoir usually has a wiper symbol engraved on it (***Figure 8.3***). To add windshield washer fluid, locate the cap and fill until the fluid almost reaches the top. When adding windshield washer fluid, take a moment to inspect the windshield wipers. The wipers should be soft and without cracks. If the wipers are streaking or skipping across the windshield they need to be replaced. See page 170 for more information on replacing wiper blades.

Figure 8.3   *Windshield Washer Fluid Reservoir*

Engine Oil

An important fluid to check is engine oil (*Figure 8.4*) because it cools, cleans, lubricates, and seals the internal engine components. Clean engine oil is gold in color, while dirty engine oil is black. Common multigrade engine oils are 5W-20, 5W-30, and 10W-30, but always refer to the your owner's manual because there are many different viscosities and brands available. Synthetic and semi-synthetic oils are also available. Some new vehicles come with synthetic oil from the factory.

Figure 8.4   **5W-20 Engine Oil Bottle**

To check the engine oil, shut off the engine, apply the parking brake, open the hood, and look for the engine oil dipstick. To get an accurate reading it is best to check the engine oil when the engine is cold. The engine oil dipstick runs through a metal tube that is usually located on the side of the engine on rear-wheel drive vehicles or on the

❓ Q & A

When to Add Oil

Q: Should I wait to add oil until it reaches the ADD mark?

A: Keep the oil at the full mark. If you allow the engine to get to the ADD mark and your engine only holds four quarts of oil, you are running the engine oil 25% low. Keeping the oil at the full mark helps in lubrication, dispenses contaminants through a larger volume of oil, and disperses heat more efficiently. Be sure not to overfill the crankcase. Engine oil contains detergents to help clean the engine. Too much oil causes foam (air bubbles) to form if the crankshaft whips the oil, lessening lubricating qualities.

front of the engine on front-wheel drive vehicles (*Figure 8.5*). Refer to your owner's manual if you have questions on the location of the engine oil dipstick. Pull out the dipstick, wipe it off with a paper towel, reinsert it completely into the tube, remove again, and note the reading.

Figure 8.5   **Engine Oil Dipstick**

The engine oil should be in the safe range (*Figure 8.6*). Most automotive engines have an oil capacity between four to five quarts (3.8 to 4.7 L). Vehicle manufacturers suggest adding oil when the engine is low one quart (≈1 L).

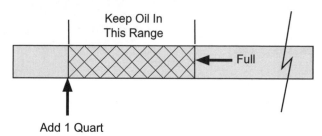

Figure 8.6   **Engine Oil Dipstick Reading**

To add engine oil, locate the oil filler cap (*Figure 8.7*) on the engine valve cover. Use a clean funnel to add the correct amount of engine oil. Give the engine oil time to flow to the oil pan. Recheck the level and correct if necessary. Do not overfill.

Figure 8.7   **Engine Oil Cap**

🚚 Trouble Guide

Excessive Oil Consumption

- Broken or worn piston rings
- Worn valve guides or seals
- Improper oil viscosity
- PCV problems

Transmission Fluid

Both automatic and manual transmissions have fluid to cool, clean, lubricate, and seal internal components. Clean automatic transmission fluid (ATF) is pinkish-red. The most common type is Dexron/Mercon® (*Figure 8.8*), but always refer to the manufacturer's recommendations.

Figure 8.8   *Automatic Transmission Fluid*

It is usually recommended to check the fluid level in an automatic transmission while it is hot. Drive the vehicle about ten minutes to warm up the transmission. To receive accurate results, most manufacturers recommend that the engine be running and that the gear selector be in park. Apply the parking brake. Locate the automatic transmission oil dipstick (*Figure 8.9*). With the engine idling, pull out the dipstick, wipe it off with a paper towel, reinsert it completely into the tube, remove again, and note the reading.

Figure 8.9   *Automatic Transmission Dipstick*

The transmission fluid should be between the full cold and the full hot marks (*Figure 8.10*). If low, use a clean funnel to pour the fluid directly into the tube. Do not overfill. It usually takes only one pint (which is ½ quart or 0.47 L) of fluid to bring the fluid level from the full cold to the full hot mark. Recheck the level and add more if necessary.

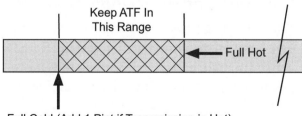

Figure 8.10   *Automatic Transmission Reading*

On a manual transmission there is usually a plug (*Figure 8.11*) on the side of the transmission housing under the vehicle. To check the fluid level you must turn the engine off, apply the parking brake, clean around the area, and then remove the plug with a wrench. The fluid should be level to the plug hole bottom. Manual transmissions take ATF, heavyweight/high-viscosity (e.g., SAE 75W-90, 75W-140, 80W-90, 80W-140, 85W-140) gear oil, or motor oil. Check your owner's manual for specifications. Fill as necessary. You may need a special adapter that fits on the bottle to transfer the fluid.

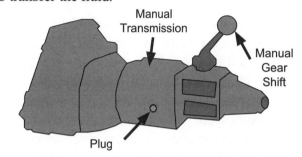

Figure 8.11   *Manual Transmission Plug*

Although a continuously variable transmission (CVT) is a type of automatic transmission, the method for checking this fluid varies. Some CVTs have a dipstick, some have two plugs, while others have three plugs. If your CVT has plugs instead of a dipstick, you need to find the fill/level plug. On plug types, the fluid should be level to the bottom of the plug hole threads (*Figure 8.12*). Review your owner's manual or contact your dealer for fluid checking and filling instructions. If the recommended CVT fluid is a proprietary formula, specific to your vehicle's make and model, you may have to buy it from the dealer. If you take your vehicle in for service, make sure the recommended CVT fluid is added. Do not assume that standard ATF is adequate for a CVT.

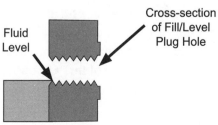

Figure 8.12   *Correct Fluid Level Check*

Coolant

Coolant (antifreeze) comes in various colors: green, orange, red, pink, yellow, and bluish-green. The most common colors are green and orange. The standard antifreeze used in vehicles before 1995 was green in color. In 1995, General Motors started using an extended life coolant, called Dex-Cool, in their engines. Dex-Cool, orange in color, was originally manufactured by Havoline for General Motors. Today, several other coolant manufacturers produce extended life coolants. Some vehicles use special coolants, so check your owner's manual for recommendations. Corrosion and head gasket damage can occur if the incorrect coolant is used. Both standard (green) antifreeze and Dex-Cool (orange) antifreeze are glycol based. The main difference between the two types of antifreeze is in the rust inhibitors and additives. Ethylene glycol, which is used in standard and extended life coolants, is a toxic substance. You may consider purchasing Quick Fill premixed or safer LowTox coolants (*Figure 8.13*).

Figure 8.13   *LowTox and Premix Coolants*

❓ Q & A

Antifreeze or Engine Coolant

Q: What is the difference between antifreeze and engine coolant?
A: Antifreeze and engine coolant are commonly used interchangeably. Antifreeze is the actual product that is added to water to make engine coolant. Generally a 50% water to 50% antifreeze is the most common mixture for freeze and boilover protection used in engines.

When checking coolant level, the engine must be cool. First, check the level in the coolant recovery tank (*Figure 8.14*), also known as an expansion tank. The recovery tank is usually translucent with a "full cold" and a "full hot" mark. If adding, remove the cap and add a 50% water to 50% antifreeze mixture.

Figure 8.14   *Coolant Recovery Tank*

Second, check the level in the radiator. This requires removing a cool radiator cap (*Figure 8.15*) and looking into the radiator. *Warning: Never remove a hot radiator cap – severe burns could result.* The fluid should be at or near the top. Add a 50/50 mixture as needed. Reinstall the cap. *Note: On some engines the pressure cap is on the coolant recovery tank.*

Figure 8.15   *Radiator Cap*

✓ Tech Tip

Environmentally Friendly Coolant

Ethylene glycol based coolants are toxic and can be fatal to animals if ingested. Some coolant manufacturers are formulating more environmentally friendly coolants. Antifreezes that are propylene glycol based are safer if spilled or accidentally ingested.

Brake Fluid

Brake fluid (*Figure 8.16*) provides the transfer of hydraulic pressure to the wheels. Clean brake fluid is clear in color (except DOT 5, which is often dyed purple). The most common type of brake fluid is DOT 3, but DOT 4, DOT 5, and DOT 5.1 are also available. Always refer to your manufacturer's recommendations because brake system damage can occur with the incorrect type. *Warning: Use extreme caution when handling. Brake fluid is harmful to your eyes and if spilled on a vehicle's finish, it will strip paint.*

Figure 8.16   *Brake Fluids*

The brake master cylinder that houses the fluid is usually mounted on the driver's side firewall in the engine compartment. Most vehicles today have a plastic translucent reservoir (*Figure 8.17*) with a "min" and "max" line. Some fluid level drop may be normal. As the brake pads wear the level will fall as more fluid fills the brake caliper pistons or wheel cylinders. To add brake fluid, park on a level surface, turn the engine off, clean around the cap and reservoir, remove the cap, and add as necessary. When reinstalling the cap, make sure that the rubber gasket seats properly.

❓ Q & A

Brake Fluid Mix-Up

Q: I poured windshield wiper fluid in my brake fluid reservoir. What should I do?
A: If you have not driven or pressed on your brakes you may be able to replace the fluid just at the brake master cylinder. However, if you have driven your vehicle, your braking system will need to be flushed (all of the brake fluid completely removed) and refilled. If contaminated fluid is left in the braking system, it could end up ruining brake components – leading to brake failure. To be on the safe side, have the vehicle towed to your dealer, tell them what you did, and get their recommendation.

Clutch Fluid

Vehicles that have manual transmissions with hydraulic clutches have a clutch master cylinder fluid reservoir. It is usually mounted next to the brake master cylinder (*Figure 8.18*). Clutch fluid is commonly DOT 3 brake fluid, but always check your owner's manual. To check the clutch fluid, turn the engine off and look through the translucent reservoir. It should be at or near the top. To add clutch fluid, park on a level surface, turn off the engine, remove the cap, and add as necessary. When reinstalling the cap, make sure that the rubber gasket seats properly.

Figure 8.17   *Brake Fluid Reservoir*

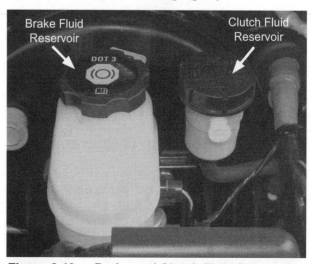

Figure 8.18   *Brake and Clutch Fluid Reservoirs*

Differential Fluid

Rear and front axle housings, which contain the axles and differential gears, also require fluid. This fluid check is performed on rear-wheel drive (RWD) and four-wheel drive (4WD) vehicles. The process is similar to checking manual transmission fluid. Remove the check plug (*Figure 8.19*), check the level, and fill as necessary. On most vehicles the oil should be at the bottom of the plug hole, but check your owner's manual for the required level.

Check Plug

Figure 8.19   *Axle Housing Check Plug*

Gear oil (e.g., SAE 75W-90, 75W-140, 80W-90, 80W-140, 85W-140) is the most common differential fluid (*Figure 8.20*). Some differentials use limited slip additives. Always check your owner's manual for the specific fluid.

Figure 8.20   *Gear Oil*

✓ Tech Tip

Fluid Specification Requirements

Do not add fluid unless you are sure the fluid meets the specification requirements as stated in the owner's manual. Adding incorrect fluids could void manufacturer's warranties and lead to premature component failures.

Power Steering Fluid

Most vehicles today have power steering. The power steering pump is located off an engine drive belt. The cap and the dipstick are commonly one unit (*Figure 8.21*). The stick usually has a full hot and a full cold line.

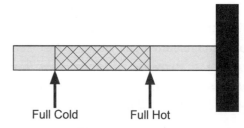

Full Cold   Full Hot

Figure 8.21   *Power Steering Dipstick and Cap*

To check the fluid, shut off the engine, locate the power steering fluid reservoir (*Figure 8.22*), remove the dipstick, wipe it off, reinstall, remove again, and note the reading.

Figure 8.22   *Power Steering Fluid Reservoir*

Using a clean funnel, add fluid as necessary. Power steering fluid (*Figure 8.23*) can be clear, gold, or red. Check your owner's manual for specifications.

Figure 8.23   *Power Steering Fluid*

Battery Electrolyte

The electrolyte in a lead acid battery is a mixture of sulfuric acid and distilled water. On some vehicles the battery is sealed so the electrolyte cannot be checked. Refer to your owner's manual or read the top of the battery to determine if it is a maintenance or maintenance-free battery. On maintenance batteries some of the water may evaporate over time. To check the electrolyte level, take off your rings and watch, put on safety goggles and gloves, and then remove the cell caps (*Figure 8.24*). Shine a flashlight into the cells and inspect the level in each cell.

Cell Cap   Cell Cap

Figure 8.24   *Battery Cell Caps*

Commonly a split ring indicator in each cell identifies the correct electrolyte level. Add only distilled water to any cell that is low, making all cell levels equal. Be sure the electrolyte covers the plates. Do not overfill. Replace the caps.

Warning: Wash hands thoroughly to remove any battery acid after removing gloves (Figure 8.25).

Figure 8.25   *Battery Warning Label on Cell Cap*

Summary

Fluids in the automobile have critical functions. Fluids that are neglected and run low for long periods of time add stress to components and can cause premature damage. Practice preventative maintenance by checking fluid levels frequently. Always refer to your owner's manual to identify the correct type of fluid for your specific vehicle. Using incorrect fluids can harm vital systems and could cause a hazardous situation while driving. Most of the fluids used in automobiles are toxic. Antifreeze has a sweet taste to animals and can be fatal if ingested. Dispose of all fluids properly. Always wash your hands thoroughly after checking and adding fluids.

💰 Price Guide

Antifreeze
↳ $4.00 to $8.00 a gallon
Automatic Transmission Fluid (ATF)
↳ $1.50 to $2.50 a quart
Brake Fluid/Clutch Fluid
↳ $1.50 to $3.00 a 12 oz. bottle
Distilled Water
↳ $0.50 to $1.50 a gallon
Manual Transmission Fluid/Differential Fluid
↳ $2.00 to $4.00 a quart
Oil
↳ $1.00 to $2.50 a quart
Power Steering Fluid
↳ $1.50 to $3.00 a pint
Windshield Washer Fluid
↳ $1.00 to $2.00 a gallon

Note:
1 gal = 3.785 L
1 qt = 0.946 L
1 pt = 0.473 L
12 oz = 0.355 L

🚗 Activities

Fluid Level Check

- Fluid Level Check Activity
- Chapter 8 Study Questions

Activities can be accessed in the Auto Upkeep workbook or online at www.autoupkeep.com.

🎓 Career Paths

Quick Lube Technician

Education: Technical Training or Experience
Median Income: $22,000
Job Market: Average Growth
Abilities: Time management, customer service skills, and basic hands-on maintenance experience.

CHAPTER 9

ELECTRICAL SYSTEM

FUEL FOR THOUGHT
- What is the purpose of an automotive battery?
- What is the difference between voltage, current, and resistance?
- Why is it important to replace a blown fuse with the correct amperage rating?

Introduction

The automotive electrical system consists of wires, lights, motors, circuits, fuses, relays, and switches. Even though the electrical system is extremely complex, there are still many repairs that you can do without taking your vehicle to a service facility. A simple thing like a headlight burning out can stop you from driving safely down the road. This chapter provides the basics on how to maintain, test, and repair electrical system components.

Objectives

Upon completion of this chapter and activities, you will be able to:
- Define electricity in terms of voltage, current, and resistance.
- Identify and describe the components in the starting and charging system.
- Explain battery performance ratings.
- Identify the importance of fuses in the electrical system.
- Test the starter and alternator.
- Clean and test a battery safely.

Electrical Terms

Electricity is defined as the movement of electrons in a conductor. Copper is a well known conductor. Electrons orbit the nucleus of an atom much like the moon goes around the earth. Electricity flows through a conductor, which is usually in the form of a wire covered by an insulator (*Figure 9.1*). An insulator, such as plastic, is something that restricts the flow of electrons. Before discussing the electrical system, you need to be able to identify and describe three main terms:
- Voltage
- Current
- Resistance

Figure 9.1   ***Cross-section of Stranded Wire***

Voltage

A volt is the measure of voltage or pressure pushing electrons. Compare this to a faucet in your home. When the faucet is off there is still potential to flow, but the valve holds back the pressure. Voltage is the electrical pressure that causes current to flow. In technical terms, one volt is the amount of pressure required to move one ampere of current through a resistance of one ohm. (Amps and ohms will be discussed later.) Most vehicles have 12-volt systems, while most homes have 120-volt systems. Another difference in most home and vehicle electrical systems is the current. Automotive batteries provide DC (Direct Current) while homes use AC (Alternating Current).

Current

Amperage is the unit used to measure electrical current. Current can be described as the quantity of electrons moving through a conductor. There are two types of electrical current: Direct Current (DC) and Alternating Current (AC). In DC systems the electrons are moving through the conductor in one direction. In AC systems the electrons change direction at a given rate. The alternator in a vehicle generates AC, but then converts the current to DC to recharge the battery.

Resistance

An ohm (Ω) is a measure of electrical resistance. The resistance in a circuit is usually a load such as a light, radio, electrical motor, or sensor. For example, there needs to be resistance in the filament of a light bulb for it to produce light. Ohm's Law shows the direct relationship between volts, amps, and ohms. Ohm's law states Voltage = Current x Resistance. This simple mathematical equation can be used to find any unknown variable if the other two variables are known.

> ▤ **Calculations**
>
> **Ohm's Law Formula (E = I x R)**
> Voltage (E) = Current (I) x Resistance (R)

Battery

A vehicle battery stores chemical energy, supplies electrical energy to the starter when the engine is cranking, and supplements the alternator in running accessories (e.g., lights and radio). The battery is the heart of the electrical system with primary functions in the starting, charging, and ignition systems. This section focuses on:

- 12-Volt Systems
- Battery Style
- CCA and CA Performance Ratings
- Battery Maintenance
- Higher Voltage Systems

12-Volt Systems

Most automotive batteries are lead acid 12-volt DC. Each of the six cells in a 12-volt DC battery produces 2 to 2.1 volts. A fully charged 12-volt battery will actually have approximately 12.6 volts.

Battery Style

When purchasing an automotive battery it is important to identify the correct battery for your vehicle. Many new batteries have top and side dual mount systems (*Figure 9.2*). Check to see how your old battery mounts in your vehicle and make sure the new one mounts safely. Batteries commonly last about five years.

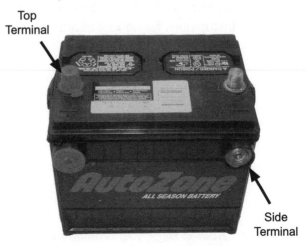

Top Terminal

Side Terminal

Figure 9.2   *Dual Mount Battery*

CCA and CA Performance Ratings

Besides being the correct physical size, a battery must meet the amperage requirements to start the engine and run accessories. When comparing batteries from different vendors make sure you are comparing the same type of rating. Battery manufacturers basically use two ratings: cold cranking amps (CCA) and cranking amps (CA) (*Figure 9.3*). A battery that is rated with cold cranking amps has been tested to deliver the specified number of amperes at 0ºF (-18ºC) for a duration of 30 seconds. A battery that is rated with cranking amps has been tested to deliver the specified number of amperes at 32ºF (0ºC) for a duration of 30 seconds.

Figure 9.3   *Battery Rating Label*

Battery Maintenance

Many permanently sealed maintenance-free lead acid batteries have a hydrometer built right into the battery casing. An indicator (*Figure 9.4*) on the top of the battery identifies a battery's charge condition. Instructions for understanding the indicator are usually next to the indicator window.

Figure 9.4   *Built-in Battery Hydrometer Indicator*

If a lead acid battery is not maintenance-free, use a hydrometer to check the battery electrolyte (*Figure 9.5*). See the Battery Activity for instructions on how to check the electrolyte.

State of Charge Electrolyte Temperature 80ºF (26.7ºC)	Approximate Specific Gravity	Volts	Approximate Electrolyte Freezing Point	
			ºF	(ºC)
100%	1.265	12.6	-77	(-67)
75%	1.225	12.4	-35	(-37)
50%	1.190	12.2	-10	(-23)
25%	1.155	12.0	5	(-15)
Discharged	≤ 1.120	≤ 11.7	20	(-7)

Figure 9.5   *Battery Electrolyte Readings*

Warning: Never recharge a battery that has a low electrolyte level or is frozen. Maintenance and maintenance-free batteries also need to have corrosion removed periodically. See page 169 for procedures on cleaning a battery and minimizing future corrosion.

Higher Voltage Systems

As electrical energy demands increase on cars, other higher voltage systems are beginning to appear, especially on hybrids. Some hybrids use Nickel Metal Hydride (NiMH) batteries with step up converters for even more volts (*Figure 9.6*). *Warning: Do not open NiMH batteries.* Automotive and battery manufacturers continue to develop and look toward more advanced technology to power hybrids, such as lithium-ion (Li-ion) batteries.

2007 Toyota Hybrid Vehicles	Voltage NiMH Battery	Electric Motor Max Voltage
Highlander	288V DC	650V
Prius	201.6V DC	500V
Camry	244.8V DC	650V

Figure 9.6   *High Voltage Hybrid Vehicles*

🚛 Trouble Guide

Common Starting Problems

- Discharged battery
- Corroded battery terminal
- Corroded electrical connections
- Worn out starter or solenoid
- Shorted circuit or broken wire

Starting System

The starting system (*Figure 9.7*) converts chemical energy (molecular energy) to electrical energy (electrons moving through a conductor) to mechanical energy (energy of motion). The starting system basically consists of five components:

- Battery
- Ignition Switch
- Solenoid
- Starter
- Park/Neutral Safety Switch

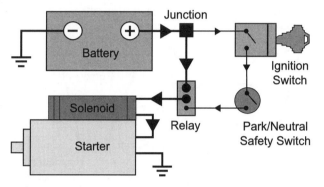

Figure 9.7 *Starting System Components*

Battery

In the starting system, the battery converts chemical energy to electrical energy when the operator closes the circuit by engaging the ignition switch to start the vehicle.

Ignition Switch

The ignition switch is turned (or on some newer vehicles pushed) to start a vehicle. The ignition switch completes the circuit, allowing electrical current to flow to the starter solenoid when it is in the start position.

✓ Tech Tip

Safe Starts

When parking always apply the parking brake. When starting, leave the parking brake on while also firmly pressing on the brake pedal to minimize the risk of the vehicle moving upon start-up. Also engage the clutch on manual transmission vehicles when starting.

Solenoid

A solenoid is an electromechanical switch. A small amount of current from the ignition switch energizes a coil in the solenoid creating a magnetic field. The magnetic field closes the circuit for a higher current to go from the battery to the starter. A solenoid that mounts directly on the starter mechanically engages the starter pinion gear with the engine's flywheel gear. Some starting systems utilize a starter relay. A relay, like a solenoid, needs a small amount of current to open and close a high current circuit.

Starter

Current from the solenoid travels to the starter. The starter (*Figure 9.8*) converts that electrical energy to mechanical energy which cranks over the engine. A small gear on the starter meshes with the engine's flywheel gear. The flywheel is connected to the crankshaft. The starter is usually mounted on the underside of the engine. As the starter turns the flywheel, the crankshaft turns and the pistons move up and down. This movement, along with air, fuel, and ignition, begins the combustion process.

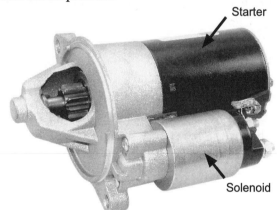

Figure 9.8 *Starter and Solenoid*

Park/Neutral Safety Switch

The park/neutral safety switch only allows current to flow in the starting system if the clutch is depressed (manual transmission) or if the gear is in park or neutral (automatic transmission) to prevent the vehicle from being started while in gear.

Charging System

The charging system (*Figure 9.9*) is somewhat a reverse of the starting system. The charging system converts mechanical energy to electrical energy to chemical energy. The charging system keeps the battery charged and provides power for a vehicle's electrical accessories. The main components of the charging system are:

- Battery
- Drive Belt
- Alternator
- Voltage Regulator
- Powertrain Control Module

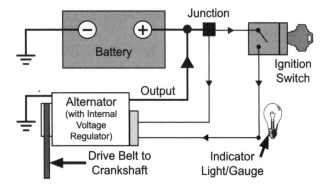

Figure 9.9   ***Charging System Components***

Battery

The battery is also part of the charging system. The battery converts electrical energy to chemical energy during charging and then converts chemical energy to electrical energy during starting. The battery stores energy for future use.

✓ Tech Tip

Buying New Belts

When buying a new belt check the following: the number of accessories the belt goes around, if it is "v" or serpentine, and if the old belt has factory numbers on it to assist in cross-referencing.

Drive Belt

The drive belt turns the pulley on the alternator. Sometimes also referred to as a fan belt, the drive belt may connect to other accessories such as the power steering pump, water pump, fan, air conditioning compressor, and air pump. A drive belt diagram is commonly located on an engine compartment label (*Figure 9.10*).

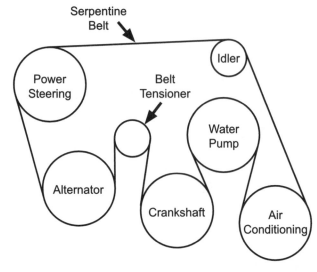

Figure 9.10   ***Example of Drive Belt Routing***

Belts come in two types: serpentine and "v". A serpentine belt (*Figure 9.11*), also called a multi-ribbed belt, is flat on one side and has grooves that run parallel with the belt on the other side.

❓ Q & A

Automatic Belt Tensioner

Q: I had to replace the serpentine belt twice in one year. What could be the problem?
A: The problem could be a worn automatic belt tensioner and/or idler pulley. The belt tensioner keeps the belt tight and vibrations to a minimum. If the bearing on the tensioner is worn, the belt may get out of alignment causing side wear and fraying. If the spring on the tensioner is worn, the belt can slip, glazing the belt's surface. Glazing leads to belt squealing.

Commonly, serpentine belts will have 2 to 8 grooves on one side. Serpentine belts are usually ½ to 1 inch (1.27 to 2.54 cm) wide depending on the number of grooves and automotive application.

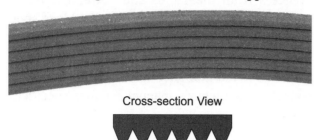

Cross-section View

Figure 9.11   *Serpentine Belt*

In contrast, a v-belt (***Figure 9.12***) is usually less than ½ inch (1.27 cm) in width and has a cross-section that looks like a "v".

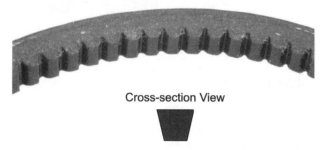

Cross-section View

Figure 9.12   *V-Belt*

Alternator

The drive belt rotates the alternator pulley, which then turns a shaft in the alternator. The alternator (***Figure 9.13***) converts mechanical energy to electrical energy. Initially it converts the electricity to alternating current (AC), but the end result is direct current (DC). Diodes are used in the alternator to make the conversion from AC to DC.

Figure 9.13   *Alternator*

⏱ Servicing

Replace Belts

- Serpentine belt 5 years/60,000 miles
- V-belt 4 years/48,000 miles

Voltage Regulator

The voltage regulator is commonly located in or near the alternator. It basically does what the name suggests; it regulates the electrical pressure (voltage). Common voltage from the regulator while the engine is running is 14.5 volts. If the regulator does not hold electrical pressure at or near 14.5 volts, the battery could be overcharged or undercharged by the alternator.

Powertrain Control Module

Newer vehicles may use computer regulation instead of a standard voltage regulator. Voltage regulated with a powertrain control module (PCM) or other control module is much more precise and efficient. The vehicle's computer will also be able to track problems for easier troubleshooting.

✓ Tech Tip

Buying a New Alternator

When buying a new alternator, check the following: number of accessories (e.g., power windows, rear window defrosters, power seats), the wiring hookup, type of pulley, and the amperage rating stamped on the housing.

🚛 Trouble Guide

Common Charging Problems

- Belt is torn, glazed, cracked, or loose
- Worn out alternator or regulator
- Shorted circuit or broken wire
- Corroded battery

Fuses

Fuses are used in electrical circuits to safeguard the vital components. A fuse has a sacrificial metal strip that will melt if too much current is trying to get to the intended load. A junction block, fuse panel, or electrical center containing fuses can be found under the hood, under the dash, on the driver's side edge of the instrument panel, or in the glove box. There may be more than one panel and some fuses may be in-line, especially on aftermarket installed accessories. Fusible links are also popular within automotive electrical circuits. A cover on the junction block often identifies the purpose of each fuse (***Figure 9.14***). If the cover is unclear, refer to your owner's manual for a fuse diagram. Always have the ignition key in the off position before working on any electrical component. This section focuses on:

- Fuse Types and Ratings
- Blown Fuse
- Flashers, Relays, and Circuit Breakers
- Fusible Links

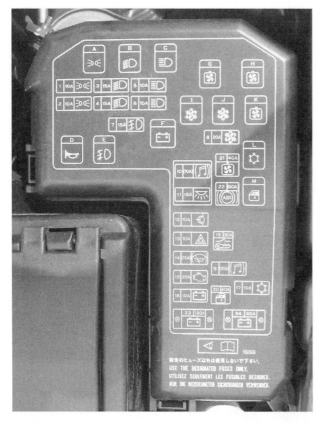

Figure 9.14   **Fuse Junction Block**

Fuse Types and Ratings

Fuses can be broken down into two types: glass cylinder and blade style (***Figure 9.15***). Most vehicles from the 1980s and newer use blade style fuses. Some vehicles use smaller blade style fuses called mini-fuses. Fuses are rated in amps such as: 3, 5, 10, 15, 20, 25, 30, etc. Maxi-fuses are often found in higher current circuits. Always consult your owner's manual for fuse specifications.

Glass Cylinder Style

Blade Style

Figure 9.15   **Automotive Fuses**

Blown Fuse

When experiencing an electrical problem the first and easiest check is to look for a blown fuse *(Figure 9.16)*. Look through the plastic part of the fuse to identify if it is blown. There is a wire filament in the fuse. If it is broken, you have found your problem. A fuse is rated so it is the weakest link in the electrical circuit to protect all of the components within that circuit. ***Warning: Never replace a blown fuse with a larger amperage rated fuse and never bypass the fuse completely by using a jumper wire or steel stock. Severe electrical damage could result.***

Sacrificial Strip

Blown Fuse

Figure 9.16   **Good and Burned Out Fuse**

Trouble Guide

Fuse Continues to Blow

- Shorted circuit
- Accessory pulling too much current
- Wrong fuse rating

Flashers, Relays, and Circuit Breakers

Electrical panels and junction blocks contain fuses, flashers, relays, and circuit breakers. Flashers are what cause turn signals and hazard lights to blink or flash. Flashers are classified into three types: thermal/bimetal (*Figure 9.17*), hybrid, and solid state/electronic.

Figure 9.17   *Thermal Flasher*

Relays are used to allow a small current to control a circuit requiring a high current. Headlights and other high current components may be on circuit breakers that can reset automatically after they have cooled (*Figure 9.18*). Like fuses, when any of these circuit components go bad, they should be replaced.

Relay   Fuse   Circuit Breaker

Figure 9.18   *Electrical Panel*

? Q & A

Turn Signal Flasher

Q: My turn signals don't flash on either side, but the bulbs are OK. What is wrong?
A: If your bulbs are OK, but don't flash, then the turn signal flasher may be faulty. Check your owner's manual for the location.

Fusible Links

Some circuits have fusible links. A fusible link is a type of circuit protector. It is a short piece of wire that has a smaller diameter than the rest of the circuit. If too much current runs through the circuit, the wire overheats and melts, opening the circuit. When a circuit is open, no electricity can flow. The fusible link has a nonflammable insulation that bubbles to indicate to the technician that it has blown.

✓ Tech Tip

Orange Cables

Cables that are orange carry high voltage. Be extra careful around them. For safety the high voltage system integrity is monitored by sensors and the computer constantly. If there is a malfunction, problem, or an airbag deploys the high voltage supply cuts off. *Warning: Do not work on or near the high voltage system. High voltage can kill.*

💰 Price Guide

Alternator
↳ $30.00 to $150.00
Battery 12-volt DC
↳ $40.00 to $80.00
Drive Belt "V"
↳ $4.00 to $10.00
Drive Belt Serpentine
↳ $20.00 to $40.00
Fuse
↳ $0.50 to $3.00 each
Headlight - Sealed Beam or Composite
↳ $3.00 to $8.00 each
Miniature Light Bulb
↳ $1.00 to $2.00 each
Powertrain Control Module (Computer)
↳ $300.00 to $800.00
Starter
↳ $30.00 to $150.00

Lights

Lights are an important safety feature. Without them we could not see at night or notice when someone is braking, turning, or changing lanes. Some lights are controlled by sensors so they automatically illuminate in low-light conditions. Other lights are turned on by manual switches. As a safety feature, daytime running lights (DRL) make it easier for approaching drivers to see each other. When a light has the word *halogen* printed on it, inside the bulb is a gas, which results in a brighter light. Lights burn out with age. When replacing bulbs, use the number on the bulb as a guide. This is not true for most automotive replacement parts, but it is true for headlights and other bulbs. It is recommended to replace blown out headlights in pairs. See page 168 for the procedure on how to replace a headlight. Miniature light bulbs (e.g., taillights, brakelights, sidemarkers) are designed as bayonet or push-in (*Figure 9.19*).

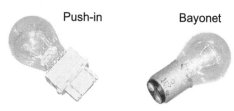

Push-in   Bayonet

Figure 9.19   *Automotive Miniature Bulbs*

❓ Q & A

Bulb Keeps Burning Out

Q: What would cause my headlight bulb to blow out frequently?

A: Make sure the headlight lens does not have any cracks. If moisture is getting in it will burn out quicker. Also check to make sure the electrical socket is not corroded. If it is, use an electrical cleaner and then put a dab of dielectric grease in the socket. Make sure if you are replacing a composite style headlight bulb that you do not touch the glass part. Oil from your fingers may shorten the life of the bulb.

Headlights usually come in two types: composite and sealed beam (*Figure 9.20*). Composite headlights are integrated aerodynamically into a vehicle's body. Their housing consists of a reflective surface covered by a lens. When a composite style headlight burns out only the bulb needs to be replaced. Sealed beam headlights come as a unit with the bulb sealed inside. When replacing a sealed beam headlight, do not remove the adjusting screws. Headlights should be checked and adjusted so they provide the proper visibility and courtesy to other drivers on the roadway.

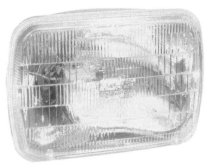

Sealed Beam Bulb   Composite Bulb

Figure 9.20   *Automotive Headlights*

🖱 Web Links

Electrical Related Sites

AC Delco
↳   www.acdelco.com
AutomotiveLightingUSA.com
↳   www.automotivelightingusa.com
Bando USA
↳   www.bandousa.com
Cooper Bussmann
↳   www.bussauto.com
Dayco Belts
↳   www.daycoproducts.com
Exide Batteries
↳   www.exide.com
Gates Corporation
↳   www.gates.com
Goodyear
↳   www.goodyearbeltsandhose.com
Interstate Batteries
↳   www.interstatebatteries.com

Computer

Advances in vehicles today are often only possible with the integration of computer technology. At least one computer, microprocessor, or electronic control module provides accurate and instant commands to almost every major mechanical or electrical system (e.g., ignition, fuel, emission, transmission, brake, safety restraint, navigation, and traction control). The main computer is commonly called the engine control unit (ECU), electronic engine control (EEC), electronic control module (ECM), or the powertrain control module (PCM). Sensors are constantly inputting raw information, in the form of electrical signals, into the central processing unit where the data is analyzed and processed (*Figure 9.21*).

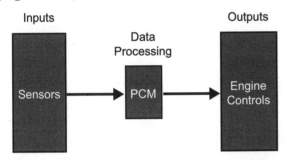

Figure 9.21   **PCM Operation**

The type and number of sensors on a specific vehicle varies. The computer monitors and adjusts engine controls by continuously performing self checks to make sure the engine is running efficiently. When something is not working properly a trouble code will normally be stored in the computer. The check engine light will go on if a code is stored. A scan tool is used to retrieve stored on-board diagnostics (OBD) codes. See page 165 to learn more about OBD. Most computers never need maintenance, but if they fail they will need to be replaced. Often the problem is sensor input. If you are having trouble with diagnosis take your vehicle to the dealer. A computer is covered under an extended federal emission warranty.

Summary

The electrical system may seem quite complex to the do-it-yourselfer, but there are simple ways to maintain it and save money. Start by keeping your battery maintained. The starting system converts chemical energy to electrical energy to mechanical energy in order to start the engine. The charging system converts mechanical energy to electrical energy to chemical energy to recharge the battery. Fuses are over-current protection devices. Lights are used in many places on the automobile and periodically need replacing. The electrical system activities will assist you in testing and replacing automotive electrical system components. Keep in mind that integrated computer technology can help you keep your vehicle running smoothly and help diagnose problems with trouble codes.

🚗 Activities

Electrical System

- Battery Activity
- Charging Activity
- Starting Activity
- Chapter 9 Study Questions

Activities can be accessed in the Auto Upkeep workbook or online at www.autoupkeep.com.

🎓 Career Paths

Electrical Engineer

Education: Bachelor's Degree and/or ASE Cert.
Median Income: $55,000
Job Market: Average Growth
Abilities: Apply math, science, technology, and ingenuity to solve electrical problems.

CHAPTER 10

LUBRICATION SYSTEM

FUEL FOR THOUGHT
- What is the function of engine oil in the lubrication system?
- How are oils rated?
- What are synthetic oils?

Introduction

The engine is the heart of a vehicle with hundreds of moving parts that must be lubricated. While the engine burns fuel, it also takes in outside air. Road dust and dirt are brought in with this air. While most of the air is cleaned, some dust may get by the air filter. In addition, incomplete combustion adds carbon deposits to the oil. Water can also come in contact with the oil from humidity in the air and gaskets leaking. All of these factors can lead to engine oil failure. Engine oil, processed from crude oil, is the substance that keeps your engine going day after day. It is extremely important to keep the oil clean and at the correct level to prevent engine oil failure.

Objectives

Upon completion of this chapter and activities, you will be able to:
- Define the purpose of engine oil.
- Explain oil service and viscosity ratings.
- Discuss the advantages and disadvantages of synthetic oils.
- Discuss the importance of oil filters.
- Change the oil and filter on a vehicle.

Web Links

Motor Oil Companies

AMSOIL Inc.
↳ www.amsoil.com
BP
↳ www.bplubricants.com
Castrol
↳ www.castrol.com
Chevron
↳ www.chevron.com
Havoline
↳ www.havoline.com
Mobil Oil
↳ www.mobil.com
Pennzoil
↳ www.pennzoil.com
Phillips Petroleum Company
↳ www.phillips66.com
Quaker State
↳ www.quakerstate.com
Valvoline Oil
↳ www.valvoline.com

Purpose of Engine Oil

Without oil an engine would not run. Engine oil:
- Lubricates
- Cools
- Cleans
- Seals

Lubricates

The most important function of engine oil is to lubricate. Within the engine there are hundreds of little parts rubbing up against each other. This rubbing creates friction. Friction is the force that resists motion between two bodies in contact. Friction creates heat (thermal energy). Engine oil molecules are like little ball bearings (***Figure 10.1***). The oil molecules have a tendency to stick to metal surfaces, but have less of a tendency to stick to each other. Oil decreases resistance and friction between two sliding bodies, resulting in a reduction of engine wear.

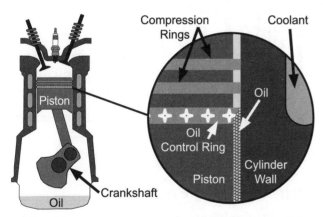

Figure 10.1   *Oil Lubrication in Engine Cylinder*

Cools

While engine oil does reduce friction, it cannot eliminate it. Friction would build up undesirable heat without engine oil. Overheating can damage engine components. Engine oil is pumped throughout the engine, moving into various parts, and then back to the oil pan. In the oil pan or through an engine oil cooler, heat is dissipated to the outside air. Engine oil helps cool your engine in this process.

Cleans

Conventional gasoline-fueled vehicles are not very efficient. Approximately 15% of money spent on fuel is used for propulsion (movement) or running accessories, like the A/C. Inefficiency in the internal combustion engine causes unburned deposits to build up in the engine. Dirty air may also come in through the air filter during the intake process. While the engine oil is lubricating all the critical engine components, it also cleans by removing particles of carbon and other contaminants. As the oil is pumped throughout the engine, the dirty particles are screened out by the oil filter. Clean engine components help ensure proper lubrication.

Seals

During engine operation, the pistons are rapidly moving up and down. Engine oil is also moving up and down with the pistons. Not only does engine oil lubricate, cool, and clean; it also seals between vital components. Engine oil seals between pistons and the cylinder walls to reduce blow-by. Blow-by is the gas that escapes past the piston rings and into the crankcase, causing power loss and piston wear. Engine oil acts as a seal between components that are separated by gaskets. For example, you should put a thin film of oil on the oil filter gasket before installation to seal the connection between the filter and engine.

? Q & A

Oil Recycling

Q: Why is it important to recycle used motor oil and where do I take it?

A: According to the Environmental Protection Agency (EPA), improperly dumping oil from one oil change can contaminate one million gallons of groundwater. Many service centers that perform oil changes are required to accept used motor oil from do-it-yourselfers. Call local garages or your county's environmental services department for collection locations. To find out more about motor oil recycling, go online to www.epa.gov or www.earth911.org.

Understanding Oil Ratings

Reading and understanding an oil bottle can be challenging. The oil ratings you need to become familiar with are (*Figure 10.2*):

- Society of Automotive Engineers (SAE)
- American Petroleum Institute (API)
- Energy Conserving
- International Lubricant Standardization and Approval Committee (ILSAC)
- European Automobile Manufacturers' Association (ACEA)

Figure 10.2   *Bottle of Oil with Ratings*

Society of Automotive Engineers

SAE rates engine oil viscosity. Viscosity is defined as the resistance to flow. Engine oil is available in single (e.g., SAE 30) and multigrade (e.g., SAE 5W-30) viscosity ratings. An oil that has two numbers in the rating is called a multigrade oil. Multigrade oils have been tested at various temperatures, and thus, can be used in a wide range of climates (*Figure 10.3*).

✓ Tech Tip

Oil Warning Light

The oil light comes on when your engine has little or no oil pressure. Without oil pressure, severe engine damage can result. If the light stays on for more than 5 seconds, turn the engine off and check your oil. If it is at the correct level and the light still stays on, do not run the engine. Have a qualified service technician look into the problem.

The W after a rating signifies that the oil has been tested for a winter weather temperature at 0°F (-18°C). If there is not a W after the number the oil was tested at 210°F (99°C). The higher the viscosity number the thicker the oil. 5W-30 oil acts like SAE 5 when cold and SAE 30 when warm. It is thin enough when the engine is cold to get to all of the components and thick enough when the engine warms up to protect against engine wear. This is why multigrade oils have become so popular – they meet the viscosity ratings in multiple temperature ranges. Common engine oil viscosity ratings for newer vehicles are 5W-20 and 5W-30, but always check the owner's manual for the manufacturer's recommendations.

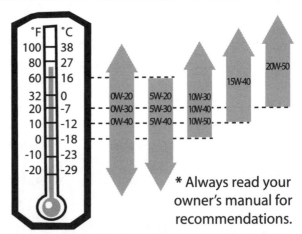

Figure 10.3   *Engine Oil SAE Viscosity Ratings*

❓ Q & A

Wrong Oil in Engine

Q: What will happen if I use 10W-30 instead of the recommended 5W-30?

A: The difference between 5W-30 and 10W-30 is the viscosity (thickness). Many new cars now recommend using 5W-30 all year long, while others indicate that it is OK to use 10W-30 in warm climates. The lower viscosity oil (5W-30) circulates quicker throughout the engine when it is cold. Check your owner's manual and see if the manufacturer allows the use of 10W-30 during warmer climatic conditions. Using the incorrect viscosity of oil may void the warranty.

American Petroleum Institute

API rates the engine oil service (*Figure 10.4*). SA, SB, SC, SD, SE, SF, SG, SH, SJ, SL, and SM are API rated engine oils. The first letter "S" stands for spark ignition (gasoline) engines. The later the second letter is in the alphabet, the newer and more advanced the oil. For example, SC oil was used in vehicles in the 1960s. Sometimes you'll see designations such as CJ-4. The C stands for compression ignition (diesel) engines.

Gas Engine (Spark Ignition)	Diesel Engine (Compression Ignition)
SM	CJ-4

Figure 10.4   ***Engine API Ratings as of 2006***

Newer engines are requiring more strenuous standards. When the American Petroleum Institute determines that current oils cannot meet newer engine needs or when current technology can improve engine oil qualities, it establishes a new set of standards. The key is that SM oils replace all the previous oils and can be used in any spark ignition engines with any of the previous letter designations. Look for the API symbols (*Figure 10.5*) when identifying the correct engine oil for your vehicle. Over time, API will come out with more advanced oil standards to replace SM oils.

Figure 10.5   ***API Symbols***

Web Links

Oil Rating Related Sites

American Petroleum Institute
↳   www.api.org
Society of Automotive Engineers
↳   www.sae.org

Energy Conserving

Energy conserving oils have increased additives to lower friction between components. By lowering the friction, the engine becomes more efficient which in turn improves fuel economy.

ILSAC

The International Lubricant Standardization and Approval Committee (ILSAC) was formed in the 1990s by Japanese and American automotive manufacturers. ILSAC develops and identifies standards for gasoline-fueled (GF) engine oils. In 2004, ILSAC developed the GF-4 standard.

ACEA

The European Automobile Manufacturer's Association (also known as Association des Constructeurs Européens d'Automobiles - ACEA) develops oil ratings. Read your owner's manual for the standard that is right for your engine.

Synthetic Oil

Synthetic oils are formulated from various chemicals and hydrocarbons to improve engine service and viscosity ratings. Even though synthetic oils have been used by military organizations since World War II, they have become more common in the automotive sector since the 1990s. Synthetic oils have advantages and disadvantages (*Figure 10.6*). Some vehicles come standard from the factory with synthetic oil in their engines.

Advantages of Synthetic Oil
• Low levels of impurities.
• Increased lubricating qualities improves fuel mileage.
• Resists sludge from forming.
• Decreases oil consumption.
• Maintains lubricating abilities for longer oil change intervals.
• Flows well in extreme cold and during initial start up.
• Protects at extremely high temperatures.

Disadvantages of Synthetic Oil
• Higher cost.
• Most manufacturer warranties require regular oil change intervals that reflect conventional oil use.

Figure 10.6   ***Synthetic Oil Factors***

Oil Filters

As oil circulates through the engine, it is cleaned by an oil filter. The oil filter should be replaced every time your engine oil is changed. Oil filters (*Figure 10.7*) are composed of paper screening materials that collect contaminants from the engine oil. Once the contaminants are removed from the engine oil, the oil is recirculated through the engine.

Figure 10.7   *Oil Filter*

 Servicing

Oil and Filter

- Change every 3 months or 3,000 miles or as recommended by the manufacturer

Web Links

Oil Related Sites

AC Delco
↳   www.acdelco.com
Champion Laboratories Inc.
↳   www.champlabs.com
Citgo Lubricants
↳   www.citgo.com
Exxon Lubricants
↳   www.exxon.com
Fram Filters
↳   www.fram.com
Motorcraft
↳   www.motorcraft.com
Wix Filters (Division of Dana)
↳   www.wixfilters.com

Changing the Oil and Filter

To help reduce wear and preserve the life of a vehicle's engine, the oil and filter must be changed (*Figure 10.8*) as recommended by the vehicle manufacturer (typically every 3,000 miles or 5,000 km).

Removing Old Oil and Filter	
1	After warming the engine to loosen contaminants and to thin the oil, shut it off and remove the ignition key.
2	Wear eye protection and disposable gloves.
3	Chock the wheels, lift the vehicle, and support it with jack stands. Or, use drive-on ramps, wheel chocks, and then jack stands. See Chapter 5 for safe lifting information. Apply the parking brake.

Figure 10.8a   *Drive-on Ramps*

4	Position an oil drain pan under the oil drain plug and filter. If the oil is extremely hot, allow it to cool some.
5	Remove oil filler cap. Loosen the oil drain plug with the correct size wrench or socket and then carefully remove it by hand.

Figure 10.8b   *Loosen Oil Drain Plug*

6	While the oil is draining (at least 5 minutes) inspect the oil plug threads, gasket, and oil pan threads for cracks, damage, or wear. Purchase a new oil plug if needed.
7	Use an oil filter wrench to remove the old oil filter and gasket. Be careful, the oil filter is full of warm oil. Set the old filter into the oil drain pan to drain.

Figure 10.8c   *Loosen Filter with Filter Wrench*

8	Use a rag to wipe off the filter mounting base, the drain plug, and the drain plug area after the engine oil has drained.

	Installing New Oil and Filter
1	Reinstall the oil plug finger tight by hand and then tighten to the recommended torque with a wrench. Do not cross-thread or overtighten.
2	Apply a thin film of clean oil on the new oil filter gasket.
3	Install the oil filter by hand by rotating it clockwise. Once the gasket contacts the engine, tighten it further according to the instructions - usually ½ to 1 full turn.

Figure 10.8d **Install New Filter**

4	Remove oil drain pan and tools from under the vehicle. Lower the vehicle if you used a jack and jack stands.
5	With the filler cap removed, use a funnel to add the correct amount and type of oil. Check owner's manual for recommendations. Reinstall the oil filler cap.

Figure 10.8e **Add Oil with Funnel**

6	Start the engine and let it idle for a minute. Check that the oil gauge or light is normal. If you used drive-on ramps remove the jack stands and carefully back down the ramps. Shut off the engine for safety and inspect the filter and oil plug for leaks.
7	If there are no leaks, wait a couple of minutes and then check the oil dipstick level. Be sure the car is on level ground to get an accurate reading. Correct if needed.
8	Clean up and properly recycle your old oil and filter.
9	Write down in your vehicle records the odometer reading and date of service.

Figure 10.8 **Oil and Filter Change Procedure**

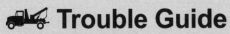 Trouble Guide

Engine Oil Leaks

- Engine oil plug loose or not sealing
- Oil filter loose or not sealing
- Other various seals or gaskets leaking

Price Guide

Conventional Oil
↳ $1.00 to $2.50 a quart
100% Synthetic Oil
↳ $4.00 to $6.00 a quart
Oil Filters
↳ $2.00 to $7.00 each

Note:
1 qt = 0.946 L

Summary

Engine oil lubricates, cools, cleans, and seals engine components. While engine oil is a vital component to the longevity of an engine and may seem extremely complex, it is not very difficult to service. When purchasing oil look for the SAE, API, and other ratings that meet the manufacturer's recommended requirements. Oil filters are used to remove contaminants from the engine oil and should be changed at oil change intervals. Synthetic oils are becoming more popular and accepted due to stringent engine tolerances. Always check your owner's manual for oil recommendations and change intervals.

Activities

Lubrication System

- Oil and Filter Change Activity
- Chapter 10 Study Questions

Activities can be accessed in the Auto Upkeep workbook or online at www.autoupkeep.com.

Career Paths

Service Writer

Education: Technical Experience or ASE Cert.
Median Income: $38,000
Job Market: Average Growth
Abilities: Diagnostic, communication, problem solving, and time management skills.

CHAPTER 11

FUEL SYSTEM

FUEL FOR THOUGHT
- How are gasoline and diesel produced?
- What is the purpose of the fuel system?
- How are gasoline prices determined?

Introduction

Most automobiles in production today depend on either gasoline or diesel. Many problems arise from using gasoline and diesel. Once these fuels are burned, they are gone forever. That is the reality of today's fossil fuel-driven society. Driving habits, maintenance procedures, and technological advances can improve the efficiency of vehicles. This chapter provides information on fuel properties, automotive fuel components, and ways to increase fuel efficiency.

Objectives

Upon completion of this chapter and activities, you will be able to:
- Explain the purpose of the fuel system.
- Describe the parts of the fuel system.
- Remove and replace an air filter.
- Remove and replace a fuel filter.
- State gasoline and diesel properties.
- Identify ways to improve fuel economy.
- Explain how fuel is priced.

Fuel System Purpose

Fuel is added to the fuel tank from a gas station. The fuel (chemical energy) is stored in the gas tank. In a gasoline engine, the fuel is then pumped to the carburetor or injection system. The carburetor or the injection system mixes the fuel with air. The cleanest burning and most fuel efficient mixture is the mass ratio of 14.7 parts of air to 1 part of fuel (i.e., stoichiometric ratio). The mixture is brought into the combustion chamber and burned. The purpose of the fuel system is to store, transfer, and then to mix the fuel with air.

Fuel System Components

The fuel system parts that will be discussed are:
- Fuel Cap
- Fuel Tank
- Fuel Pump
- Fuel Lines
- Fuel Filter
- Fuel Injectors or Carburetor
- PCV Valve
- CCV Filter
- Air Filter
- Mass Airflow Sensor
- Powertrain Control Module

Fuel Cap

The fuel (gas) cap (*Figure 11.1*) keeps the fuel from spilling out, releases the vacuum that is created as fuel is drawn into the engine, releases pressure to prevent spray (when removing the cap to refuel), and keeps foreign objects from entering the fuel tank.

Figure 11.1   *Fuel Cap*

Fuel Tank

The fuel (gas) tank, made of either steel or plastic (*Figure 11.2*), stores the fuel for later use. The most common reason for having to remove the fuel tank is replacement of a bad in-tank electric fuel pump.

Figure 11.2   *Fuel Tank*

Fuel Pump

The fuel pump, either mechanical or electric (*Figure 11.3*), supplies the engine with fuel. Mechanical fuel pumps are usually located on the engine and are commonly used with carburetor type vehicles. Electric fuel pumps are usually located in the fuel tank and are commonly used with fuel injected vehicles.

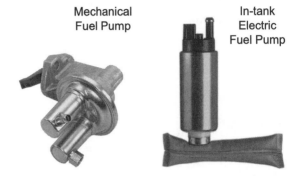

Mechanical Fuel Pump   In-tank Electric Fuel Pump

Figure 11.3   *Fuel Pumps*

Fuel Lines

Fuel lines (*Figure 11.4*), made of either steel or rubber, carry fuel to the carburetor or fuel injectors.

Figure 11.4   *Fuel Lines with In-line Fuel Filter*

✓ Tech Tip

Changing the Fuel Filter

When changing the fuel filter wear goggles to protect your eyes and disposable gloves to avoid getting fuel on your skin. All fuel system services should be done in a well-ventilated area with the engine cool. It is also important to relieve fuel pressure (follow the manufacturer's procedure). Some vehicles with fuel injection systems run as high as 85 psi (586 kPa) of fuel pressure.

? Q & A

Fuel Pump Replacement

Q: My technician told me that I need a new fuel pump. The estimate was over $500. Why does it cost so much?

A: The fuel pumps on most vehicles today are located in the fuel tank. Some pumps are purchased as a complete fuel assembly module that includes the pump and the fuel level sender. The technician has to drain and then remove the fuel tank from the vehicle to access the fuel pump. The part itself can cost over $300.

Fuel Filter

The fuel filter (*Figure 11.5*), located between the fuel tank and the carburetor or injection system, cleans the fuel entering the engine. The fuel filter may be located under the vehicle near a frame member or under the hood near the carburetor or fuel injectors. Fuel filters contain a paper type element to collect contaminants. A clogged fuel filter slows fuel delivery, lowers the performance of an engine, and causes excessive wear on the fuel pump.

Figure 11.5   **Fuel Filter**

Fuel Injectors or Carburetor

Vehicles today use fuel injectors (*Figure 11.6*) to add fuel to the air. Fuel injectors can be one of two types: throttle body or port. In a throttle body injection system, usually one fuel injector is used to supply fuel to all of the engine's cylinders. In a port injection system, there is one fuel injector for each cylinder. Older vehicles used carburetors to mix the air and fuel together.

Figure 11.6   **Fuel Injector**

PCV Valve

The positive crankcase ventilation (PCV) valve (*Figure 11.7*) reduces vehicle emissions, increases fuel economy, recirculates excess gas, decreases oil contaminants, and reduces air pressure within the engine.

Figure 11.7   **PCV Valve**

CCV Filter

The crankcase ventilation (CCV) filter (*Figure 11.8*) is usually placed inside the air filter housing and is connected to the PCV valve via a tube or hose. This filter cleans the air going into the engine's crankcase. The CCV filter is sometimes called the PCV inlet filter.

Figure 11.8   **CCV Filter**

Air Filter

Air filters (*Figure 11.9*) clean dirt and dust from the air that is being drawn into the engine. Large masses of air are drawn into the engine when fuel is burned. A dirty air filter can cause low fuel efficiency by creating a rich air-fuel mixture (choking out the engine). Dirty air can also cause premature failure to vital engine components (e.g., bearings, valves, and piston rings). The following is a general procedure for replacing an air filter (*Figure 11.10*).

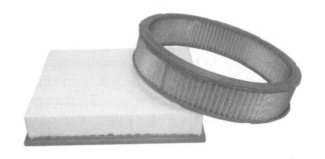

Figure 11.9   **Air Filters**

Air Filter Replacement

STEP 1	Locate the air filter housing by looking for the cold air intake system on your engine.

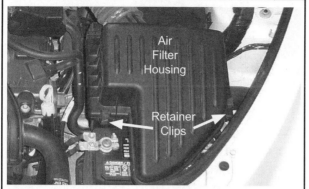

Figure 11.10a   **Locate Air Filter Housing**

STEP 2	Identify how the air filter housing cover secures the air filter. This is usually done by retainer clips or screws. Remove air intake hoses if necessary.

Figure 11.10b   **Detach Retainer Clips**

STEP 3	Remove the air filter housing cover and dirty air filter.

Figure 11.10c   **Remove Air Filter**

STEP 4	Use a vacuum to clean any dirt or debris from the air filter housing.
STEP 5	Install the new air filter and reassemble by reversing the procedure.

Figure 11.10   **Changing an Air Filter**

Mass Airflow Sensor

The Mass Airflow Sensor (MAF) is located in the cold air intake system. The MAF measures the volume (quantity) and mass (density) of air entering the engine. The MAF sends an electrical signal to the powertrain control module (PCM) to control fuel flow through the fuel injectors.

Powertrain Control Module

The powertrain control module (PCM) processes information from a variety of sensors to control the amount of fuel being injected, resulting in higher fuel economy and lower emissions.

💰 Price Guide

Air Filter
↳ $3.00 to $15.00 each
CCV Filter
↳ $3.00 to $8.00 each
Fuel Filter
↳ $3.00 to $15.00 each
Fuel Pump
↳ $20.00 to $300.00 each
PCV Valve
↳ $3.00 to $8.00 each

🕐 Servicing

Air Filter
- Change every 12,000 miles or as recommended by the manufacturer

CCV Filter
- Change every 2 years, 24,000 miles, or as recommended by the manufacturer

Fuel Filter
- Change every 2 years, 24,000 miles, or as recommended by the manufacturer

PCV Valve
- Change every 2 years, 24,000 miles, or as recommended by the manufacturer

Crude Oil Distillation

Gasoline and diesel, like various other products (e.g., cosmetics, paints, nylon, and asphalt), come from crude oil. Crude oil, a fossil fuel, is a nonrenewable energy resource. Examples of nonrenewable energy resources are coal, oil, and natural gas. Under current production and consumption rates, experts project oil to last 50-100 years. The exact time frame is uncertain. How long oil actually lasts will depend on future discoveries, technological advancements, global use, actual supply, and price. Crude oil goes through a distillation process (i.e., separating and vaporizing) at a refinery to form gasoline and diesel. At different temperatures of the distillation process (*Figure 11.11*) various products are collected.

❓ Q & A

Gasoline vs. Diesel

Q: I am buying a new ¾ ton F-250 Ford truck, but don't know if I should get one with a diesel engine or a gasoline engine. What are the main differences between the two types of engines?

A: A diesel engine is a compression ignition engine while a gasoline engine is a spark ignition engine. Diesels do not have spark plugs to ignite the fuel, resulting in lower maintenance costs. Even though gasoline engines usually produce higher horsepower, diesels turn out more torque. Torque is crucial for pulling. If the truck is used to tow or haul heavy loads, a diesel may be the better choice. Diesel engines are more fuel efficient and have a longer life, but tend to initially cost significantly more than gas engines. Gasoline engines start better in extremely cold weather.

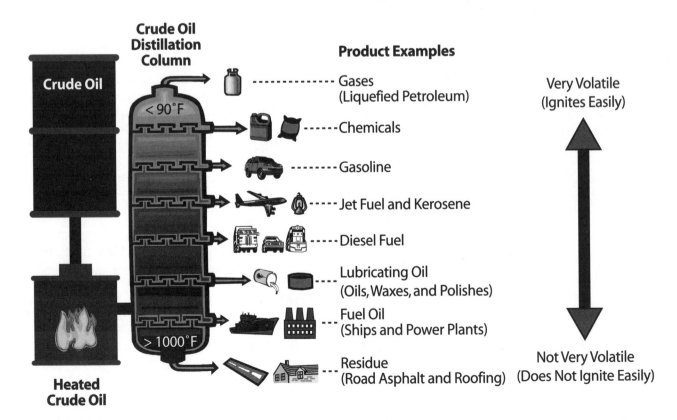

Figure 11.11

Gasoline Properties

Gasoline is a mixture of hydrocarbons (hydrogen and carbon) and is primarily used in internal combustion engines to propel most of today's automobiles. Gasoline engines are considered spark ignition engines. The fuel needs to be ignited to burn in the engine. This section focuses on:

- Octane
- Knocking
- Additives
- Oxygenates

Figure 11.12   **Common Octane Ratings**

Octane

Gas pumps are commonly labeled *regular*, *mid-grade*, or *premium*. What does this mean? For the most part, it relates to the octane rating of the gasoline. Octane is defined as a resistance to detonate. The higher the octane number, the more the fuel resists detonation under pressure. The more the fuel resists detonation, the more complete the combustion is when the fuel ignites. Usually higher compression engines need higher octane fuels. Common octane numbers are regular 87, mid-grade (or plus) 89, and premium 93 (***Figure 11.12***). The octane requirement depends on the engine design, the altitude the vehicle is driven at, and driving habits. Most automobiles require a minimum of 87 octane, but always check the owner's manual.

Knocking

Many people have experienced an engine knocking or pinging during acceleration. This sound is created when fuel ignites prematurely. Anti-knock characteristics relate directly to octane ratings. The higher the octane rating the more the fuel resists knocking. It takes a higher temperature and more compression to ignite a fuel with a higher octane. Many new car engines have "knock sensors" to identify when slight knocking begins to occur. When the sensor detects any knocking (it senses it by the vibration in the engine), a signal is sent to the car's computer to adjust the ignition timing. The timing adjustment eliminates the knock, but also compromises optimal engine performance (i.e., power and acceleration) and fuel economy. Even though a knock isn't audible to the ear, it may be occurring slightly.

❓ Q & A

Octane and High Compression

Q: If the owner's manual says to use 91 octane fuel, will it damage the engine if I use a lower octane fuel?

A: Some cars have high compression engines, requiring a mid-grade or premium fuel. The higher the octane number, the more the fuel resists "knocking" or "pinging" from premature ignition. Use the octane rating that the manufacturer suggests.

🛻 Trouble Guide

Engine Lacks Power (sluggish)

- Clogged fuel filter
- Impurities in fuel
- Fuel octane too low

Excessive Fuel Consumption

- Dirty air filter

Additives

Rust inhibitors are added to help metals resist rusting. Detergents are added to clean the fuel system. During cold weather, you can add gas-line antifreeze to gasoline to prevent fuel lines from freezing (*Figure 11.13*).

Figure 11.13   *Gas-Line Antifreeze*

Oxygenates

Oxygenates increase the octane rating in gasoline. Oxygenates include methyl tertiary butyl ether (MTBE), ethyl tertiary butyl ether (ETBE), tertiary amyl methyl ether (TAME), and ethanol. Gasoline burns cleaner when oxygenates are added, resulting in lower tailpipe emissions. Up until the late 1970s and early 1980s, tetraethyl lead was primarily used to increase octane levels. However, lead is toxic and shortened the life of catalytic converters by destroying the catalyst inside. Tetraethyl lead was phased out completely from U.S. automotive gasoline. MTBE was primarily used to replace lead and to increase the octane in fuel. Recently, MTBE has also been banned in many places. MTBE has been found to contaminate drinking water from leaking gasoline storage tanks. Now ethanol use has significantly increased to replace MTBE as a gasoline oxygenate. Oxygen in the fuel helps the air-fuel mixture burn more completely, creating less pollution. Often up to 10% of gasoline is ethanol. Ethanol is a grain alcohol, commonly made from corn or other starch-rich grains. When gasoline and ethanol are mixed, it is called gasohol. Gasohol burns cleaner, emitting less air pollutants and greenhouse gases than 100% gasoline.

Diesel Properties

Diesel fuel is not only used in semi-tractors and heavy equipment, it is also used in many diesel cars and light trucks. Diesel fuel actually has more energy per volume than gasoline. This section focuses on:

- Cetane Number
- Grades of Diesel
- Ultra-Low Sulfur Diesel

Cetane Number

The cetane number relates to how well fuel ignites. Diesel fuels have a short time delay in the cylinder before igniting. Remember from Chapter 1 that diesel engines are compression ignition engines. Diesel is ignited by heat and pressure in the combustion chamber. When compared to lower cetane number fuels, diesel fuels with a higher cetane number have a shorter time delay from when the diesel is injected into the combustion chamber to the point when it ignites. Cetane numbers of 40 to 50 are the most common.

Grades of Diesel

Two types of diesel fuels are used in cars and trucks: No. 1 and No. 2. The American Society for Testing and Materials (ASTM) classifies these two grades. In the distillation process, No. 1 diesel fuel has a lower boiling point than No. 2 and thus vaporizes easier than No. 2. Therefore, No. 1 diesel fuel is commonly used when the outside ambient temperature is abnormally low. In cold climates many gas stations commonly provide No. 1 in the extreme winter, a mixture of No. 1 and No. 2 in the fall and spring, and No. 2 in the summer. No. 2 diesel fuel has a tendency to "gel" in severely cold climates.

Ultra-Low Sulfur Diesel

Under Environmental Protection Agency's (EPA) requirements, in 2006 there was a significant reduction of sulfur in diesel fuel. Burning sulfur contributes to air pollution. One of the greatest contributors to particulate matter (soot) emissions is the sulfur content in diesel. Ultra-low sulfur diesel (ULSD) contains a maximum of 15 parts-per-million (ppm) of sulfur, as compared to low sulfur diesel that allows up to 500 ppm of sulfur. Model year 2007 and later diesel engines require ULSD (*Figure 11.14*). These engines have advanced emission systems to burn cleaner and pollute less. ULSD is compatible with pre-2007 model vehicles. The disadvantage is that older diesel engines do not have the advanced emission systems to take full advantage of polluting less.

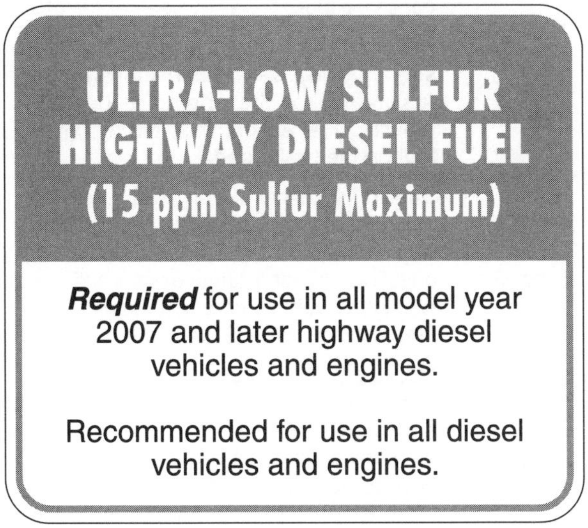

ULTRA-LOW SULFUR HIGHWAY DIESEL FUEL
(15 ppm Sulfur Maximum)

Required for use in all model year 2007 and later highway diesel vehicles and engines.

Recommended for use in all diesel vehicles and engines.

Figure 11.14   *ULSD Pump Sticker*

❓ Q & A

Clean Diesels

Q: What are "clean" diesels? When I think of diesels I think of black smoke.
A: DaimlerChrysler has produced a diesel engine called BLUETEC. These engines run on ultra-low sulfur diesel and use particulate filters, nitrogen oxide traps, and special catalytic converters to substantially reduce tailpipe emissions.

Refueling

Before refueling your automobile, check the owner's manual to be sure you put in the correct type and grade of fuel. Most automotive gasoline engines are designed to run on unleaded gasoline with an octane number of 87 or greater. Some high performance or high compression engines may require a higher octane fuel. The following is a general procedure to refilling a fuel tank (*Figure 11.15*).

Refueling Procedure	
STEP 1	As you arrive at the filling station, make sure you drive up to the fuel pump dispenser with the vehicle's fuel fill door lined up with the pump.
STEP 2	Shut off the engine and engage the parking brake. Do not smoke.
STEP 3	Open the fuel fill door. Some vehicles have a release button for the fuel fill door near the driver's seat.
STEP 4	Remove the fuel (gas) cap slowly. You may hear a hissing sound caused by the pressure in the tank equalizing with the outside pressure. Most fuel fill doors have a place to attach the fuel cap.

Figure 11.15a   *Fuel Fill Door with Fuel Cap*

STEP 5	Read and follow the instructions on the fuel pump dispenser.
STEP 6	Do not overfill or "top off" the tank. Once the pump nozzle automatically shuts off, stop refueling. Fuel needs room to expand and overfilling can cause emission system problems in the vapor recovery system.
STEP 7	Before removing the gas pump nozzle, be sure all the fuel drips out of the nozzle's end. Spilled fuel contributes to air and ground pollution.
STEP 8	Hang up the nozzle on the pump.
STEP 9	Replace the fuel cap. Most manufacturers require the cap to be tightened until 1-3 clicks are heard. Check the owner's manual. If the cap is not tightened correctly, a malfunction indicator light (e.g., check fuel cap or check engine) may illuminate. Close the fuel fill door.

Figure 11.15   *Refueling Procedure*

Improving Fuel Economy

Automobiles are not very efficient from an energy usage point of view. Losses occur in the engine, drivetrain, aerodynamics, rolling resistance, and braking (*Figure 11.16*).

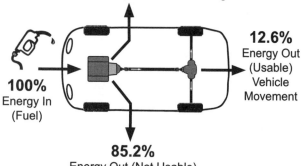

2.2%
Energy Out (Usable)
Run accessories such as Power Steering, A/C, Windshield Wipers, Radio, and Lights

12.6%
Energy Out (Usable)
Vehicle Movement

100%
Energy In (Fuel)

85.2%
Energy Out (Not Usable)
Losses through Engine and Drivetrain Inefficiency

Figure 11.16   ***Automobile Energy Usage***
Data Obtained from www.fueleconomy.gov

Several factors contribute to good fuel economy. Over time, new technology has contributed to better fuel and fuel delivery methods. There are many simple ways to improve fuel economy (*Figure 11.17*).

Web Links

Fuel Related Sites

British Petroleum
↳ www.bp.com
Chevron Corporation
↳ www.chevron.com
Conoco/Phillips
↳ www.conocophillips.com
Exxon/Mobil
↳ www.exxonmobil.com
Holley Performance Products Inc.
↳ www.holley.com
Shell Oil Company
↳ www.countonshell.com
US DOE - Fuel Economy Website
↳ www.fueleconomy.gov

Ways to Improve Fuel Economy	
Checking Tire Pressure	Low tire pressure causes more frictional resistance on the highway, reducing fuel economy and increasing tire wear. Having incorrect pressure can also increase the chances of having a dangerous blowout.
Tuning-up the Engine	A properly tuned engine (replacing ignition components such as spark plugs and replacing fuel related components such as the air filter) can improve your fuel mileage. An improperly running engine can waste up to 15% of additional fuel.
Checking the Wheel Alignment	If the wheels are not contacting the road surface properly, fuel mileage will decrease due to increased friction.
Changing the Oil as Required	Clean engine oil has better cooling, cleaning, lubricating, and sealing properties than dirty oil, allowing an engine to run more efficiently.
Limiting A/C Usage	Running extra accessories puts more load on the engine, requiring more fuel. Use the air conditioner only when necessary to conserve fuel.
Eliminating Brake Drag	If the brakes are dragging or rubbing slightly, they can cause more frictional resistance for the engine to overcome, reducing fuel economy. Avoid resting your foot on the brake pedal.
Avoiding Excessive Idling	Shut off your car if you plan to sit for an extended period of time. An engine idling for an hour can burn three gallons (11.36 L) of gasoline, creating unnecessary pollution. A well-tuned vehicle does not require a lot of fuel to start. Hybrids save fuel by shutting down at stops.
Combining Trips	Short trips increase wear on an engine and cause poor fuel economy because the engine does not have time to reach an optimal operating temperature. Combining errands will also put fewer miles on your vehicle.
Moderating Speed	It is important to avoid abrupt acceleration and deceleration. "Stop and go" traffic reduces fuel economy dramatically. Using cruise control on the highway to keep your speed constant and putting the transmission in overdrive will also increase fuel economy.
Checking the Cooling System	Running an engine too cool can lower fuel economy. The correct thermostat and periodical flushing will assure proper operation.
Removing Weight and Accessories	Clean out your trunk by removing any excess supplies. Each additional 100 lbs (45.36 kg) carried in your car decreases fuel economy by 1-2%. Also remove any accessories (e.g., ski racks) that decrease the aerodynamics of your vehicle.

Figure 11.17   ***Fuel Saving Tips***

Cylinder Deactivation

Cylinder deactivation (also known as displacement on demand, variable displacement, multiple displacement system, or active fuel management technology) uses engine control systems to shut off the air-fuel mixture to some of the engine's cylinders when all the cylinders are not needed. For example, cruising at highway speeds takes less horsepower and torque than accelerating. When additional power is not needed, the intake and exhaust valves on half the engine's cylinders close. When the valves are closed, fuel is not being burned in those cylinders.

Fuel Prices

Fuel prices became a major concern in the 1970s, but have gained attention once again. Contrary to popular belief, fuel is only marked up about 5-9% at retail outlets. Fuel prices (*Figure 11.18*) are influenced by taxes, marketing costs, distribution costs, geographical region, refinery productivity, supply, demand, crude oil prices, markup (i.e., profits), investor speculation of future prices, and world events.

Even though technology is advancing fuel efficiency, many consumers drive gas-guzzling vehicles (e.g., sport utility vehicles). Every year more and more vehicles are put on the highways, increasing the demand for fuel. If the supply of fuel decreases and fuel demand increases, prices will surely rise.

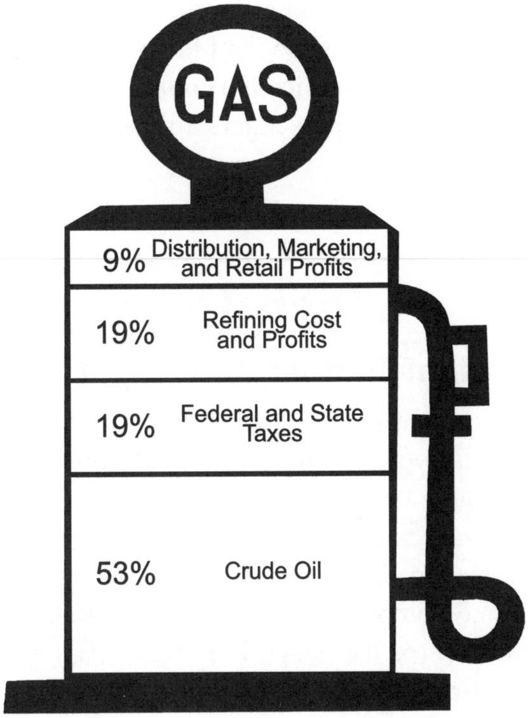

Summary

It is important to supply your engine with the fuel that the automotive manufacturer recommends. The purpose of the fuel system is to store, transfer, and then mix the fuel with air. In a gasoline engine, the lower the octane number the more likely the engine will knock. Gasoline engines are spark ignition engines. Diesel engines are compression ignition engines. Diesel fuel comes in two grades: No. 1 and No. 2. The outside temperature determines the type of diesel to use – No. 2 in warm weather and No. 1 in extreme cold weather. Various parts of the fuel system work together to supply clean fuel and air to the engine. Fuel economy can increase through tune-ups, correct tire pressure, regular oil changes, and moderating your driving habits.

9%	Distribution, Marketing, and Retail Profits
19%	Refining Cost and Profits
19%	Federal and State Taxes
53%	Crude Oil

Figure 11.18   *U.S. Fuel Price Breakdown*

Activities

Fuel System
- Fuel System Activity
- Chapter 11 Study Questions

Activities can be accessed in the Auto Upkeep workbook or online at www.autoupkeep.com.

Career Paths

Petroleum Engineer

Education: Bachelor's Degree in Engineering
Median Income: $62,000
Job Market: Average Growth
Abilities: Strong science, math, analytical, and problem solving skills in technical areas.

CHAPTER 12

COOLING SYSTEM AND CLIMATE CONTROL

FUEL FOR THOUGHT
- Why is it important for the engine to run at an optimum temperature?
- How does coolant circulate in an engine?
- How is heat transferred to the passenger compartment?

Introduction

Thousands of automobiles are stranded on the side of the road each year due to cooling system problems. Precautions can be taken to avoid this, including paying attention to the temperature gauge (*Figure 12.1*). Engine coolant carries away excess heat from the engine. Too much heat can destroy an engine, while an engine that is not at the proper operating temperature will run inefficiently. This chapter will identify and describe the importance of the cooling system, maintenance procedures, cooling system components, and passenger cabin climate control.

Objectives

Upon completion of this chapter and activities, you will be able to:
- Identify the purpose of the cooling system.
- Describe the cooling system's components.
- Define coolant properties.
- Explain how coolant flows in an engine.
- Test and service the cooling system.
- Change a passenger cabin air filter.

Figure 12.1   **Temperature Gauge**

✓ Tech Tip

Coolant Temperature Light

The coolant temperature warning light comes on when your engine has reached a potentially damaging temperature. Overheating an engine can warp and crack cylinder heads, overheat the engine oil, and cause excessive stress on engine components. If the temperature light stays on (or the gauge is in the HOT range), pull over to the side of the road and let the engine cool.

Cooling System Purpose

The cooling system is designed to do four things:
- Reach Operating Temperature Quickly
- Maintain Operating Temperature
- Remove Excess Engine Heat
- Provide Passenger Comfort

Reach Operating Temperature Quickly

Fuel is wasted every second the engine runs below the most efficient operating temperature. The powertrain control module (PCM, also known as the computer) communicates with the temperature sensor and regulates the other systems based on the coolant temperature. An engine running at the proper temperature will run cleaner (pollute less), smoother, and more efficient than an engine running too cool or too hot.

Maintain Operating Temperature

On today's computer controlled vehicles it is vital to maintain an efficient operating temperature. Too low of a temperature will cause the computer to run the vehicle with a rich air-fuel mixture. Excessively high temperatures can warp metal and crack gaskets, leading to major engine damage. Most vehicles run coolant at a temperature of around 195°F (91°C). Coolant temperature is controlled by a thermostat, which will be presented later in this chapter.

Remove Excess Engine Heat

Metal around the combustion chamber (where the fuel is ignited) can reach extremely high temperatures. Coolant circulates throughout the engine. To remove excess heat, coolant is transferred to the radiator where the movement of air dissipates the heat. A radiator fan is placed behind the radiator to draw air through the radiator fins.

Provide Passenger Comfort

Heat is transferred from engine coolant through the heater core to warm the passenger compartment.

Cooling System Components

This section focuses on:
- Radiator
- Radiator Cap
- Thermostat
- Coolant Recovery Tank
- Radiator Fan
- Radiator and Heater Hoses
- Clamps
- Water Pump
- Drive Belts

Radiator

The purpose of the radiator (*Figure 12.2*) is to remove heat from the coolant. When the temperature of the coolant reaches the opening rating of the thermostat, hot coolant enters the radiator by the upper radiator hose. The coolant runs down through various tubes. Air is drawn around the radiator tubes by a fan and by the motion of the vehicle. The air flow cools the coolant in the radiator tubes so it can be returned to the engine.

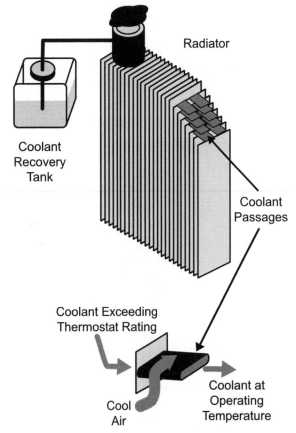

Figure 12.2   **Radiator**

Radiator Cap

The radiator cap (*Figure 12.3*) is designed to maintain a constant pressure in the cooling system. Most pressure caps are rated between 8 to 16 psi (55 to 110 kPa). Increasing pressure on the cooling system increases the boiling point of the coolant. The radiator cap allows expanding coolant to go to the coolant recovery tank. When the fluid has cooled, coolant is drawn back into the radiator through a vacuum valve in the cap.

Figure 12.3   *Radiator Cap*

Thermostat

The thermostat (*Figure 12.4*) is the brain of the cooling system. It senses the temperature of the coolant and allows the fluid to exit from the engine to the radiator. The thermostat controls the temperature in the cooling system. Thermostats are rated at a specified temperature – usually between 180-195°F (82-91°C). When an engine is cold, the thermostat is closed. Once the engine temperature reaches the thermostat rating, the thermostat opens.

Figure 12.4   *Thermostat*

 Servicing

Thermostat

- Change every 2 years or as recommended by the manufacturer

Coolant Recovery Tank

The coolant recovery tank (also called the expansion bottle) (*Figure 12.5*) holds excess coolant during the cooling system operation. As pressure and heat build up, the coolant expands and is then transferred to the recovery tank. This prevents fluid being lost during cooling system operation, while keeping the maximum amount of coolant in the system at all times. Another advantage of using a coolant recovery tank is to keep outside air from being drawn into the engine block. Air, carrying outside contaminants, can cause corrosion to cooling system components.

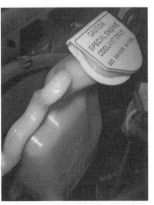

Figure 12.5   *Coolant Recovery Tank*

Radiator Fan

Radiator fans draw air through the radiator to cool the coolant. Fans are either mechanically or electrically driven. A mechanical fan is driven by a belt. An electrical fan is driven by an electric motor. Most newer vehicles use an electric fan (*Figure 12.6*) because it is more efficient and more suitable for front-wheel drive vehicles with transverse engines. Use caution when working on a vehicle with an electric fan. Electric fans can start without the engine running. Keep your fingers away from the fan area. If you need to work near an electric fan, disconnect your car's negative battery cable.

Figure 12.6   *Electric Radiator Fan*

Radiator and Heater Hoses

The upper and lower radiator hoses (*Figure 12.7*) connect the radiator to the engine. Cooled coolant is transferred from the radiator to the engine through the lower hose. Hot coolant is returned to the radiator by the upper hose. The upper hose connects to the water outlet that covers the thermostat. The lower hose connects to the water pump. Heater hoses are also used to transport heated coolant to the heater core (basically a mini-radiator) that provides heat for the passenger compartment.

Figure 12.7   *Radiator Hose*

Clamps

A variety of clamps are used to attach radiator and heater hoses under the hood. Some clamps can be tightened with a screw and others use a tension

band (*Figure 12.8*) that must be sized correctly to the hose. Use a pair of pliers to squeeze the clip ends together to remove a tension band clamp.

Clamp Clip Ends

Figure 12.8   *Tension Band Clamp*

Water Pump

The water pump (*Figure 12.9*) is attached to the engine block. Its main purpose is to keep the coolant circulating. It draws cooled coolant in from the lower radiator hose and pushes it through the engine. An engine drive belt ("v" or serpentine) or timing belt rotates most water pumps.

Figure 12.9   *Water Pump*

❓ **Q & A**

Radiator Hose Collapse

Q: Why would a radiator hose collapse?
A: You may have a faulty radiator cap. A radiator cap works to maintain a constant pressure in the cooling system. As the antifreeze mixture begins to cool after engine shutdown, a vacuum is created. If the pressure cap doesn't equalize this pressure, a radiator hose can collapse. The small vacuum valve in the radiator cap may not be working properly.

❓ **Q & A**

Water Pump "Weep" Hole

Q: My car is dripping antifreeze around the water pump. What is the problem?
A: Water pumps have a built in "weep" hole. This hole is engineered in the water pump to signal the car owner when the internal seals have failed. When the water pump is leaking from this hole it is time for replacement.

Drive Belts

Drive belts turn water pumps, mechanical fans, power steering pumps, alternators, and air conditioning compressors. Automotive drive belts (*Figure 12.10*) are connected to the crankshaft pulley that turns from the reciprocating motion of the pistons. Worn or loose belts can cause slippage. Belt slippage can lead to an engine overheating.

Figure 12.10   *Serpentine Drive Belt*

Coolant Properties

Mainly two types of coolant are sold for automotive use: standard antifreeze and extended life antifreeze (*Figure 12.11*). As presented on page 70, antifreeze is manufactured in various colors and formulas (additive packages). Always refer to your owner's manual to identify the correct antifreeze to use in your vehicle. Only use an antifreeze that is compatible with your engine. Coolant within an engine does three main things:

- Prevents Freezing and Boiling
- Lubricates the Water Pump
- Inhibits Corrosion

Figure 12.11   *Extended Life Antifreeze*

🚛 Trouble Guide

Engine Overheating

- Coolant low
- Improper coolant mixture
- Clogged radiator fins
- Faulty thermostat (stuck closed)
- Restricted radiator hose
- Fan not working
- Faulty temperature sensor
- Faulty water pump
- Drive belt loose
- Faulty radiator cap

Engine Overcooling

- Faulty thermostat (stuck open)
- Faulty temperature sensor

🖱 Web Links

Cooling System Related Sites

Gates Rubber Company
  ↳   www.gates.com
Griffin Thermal Products
  ↳   www.griffinrad.com
Hypertech Inc.
  ↳   www.hypertech-inc.com
Peak Antifreeze
  ↳   www.peakantifreeze.com
Prestone Antifreeze
  ↳   www.prestone.com
Sierra Antifreeze
  ↳   www.sierraantifreeze.com
Stant Corporation
  ↳   www.stant.com

Prevents Freezing and Boiling

Pure water can be corrosive to engine components, so it should not be used to cool an engine. Additionally, it freezes at 32ºF (0ºC) and boils at 212ºF (100ºC). If coolant freezes, it will expand and eventually crack the engine block. Also, the engine can run hotter than 212ºF (100ºC) and boiling causes problems. The solution to this is to use an antifreeze/water mixture. In most climates a 50% antifreeze to 50% water mixture is recommended all year. This will give the coolant a freezing point of -34ºF (-37ºC) and a boiling point of about 226ºF (108ºC). When the cooling system is under pressure from the radiator cap, the boiling point raises to about 265ºF (129ºC) when the mixture is 50/50 (*Figure 12.12*). In a severely cold climate, 60% antifreeze to 40% water is necessary. It is not recommended to use pure antifreeze in the cooling system. Manufacturers commonly recommend a maximum of 70% antifreeze to 30% water when using standard antifreeze. The antifreeze/water mixture carries the best properties.

Antifreeze	Water	Freezing Point		Boiling Point with 15 lb. Radiator Cap	
		ºF	(ºC)	ºF	(ºC)
50%	50%	-34	(-37)	+265	(+129)
60%	40%	-62	(-52)	+269	(+132)
70%	30%	-84	(-64)	+276	(+136)

Figure 12.12   *Freezing and Boiling Points*

Lubricates the Water Pump

The coolant mixture lubricates bearings that are located inside the water pump. As antifreeze ages, its lubricating ability lessens.

Inhibits Corrosion

Bare engine components are susceptible to corrosion. Coolant contains chemicals to minimize rust and corrosion from taking place inside the engine.

 Servicing

Coolant (Antifreeze)

- Change standard (green) antifreeze every 2 years
- Change Dex-Cool (extended life) antifreeze every 5 years
- Test once a year

? Q & A

White Smoke

Q: I have white smoke coming from the tailpipe on my car, what could be wrong?
A: Be aware that all cars, new ones included, may release a little white vapor when cold. This is caused from condensation in a car's exhaust system. Water dripping from the tailpipe is also fairly common from condensation. However if your car billows out white smoke after it is warm, you may have a problem. White smoke indicates that the engine is burning coolant. This means that coolant is getting into the cylinders and burning with the air-fuel mixture. Another indication of burning coolant would be a low coolant level in the radiator or expansion bottle. A blown head gasket, cracked block, or cracked head can cause coolant to leak into the cylinders. To prevent severe engine damage, do not continue to drive your car. Have a technician look into the problem.

🚛 Trouble Guide

Coolant Loss

- Crack in block or cylinder head
- Defective seal or gasket
- Engine overheating and boiling over
- Heater core leak
- Hole in hose
- Hole in radiator
- Loose hose clamp
- Worn water pump

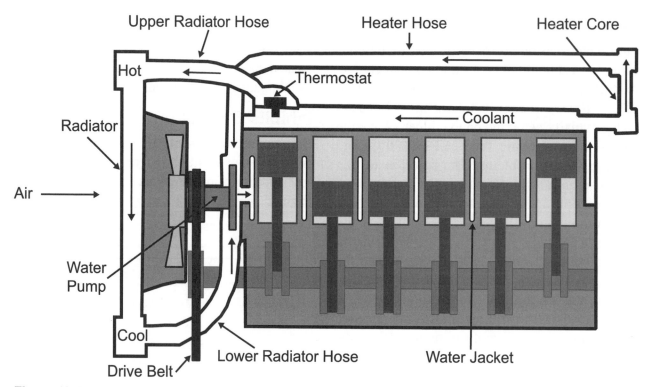

Figure 12.13   *Coolant Flow in an Inline 6 Engine*

Coolant Flow

The water pump, driven by the drive belt, forces coolant to flow throughout the engine (*Figure 12.13*). If a drive belt is slipping or not working properly the water pump will not circulate the coolant as needed and the engine will overheat. Coolant travels in passageways called water jackets (coolant voids) in the engine. Coolant, cooled from the car moving or from the radiator fan drawing in air across the radiator, flows from the radiator through the lower radiator hose, to the water pump, to the numerous water jackets

in the engine, and then to the thermostat. If the coolant has reached operating temperature, the thermostat will open and allow the coolant to pass through the upper radiator hose back to the radiator to be cooled again. If the coolant has not reached operating temperature it will recirculate through the engine until it heats up to the thermostat's rating. Some coolant is also diverted from the engine through the heater core. Heat is transferred from the heater core to the passenger compartment when the inside heater blower is turned on. Coolant is separated from the engine oil and combustion chamber by gaskets and seals placed in the joints of mated components. If any of the gaskets (*Figure 12.14*) or seals fail, coolant will leak. Some leaks can be fixed by retightening components, but most will need to be replaced.

✓ Tech Tip

Recycle Used Coolant

Used coolant is considered a hazardous waste. Bring the coolant to a service center that recycles it or wait until your community has a hazardous waste pickup day. If you have to store the coolant, do not leave it in open pans where pets or children can get into it. Coolant is toxic.

Figure 12.14   *Thermostat Gasket*

Heater Core

The heater core (*Figure 12.15*) looks like a little radiator. It is normally mounted between the engine compartment and the passenger compartment on the firewall. Coolant from a warm engine flows through the heater core and radiates thermal heat energy. When you turn on the heater fan the heat is transferred into the passenger cabin of the vehicle through the heating/air conditioning ducts. If you notice a sweet odor in your car when you turn on your heat you may have a heater core leak. If it is leaking, it drips in the heater ducts and sometimes on the floor inside the car. When the blower is turned on, the odor circulates inside the passenger compartment. Check to see if your coolant level is low if you believe you have a leak.

Figure 12.15   **Heater Core**

❓ Q & A

No Heat Inside Vehicle

Q: My car never seems to warm up inside. The heater blows plenty of air, but it is lukewarm at best. What do I need to do?

A: Your problem may be the car's thermostat. The thermostat controls the circulation of coolant in the engine. If the thermostat is stuck open, the coolant never gets a chance to warm up to the optimal temperature. Also, check to make sure your engine is not low on coolant. A clogged heater core or control valve can also restrict the circulation of coolant. Follow the manufacturer's recommendations for coolant flushes to avoid contaminants being built up in the coolant system.

Cabin Air Filter

A cabin air filter (*Figure 12.16*) is used to clean the air coming into the heating, ventilation, and air conditioning system (HVAC). This filter works similarly to a high efficiency filter in a home with a forced air furnace. It cleans the air in the HVAC system by removing pollen, dust, bacteria, and other contaminants. This cleaning increases the passenger cabin air quality. Without a filter or running the system with a dirty filter can cause the air quality inside the passenger cabin to be much worse than the outside air. The cabin air filter should be changed every 15,000 miles (≈24,000 km), depending on the air quality and road conditions where the vehicle is driven. It is commonly located near the glove box or under the hood in the outside air intake for the HVAC system. Check your owner's manual for the location. Arrows on the filter should identify the correct air flow direction for installation.

Figure 12.16   **Cabin Air Filters**

💰 Price Guide

Antifreeze
↳ $6.00 to $10.00 a gallon

Hose Clamps
↳ $0.50 to $1.00 each

Radiator Cap
↳ $7.00 to $15.00 each

Thermostat
↳ $2.00 to $8.00 each

Upper and Lower Radiator Hoses
↳ $7.00 to $15.00 each

Water Pump
↳ $30.00 to $75.00 each

Note:
1 gal = 3.785 L

Air Conditioning

The air conditioning (A/C) system (*Figure 12.17*) removes heat and humidity from the air for passenger comfort. During some weather conditions it would be dangerous to be inside a vehicle without air conditioning, especially for children and pets. The following components work together to remove heat and dehumidify the air in an orifice tube A/C system:

- Refrigerant
- Accumulator
- Compressor
- Condenser
- Orifice Tube
- Evaporator

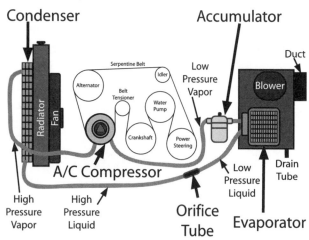

Figure 12.17   *Orifice Tube A/C System*

Refrigerant

Refrigerant is in the A/C system to remove heat. During operation the refrigerant cycles through the system changing from a liquid to a vapor (absorbs heat) and then a vapor to a liquid (dissipates heat). The most common automotive refrigerants are R-12 and R-134a. R-12 was used extensively in automobiles until the early 1990s. Releasing refrigerant into the atmosphere contributes to ozone depletion and global warming. R-134a, a more environmentally friendly refrigerant, was phased in to replace R-12. R-12 and R-134a are not compatible with each other. You should not perform air conditioning work unless you have a special machine to recover and recycle the refrigerant and you have been trained

and certified to perform this type of procedure (*Figure 12.18*). Service technicians are required by law to recover and recycle refrigerants in an effort to protect the environment.

Figure 12.18   *Refrigerant Warning Label*

Accumulator

The A/C accumulator (*Figure 12.19*) cleans and stores refrigerant. It prevents refrigerant liquid from entering the A/C compressor. Some systems use a receiver-drier instead of an accumulator. They perform similar functions. However, an accumulator is installed on the low pressure side, while a receiver-drier is installed on the high pressure side.

Figure 12.19   *Air Conditioning Accumulator*

Compressor

The A/C compressor (*Figure 12.20*) is commonly powered by the main drive belt. An electromagnetic clutch is used to engage the pulley with the compressor shaft. If the clutch circuit senses low refrigerant or another problem, the clutch will not engage. The compressor compresses and recirculates refrigerant, which is sent to the condenser. A seized compressor may cause a turning belt to squeal. Since liquid cannot be compressed, only vapor enters the compressor.

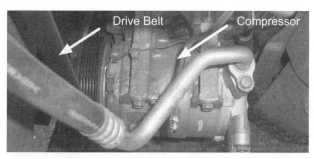

Figure 12.20   *Air Conditioning Compressor*

Condenser

After the refrigerant in the evaporator absorbs heat from the air, the refrigerant is circulated by the compressor to the condenser to release that heat. The condenser, a heat exchanger, looks very similar to a radiator and is normally located in front of the radiator. If the air conditioner is not getting as cool as you think it should, make sure there is nothing in the condenser fins restricting air flow.

Orifice Tube

The orifice tube controls the refrigerant flow from the condenser to the evaporator. It changes the refrigerant from a high pressure liquid to a low pressure liquid.

Evaporator

The compressed refrigerant travels from the condenser to the evaporator, a heat exchanger, where heat is absorbed from the surrounding air. When you turn on the air conditioner blower this cooled air is transferred to the passenger cabin through the ducts. If the air recirculation switch is on, air will be pulled from inside the cabin making the system more efficient once the inside air is already cooled. Otherwise fresh air is pulled in from outside the vehicle. A drain tube (*Figure 12.21*) on the evaporator allows condensation from humidity in the air to drain from the evaporator. The drain often leaves a water puddle on the ground that may look like a leak, especially if the A/C has been running on a humid day. If the drain becomes clogged it should be cleaned by probing it with a long dull object. If left clogged, the water can eventually work its way out onto the interior floorboards.

Figure 12.21   *Evaporator Drain Tube*

Summary

The cooling system is extremely important to the operation of the engine. The cooling system maintains efficient engine-operating temperature, removes excess heat, brings the engine up to operating temperature as quickly as possible, and provides warmth to the passenger compartment. Antifreeze prevents the coolant from freezing, increases the boiling temperature, lubricates components within the engine, and reduces the likelihood of corrosion. The heater core transfers heat from the engine to warm the passenger cabin. A cabin air filter cleans the air that blows through the cabin vent system and should be considered a required maintenance item. If your A/C doesn't work, take it to an ASE certified technician that has the proper equipment to find, repair, and recycle the refrigerant if necessary.

 Activities

Cooling System and Climate Control

- Air Conditioning Activity
- Cabin Air Filter Activity
- Cooling System Activity
- Chapter 12 Study Questions

Activities can be accessed in the Auto Upkeep workbook or online at www.autoupkeep.com.

🎓 **Career Paths**

Heating and A/C Technician

Education: Technical Training and ASE Cert.
Median Income: $40,000
Job Market: Average Growth
Abilities: Understands system controls, testing equipment, and environmental regulations.

IGNITION SYSTEM

FUEL FOR THOUGHT

- What is required for an engine to run?
- How have ignition system advancements reduced required maintenance intervals?
- Why is it important to set the correct gap on a spark plug?

Introduction

The engine in a vehicle needs three things to run: fuel, air, and ignition. Fuel is ignited by an electric spark in gas engines. Diesel engines use heat from compression to ignite the air-fuel mixture. This chapter focuses on gasoline engines. Chapter 11 presented how the engine receives fuel and air, now it is time for the ignition. The ignition system on vehicles has changed over the years, but its purpose has been the same – to ignite the air-fuel mixture. The ignition converts chemical energy of the fuel into wanted mechanical energy of motion and wasted thermal energy. This chapter gives you the knowledge to identify and perform basic maintenance procedures on a vehicle's ignition system.

Objectives

Upon completion of this chapter and activities, you will be able to:

- Define the purpose of the ignition system.
- Identify ignition system generations.
- Define and discuss the importance of the ignition system components while relating them to their respective generation.
- Test and perform basic service procedures on the ignition system.

Ignition System Purpose

As mentioned earlier, fuel, air, and ignition must all be present for the engine to run. The purpose of the ignition system is to:

- Step Up Voltage
- Ignite the Air-Fuel Mixture

Step Up Voltage

One of the purposes of the ignition system is to step up voltage. Basic electrical principles were presented in Chapter 9. You know now that standard automotive batteries have a surface voltage of about 12-volts DC. This is sufficient for running accessories such as lights and radios, but not powerful enough to ignite the air-fuel mixture within the combustion chamber. Common voltages at the spark plug can range from about 10,000 to 100,000 volts. These high voltages are created with a coil, a step up transformer.

Ignite the Air-Fuel Mixture

Automotive engines are considered four-stroke engines (intake, compression, power, and exhaust). To get to the stroke that is wanted, the power stroke (the one which gives the vehicle power to move), the engine must cycle through the other necessary strokes. Most automotive engines have four to eight pistons working together to provide the mechanical energy. Not only does the ignition system have to ignite the air-fuel mixture, it also needs to ignite it at the correct time. Some of the ignition system components carry low voltage (12-volts) while others support high voltages (10,000 to 100,000 volts). The ignition system is designed to monitor and control the ignition to make the vehicle run smoothly.

🚚 Trouble Guide

Engine Rotates, but No-Start

- Moisture on ignition components
- Worn or incorrectly gapped spark plugs
- Faulty ignition module or coil
- Cracked, burned, or corroded distributor cap or rotor

💰 Price Guide

Battery
↳ $40.00 to $80.00 each
Coil Packs
↳ $100.00 to $200.00 per set
Distributor Cap and Rotor
↳ $15.00 to $30.00 per set
Ignition Coil
↳ $50.00 each
Ignition Module
↳ $40.00 to $200.00 each
Spark Plug Wire Set
↳ $20.00 to $80.00 per set
Spark Plugs
↳ $1.00 to $5.00 each

Ignition System Generations

Over the years automotive manufacturers have come a long way in making the "power" (ignition) stroke more efficient through advancements in technology. The purpose over time has been the same: to increase the voltage to induce a spark. Modern technology has made the power stroke more reliable and efficient. It should be noted that the following dates of the ignition generations are approximated. Depending on the automotive manufacturer, the implementation time of the ignition system generation may vary. The generations of the ignition system are commonly divided into the following eras:

- Conventional Ignition System
- Distributor Ignition (DI) System
- Electronic Ignition (EI) System

Conventional Ignition System

The conventional ignition system was common in vehicles from about 1920 to the mid 1970s. This system is considered a mechanical type ignition system. Tune-ups during this age were frequent – sometimes every 5,000 to 10,000 miles (≈8,000 to 16,000 km). Common components in the conventional ignition include the battery, ignition coil, contact points and condenser (***Figure 13.1***), distributor cap and rotor, spark plug wires, and spark plugs.

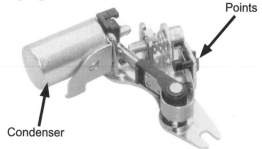

Points

Condenser

Figure 13.1   *Contact Points and Condenser*

Distributor Ignition (DI) System

The distributor ignition system was common in vehicles from about 1975 to the early 1990s. Tune-ups during this age were required about every 25,000 miles (≈40,000 km). Common components in the distributor ignition system include the battery, ignition coil, ignition module, distributor cap, distributor rotor, spark plug wires, and spark plugs. The main advantage over the conventional ignition was the elimination of the contact points that physically rubbed on the distributor shaft. This elimination decreased the number of components that needed servicing. The ignition module in this system controls the spark.

Electronic Ignition (EI) System

Electronic ignition systems (also known as distributorless, direct, or computer-controlled coil ignition systems) were actually introduced in the mid 1980s, but really became popular in the early 1990s. Tune-up intervals on the electronic ignition systems vary, but some manufacturers boast up to 100,000 miles (≈160,000 km). Common components in the electronic ignition system include the battery, individual ignition coils, electronic control module, spark plug wires, spark plugs, crankshaft sensor, and camshaft sensor. The advantages over the distributor ignition are the elimination of a mechanical distributor, increased voltage at the spark plug, better timed spark, and a more efficient running engine.

Web Links

Ignition System Related Sites

Autolite Spark Plugs
↳ www.autolite.com
MSD Ignition (Autotronic Control Corp.)
↳ www.msdignition.com
Mr. Gasket Company (ACCEL Wires)
↳ www.mrgasket.com
NGK Spark Plugs
↳ www.ngksparkplugs.com
SparkPlugs.com
↳ www.sparkplugs.com
SplitFire Spark Plugs
↳ www.splitfire.com
Standard Motor Products Inc.
↳ www.smpcorp.com

Ignition System Components

Changing technology has made major advancements in many parts of the ignition system. Over time some components were eliminated, others were added, while others stayed pretty much the same (***Figure 13.2***). The following are common ignition system components:

- Battery
- Distributor Cap and Rotor
- Ignition Module
- Ignition Coil or Coil Packs
- Spark Plug Wires
- Spark Plugs
- Crankshaft and Camshaft Sensors
- Powertrain Control Module

Component	Conventional Generation	Distributor Generation	Electronic Generation
Battery	YES	YES	YES
Contact Points/ Condenser	YES	NO	NO
Coil or Coil Packs	YES	YES	YES
Ignition Module	NO	YES	YES
Distributor Cap/Rotor	YES	YES	NO
Spark Plug Wires	YES	YES	YES (Except Coil-on-Plug)
Spark Plugs	YES	YES	YES
Crank/ Camshaft Sensors	NO	Sometimes	YES
Powertrain Control Module	NO	YES	YES

Figure 13.2 ***Ignition System Components***

Trouble Guide

Engine Misses

- Faulty spark plug wires
- Worn spark plugs
- Worn distributor cap or rotor

Battery

The battery, used in all three ignition generations, is a critical component in the electrical, starting, charging, and the ignition systems. Electrical energy must be present to ignite the air-fuel mixture. The problem is that a 12-volt DC battery does not have enough voltage to create the spark that is necessary in the combustion chamber, but it is the beginning point of power.

Distributor Cap and Rotor

The distributor cap and rotor (*Figure 13.3*), used on conventional and distributor ignition systems, distributes or sends high voltage to each spark plug. The rotor rotates inside the cap, connecting and sending high voltage to one terminal at a time.

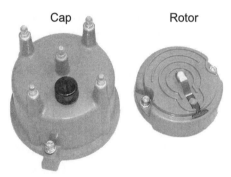

Cap   Rotor

Figure 13.3   *Distributor Cap and Rotor*

Ignition Module

The ignition module (*Figure 13.4*), used on distributor and electronic ignition systems, is basically a switch that turns the low voltage from the battery on and off to the ignition coil(s). It is a transistor that is timed and controlled by the powertrain control module (computer). In conventional ignition systems, contact points controlled the spark mechanically.

Figure 13.4   *Ignition Module*

Ignition Coil and Coil Packs

The ignition coil, used on all three generations, steps up low voltage to the high voltage needed to ignite the air-fuel mixture. Some engines have only one coil (*Figure 13.5*), while others have a coil for each cylinder. The electronic generation has coil packs. These packs are a series of coils to induce voltage for each individual cylinder.

Figure 13.5   *Ignition Coil*

Some electronic ignition systems use "coil-on-plug" (COP) (*Figure 13.6*) technology. They eliminate spark plug wires by just using boots to directly connect the spark plugs to the coils. The COP ignition system is more reliable because high voltage plug wires often cause problems over time.

COP

Figure 13.6   *Ignition Coil-on-Plugs*

 Servicing

Distributor Cap and Rotor
- Change every 25,000 to 50,000 miles

Ignition Coils
- Change when faulty

Spark Plug Wires

Spark plug wires (*Figure 13.7*) are used on all generations of ignition systems, except coil-on-plug systems. On the conventional and distributor ignition systems, spark plug wires connect the distributor to the spark plugs at each cylinder. In the electronic ignition system, the spark plug wires connect the coil packs to the spark plugs. The spark plug wires carry high voltage electricity.

Figure 13.7   *Spark Plug Wires*

✓ Tech Tip

Changing Spark Plug Wires

Changing spark plug wires is relatively easy. Keep in mind that engines have certain firing orders that cannot be mixed up. Remove and replace only one wire at a time to avoid mixing up the wires. Route the wires away from the exhaust manifold because the outer insulation can burn. It is also a good practice to use dielectric grease in the boot end of each spark plug wire to inhibit corrosion.

Servicing

Spark Plugs

- On conventional ignition systems, every 10,000 miles
- On distributor ignition systems, every 25,000 miles
- On electronic ignition systems, every 50,000 to 100,000 miles

Spark Plugs

The spark plug (*Figure 13.8*), used in all generations of ignition systems, completes the high voltage circuit. Spark plugs can be found at the end of spark plug wires or under coil packs on coil-on-plug systems. Spark plugs are screwed into the engine head so their electrodes at the tip are exposed to the combustion chamber. Voltage at the spark plug needs to be great enough to arc across the gap between the electrodes, thus creating a spark. This spark is what ignites the air-fuel mixture. Most engines have one spark plug per cylinder. The center electrode on a spark plug is commonly made of copper, platinum, or iridium. The gap between the center electrode and the ground electrode is usually between 0.020 to 0.080 of an inch (0.51 to 2.03 mm). Always check the service manual or the vehicle emission control information sticker under the hood for the gap setting. Some technicians use anti-seize compound on spark plug threads to prevent seizing that can result when different metals come in contact with one another, especially on vehicles with aluminum heads. Check vehicle and spark plug manufacturers' recommendations before applying. *Note: Using anti-seize compound can cause overtightening due to the increased thread lubrication. Some threads are engineered with corrosion protection, so applying anti-seize compound is not recommended.*

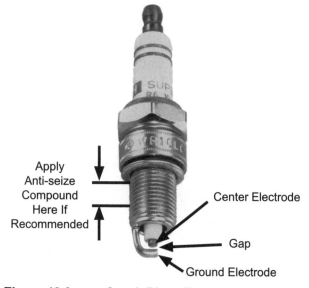

Apply Anti-seize Compound Here If Recommended

Center Electrode

Gap

Ground Electrode

Figure 13.8   *Spark Plug, Electrodes, and Gap*

Crankshaft and Camshaft Sensors

The crankshaft and camshaft sensors are used on electronic ignition systems and some recent distributor ignition systems. They keep track of piston and valve positions in the engine to efficiently time the spark. The crankshaft position sensor relays information about the crankshaft position and engine speed. The camshaft position sensor signals which coil needs to fire and sequences fuel injection timing.

Powertrain Control Module

Advanced integration of the powertrain control module (PCM), also known as the computer, is increasingly evident in the electronic ignition system. The PCM has earned the vital role of controlling the ignition spark. The PCM precisely determines when the spark is needed to ignite the air-fuel mixture. Operating conditions are input by crankshaft, camshaft, throttle position, knock, and various other sensors. Engine speed in revolutions per minute (RPM), throttle position, and coolant temperature are some of the data collected, compared, and used to determine the spark timing. The PCM monitors inputs from the sensors and then makes adjustments as needed so the engine can operate as efficiently as possible. An ignition timing malfunction may be a sign of a loose, dirty, or worn sensor not sending the correct input to the PCM.

Summary

The ignition system is designed to ignite the air-fuel mixture in the combustion chamber. Ignition systems have gone through three main generations: conventional, distributor, and electronic. Even though the ignition system may seem complex with sensors and control modules, there are things that the do-it-yourselfer can do to maintain and tune-up the engine to make it run smoothly.

? Q & A

Spark Plug Gap

Q: What does it mean to gap a spark plug?
A: When you gap a spark plug you set the distance between the electrodes. The side electrode, also called the ground electrode, is the piece that protrudes out and makes an "L" shape. The center electrode is the piece that is in the center of the plug. The distance between the two electrodes has to be exact for the spark to fire correctly; otherwise the engine will not run efficiently. To gap a spark plug insert a wire gap gauge between the electrodes and adjust to the correct gap distance. The correct gap distance should be on the vehicle emission control information sticker in the engine compartment.

Activities

Ignition System

*   Ignition System Activity
*   Chapter 13 Study Questions

Activities can be accessed in the Auto Upkeep workbook or online at www.autoupkeep.com.

🎓 Career Paths

Electrical/Electronics Technician

Education: Technical Experience or ASE Cert.
Median Income: $40,000
Job Market: Average Growth
Abilities: Problem solving, understands schematics, and use of electronic test equipment.

SUSPENSION, STEERING, AND TIRES

FUEL FOR THOUGHT

- What would it feel like to ride in a vehicle that did not have a suspension system?
- Why might the steering wheel of a vehicle pull to one side?
- How are tires designed to help you determine when they are worn out?

Introduction

Most of the roads that we drive on are not perfectly smooth and straight. S-curves, potholes, speed bumps, construction zones, and weather conditions make it necessary for vehicles to have control mechanisms. A properly working suspension and steering system gives the operator and passengers of the vehicle a smooth and pleasant ride. Shocks, struts, springs, and tires all assist in controlling the automobile by keeping the tires in contact with the road. This chapter presents information about suspension, steering, and tires.

Objectives

Upon completion of this chapter and activities, you will be able to:
- Define the purpose and identify the functions of the suspension system.
- Define the purpose and identify the functions of the steering system.
- Discuss the importance of tires and explain their ratings.
- Inspect suspension and steering components.
- Inspect and rotate tires.

Suspension System Purpose

The suspension system helps to control the up and down movement of the vehicle. During braking or going over bumps the suspension system helps provide stability, safety, and control of the vehicle.

✓ Tech Tip

Bounce Test

The bounce test is one generic method to test suspension components. To test the shocks and/or struts on a vehicle push down as hard as you can on the end of the vehicle that you want to test and then let go. The vehicle should come to a rest after one cycle. If it cycles more than once, the shocks, struts, or springs could be worn out. This test should be made in conjunction with a visual inspection.

Servicing

Lubricate Grease Fittings (Zerks)
- At every oil change

Suspension Components

The suspension components consist of many parts, all of which are attached to and become a part of the chassis. The chassis consists of some or all of the following components:

- Frame or Unibody
- Shocks
- Springs
- Struts

Frame or Unibody

The vehicle must have a foundation to build the rest of the vehicle upon. Some vehicles have a ladder type steel frame that runs the length of the vehicle. Others have partial frames, called unibodies, that connect the body and frame into one unit.

Shocks

The shocks (*Figures 14.1*) on a vehicle reduce the up and down motion that is produced from going over bumps on the highway. One end of the shock absorber is connected to a stationary part on the frame or unibody, while the other is connected to a suspension component that moves. The shock absorber contains a gas, fluid, and/or compressed air to reduce the number of oscillations (up and down motions) that are produced from driving on uneven roads. Excessive oil leakage around the shock is a sign that it needs replacement.

Figure 14.1   **Shock**

Springs

Springs work in conjunction with the shocks to help absorb the irregularities in the road surface. Springs come in coil and semi-elliptical shapes.

Trouble Guide
Body Rolls Around Corners

- Defective shocks, struts, or springs

Coil springs (*Figure 14.2*) are common on the front and rear of a number of vehicles. Vehicles with automatic leveling systems use compressed air springs.

Figure 14.2   **Coil Spring**

Semi-elliptical springs, usually called leaf springs (*Figure 14.3*), are common on the rear of trucks.

Figure 14.3   **Leaf Springs**

Struts

Struts (*Figure 14.4*) are a structural part of the suspension and/or steering system. Struts basically eliminate the need for individual shocks and springs on the front and/or rear of a vehicle. They do this by integrating the shock, spring, and upper control arm into one unit, reducing the overall weight and space. Some vehicles have struts in the front and shocks and springs in the rear, while others have struts at each wheel.

Figure 14.4   **Strut**

Steering System Purpose

The steering system controls the directional movements of the vehicle. The steering system, in conjunction with the suspension system, provides control and stability of the vehicle. The motion the operator makes at the steering wheel is transferred to the front wheels.

Web Links

Suspension, Steering, and Tire Related Sites

Bridgestone/Firestone Tires
↳ www.firestone.com
Cooper Tires
↳ www.coopertires.com
Dunlop Tires
↳ www.dunloptire.com
Goodyear Tires
↳ www.goodyear.com
Kelly Springfield Tires
↳ www.kelly-springfield.com
Michelin Tires
↳ www.michelin.com
Monroe Shocks and Struts
↳ www.monroe.com
Federal-Mogul
↳ www.federal-mogul.com
Performance Suspension Technology
↳ www.p-s-t.com
Pirelli
↳ www.us.pirelli.com
Rubber Manufacturers Association
↳ www.rma.org
Tenneco Automotive
↳ www.tenneco-automotive.com
TireRack.Com
↳ www.tirerack.com
Toyo Tires
↳ www.toyo.com
Uniroyal Tires
↳ www.uniroyal.com

Steering System Components

Some of the steering system components are connected to the frame of the vehicle while others need to move with the suspension. The following are some of the basic steering system components:
- Steering Wheel
- Steering Linkage
- Power Steering Pump

Steering Wheel

The steering wheel is how the operator controls the direction of a vehicle. Slight movements of the steering wheel can easily turn a 2,000+ pound (900+ kg) vehicle. The steering wheel is connected to the wheels by steering linkage. Performing work on the steering wheel or column can be dangerous on vehicles equipped with airbags. Make sure you follow all manufacturer precautions.

Trouble Guide

Hard Steering
- Low power steering fluid
- Loose belt

? Q & A

Wheel Alignment

Q: Should an alignment be part of regular maintenance?
A: Get an alignment when one or more of the following conditions occurs: the vehicle hit a curb or other obstruction; steering wheel is pulling one way; one or more tires are wearing abnormally; when replacing the tires; after an accident or going in the ditch; or, when suspension or steering components have been replaced. The correct alignment will increase the life of the tires, increase fuel economy, and provide for safer driving.

Steering Linkage

Steering linkage connects the steering shaft from the steering wheel to control the wheels on the highway. The parallelogram system (*Figure 14.5*), also called a pitman arm or recirculating ball system, is commonly used on trucks, SUVs, and large cars.

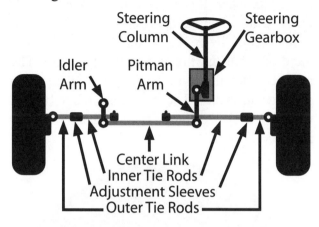

Figure 14.5   ***Parallelogram Steering Linkage***

Most front-wheel drive cars incorporate a rack and pinion system (*Figure 14.6*) that works in conjunction with a strut type suspension system to reduce space and weight. The rack, a flat piece with teeth, is connected to the tie rods. The pinion is connected to the steering shaft from the steering wheel. As the operator turns the steering wheel, the pinion turns, moving the rack to turn the vehicle.

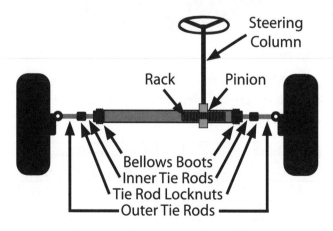

Figure 14.6   ***Rack and Pinion Steering Linkage***

Power Steering Pump

Power steering reduces the amount of effort that a driver needs to exert when steering. A power steering pump, which is commonly driven by a belt on the engine, provides fluid pressure to ease the force required by the operator to turn the steering wheel. It is necessary to periodically check the power steering pump reservoir fluid level. If there is a howling sound when turning the steering wheel the power steering fluid is most likely low. Some power steering systems are not mechanically belt driven. Electric Power Steering (EPS) is becoming more popular, especially in hybrids. EPS systems allow the driver to have power steering even if the vehicle stalls or is shut down intentionally at stops (e.g., hybrids). It is estimated that using an EPS system increases fuel efficiency by 1-3% by reducing weight and mechanical losses. Being electrical, it also has built in self diagnosis features.

🚚 Trouble Guide

Vehicle Pulls to One Side

- Uneven tire pressure
- Defective tire
- Wheels out of alignment
- Brake caliper stuck

💰 Price Guide

Radial Tires
↳ $40.00 to $250.00 each

Shocks
↳ $50.00 a pair

Struts
↳ $150.00 a pair

Tire Repairs
↳ $10.00 to $20.00 including labor

Wheel Alignments
↳ $40.00 to $80.00 labor

Tire Classifications

The tires on a vehicle provide the connection to the road surface. They are part of both the steering and suspension system and are a critical component to driving safely. Tires are designed to give passengers a comfortable ride and the needed traction (adhesive friction) to control the vehicle. Tires make driving safe during acceleration, cornering, and braking. This section focuses on:

- Tread Design
- Tire Sizes
- Tire Plies
- Tire Grading
- Light Truck Tire Load Range
- Run Flat Tires

Tread Design

Tires are generally classified as all-season or snow tires. All-season tires will meet most consumer demands throughout the year. Snow tires have a more aggressive tread and are more flexible than all-season tires. This gives snow tires superior traction in the winter. Even though an all-season radial may have a "M+S" (mud and snow) designation, it is not truly a snow tire. A certified snow tire will have a snowflake-on-a-mountain icon (*Figure 14.7*) on the tire's sidewall.

Figure 14.7   *Snowflake-on-a-Mountain Icon*

Tire Sizes

Tires come in a variety of sizes depending on vehicle size and weight. It is important to replace the tires on a vehicle with the size recommended by the manufacturer. Having tires too big or too small will influence how a vehicle handles and may cause the speedometer to be inaccurate. The following is an example of a tire size: P205/55R16 89H (*Figure 14.8*). The first letter can start with a P, LT, T, or ST. P stands for

passenger, LT stands for light truck, T stands for temporary, and ST stands for special trailer. ST tires should only be used on trailers. Most cars will have passenger tires. Light trucks can come with either passenger or light truck type tires. The 205 stands for the tire width in millimeters. The 55 stands for the aspect ratio or profile of the tire. It compares the cross-sectional height to the cross-sectional width. A lower number will result in an overall lower, wider tire. The next letter R identifies that the tire is a radial type tire. The number after the R represents the wheel (rim) diameter in inches. The tire below fits a 16-inch wheel. Wheel sizes range from 12 inches to over 20 inches.

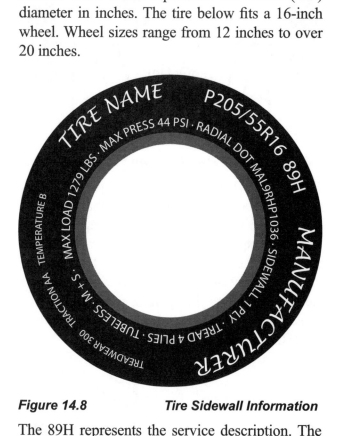

Figure 14.8   *Tire Sidewall Information*

The 89H represents the service description. The service description identifies the load index and speed rating of the tire (*Figure 14.9*).

Load Index			Speed Rating		
Index	lbs	kg	Rating	mph	km/h
81	1019	462	S	112	180
85	1135	515	T	118	190
89	1279	580	U	124	200
93	1433	650	H	130	210
97	1609	730	V	149	240
101	1819	825	W	168	270

Figure 14.9   *Service Description Examples*

Tire Plies

Steel belted all-season radial tires are the most common type of tire. They consist of steel wires running around the tire. Radial ply cords run from the bead (where the tire attaches to the wheel rim) on one side to the bead on the other side. Other belts are also directly under the tread for added stability.

Tire Grading

All passenger (P) vehicle tires have UTQG (uniform tire quality grading) ratings established by the United States Department of Transportation (DOT). These have been set to help consumers compare tire brands and types. The three UTQG ratings (*Figure 14.10*) are treadwear, traction, and temperature. The treadwear rating, given as a number, is based on the wear rate of the tire when tested in a controlled setting. For example, a tire graded 300 should last twice as long as a 150 tire. Traction ratings, shown as *AA*, *A*, *B*, or *C*, represent a tire's ability to grip the road on a wet surface. An *AA* rating has superb traction, an *A* rating has excellent traction, a *B* rating has good traction, and a *C* rated tire has poor traction. The third rating, temperature, represents a tires ability to resist high temperatures. These are rated as being *A*, *B*, or *C* – where *A* can withstand the highest temperature.

Ratings	BEST	⇔		POOR
Treadwear	500+			100
Traction	AA	A	B	C
Temperature	A		B	C

Figure 14.10　　　　　　　　*UTQG Ratings*

Light Truck Tire Load Range

The load range, ply rating, and maximum inflation pressure determines the load that the tire can carry. Light truck tire sizes are often available in several load ranges (*Figure 14.11*).

Load Range	Ply Rating	Max PSI	Max kPa
B	4	35	241
C	6	50	345
D	8	65	448
E	10	80	552
F	12	95	655

Figure 14.11　　　　　　　*Light Truck Tire Load Range*

Run Flat Tires

Tire technology continues to advance. When some tires are punctured, they have the ability to maintain mobility. Three technologies that are emerging are self-sealing, self-supporting, and tire/wheel combination systems. Self-sealing tires have a special lining inside that will permanently seal most small nail or screw punctures. Self-supporting tires are designed with a stiff internal construction, generally carrying the weight of a vehicle for about 50 miles (80 km) even if the tire loses all air pressure. Tire/wheel combination systems use a special tire and wheel assembly that has a support ring to carry the weight of the vehicle if the tire loses air pressure. These tire and wheel assemblies allow the vehicle to be driven about 125 miles (201 km) with no air pressure.

✓ Tech Tip

Buying Tires

When pricing tires, make sure you include mounting, balancing, disposal, and road hazard insurance (if desired, to cover tire replacement costs if it is damaged beyond repair). It is also recommended that new valve stems are installed. Over time, this little (but important) component also wears from the weather. Always replace tires in pairs or complete sets.

🚚 Trouble Guide

Vibration

- Out of balance tire
- Tire has broken belts

Tire Care and Maintenance

Inspecting your tires on a regular basis will help you identify their condition. Many things can cause abnormal tire wear (*Figure 14.12*): underinflation, overinflation, worn steering components, worn suspension components, tires out of balance, and tire misalignment (e.g., camber or toe). This section focuses on:

- Tire Wear Indicator Bars
- Tire Rotation
- Tire Repairs
- Tire Pressure Monitoring System

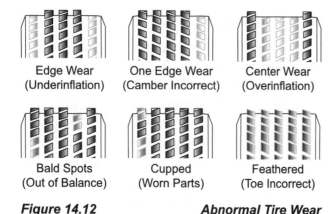

Edge Wear (Underinflation)   One Edge Wear (Camber Incorrect)   Center Wear (Overinflation)

Bald Spots (Out of Balance)   Cupped (Worn Parts)   Feathered (Toe Incorrect)

Figure 14.12   *Abnormal Tire Wear*

Tire Wear Indicator Bars

The design of tire tread, the part of the tire that contacts the road, determines how well a tire will act on different road conditions, such as ice, water, mud, and snow. A tire with very little tread is more likely to lose traction or hydroplane when roads are wet. Hydroplaning occurs when the tire is lifted off the road by a thin film of water. Tire wear indicator bars (*Figure 14.13*) run perpendicular to the tread providing a visual, tool free inspection of tread depth. Tread depth is measured in 32nds of an inch or in millimeters. A tire is legally worn out when tread reaches 2/32nds of an inch (1.6 mm), the same level as the indicator bars. Inspect your tires regularly to make sure they have plenty of tread.

Wear Indicator Bars

Figure 14.13   *Wear Indicator Bars*

Tire Rotation

Rotating tires improves tire life. Check your owner's manual for the rotation pattern (*Figure 14.14*). Be aware that some tires are directional, designed to roll in one direction. An arrow on the sidewall indicates the forward rotation on directional tires.

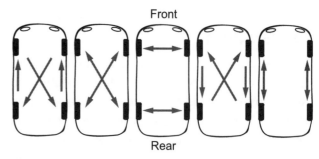

Front

Rear

Figure 14.14   *Example Tire Rotation Patterns*

It is important to torque the lug nuts in a star pattern (*Figure 14.15*) with a torque wrench. Torque refers to getting all of the lug nuts to the same tightness. Over tightened lug nuts will make it difficult to change the tire in the future, while under tightened lug nuts may loosen up and cause the wheel to come off. In addition, unevenly tightened lug nuts can warp brake drums and rotors. See the Tire Inspection and Rotation Activity for additional information about completing tire rotations.

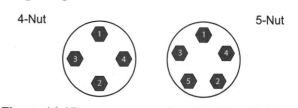

4-Nut   5-Nut

Figure 14.15   *Lug Nut Star Patterns*

🚚 Trouble Guide

Excessive Tire Wear

- Incorrect tire pressure
- Excessive speeds in turns
- Excessive braking
- Tires out of balance
- Suspension/steering components excessively worn
- Alignment incorrect

Tire Repairs

A quality and safe tire repair requires a patch/plug combination to seal and fill a puncture. When a tire is removed from the rim the reassembled wheel should be rebalanced after making the repair. Only small holes in the tread can be repaired. The sidewall experiences too much stress from expansion and contraction as the tire rotates down the highway and therefore should not be repaired.

Tire Pressure Monitoring System

Correct tire pressure is critical to tire wear and vehicle handling. A tire pressure monitoring system (TPMS) is used to alert the driver if any tire is significantly low on pressure (*Figure 14.16*). Vehicles that have a gross vehicle weight ratio of less than 10,000 pounds (4,536 kg) and manufactured on or after September 1st, 2007 are required by the National Highway Traffic Safety Administration to have a TPMS. Automotive manufacturers have had several years to phase in this technology, so your vehicle may have a TPMS already. Before having tire service completed, make sure the service facility is familiar with protecting sensors and resetting the TPMS.

Figure 14.16   *Tire Pressure Monitor Indicator*

It is still a good idea to check the pressure in your tires at least once a month. Locate the vehicle's tire placard (*Figure 14.17*) for the recommended tire pressure. Tire pressure is based on tire type, vehicle weight, and ride performance desired. The tire placard should be on the driver's side door. Use a high quality air gauge and remember

to replace the valve stem caps. Always check when tires are cold and before long trips. See page 49 for the procedure to check tire pressure.

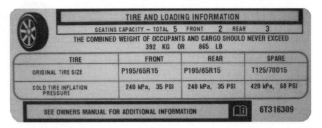

TIRE AND LOADING INFORMATION			
SEATING CAPACITY – TOTAL 5 FRONT 2 REAR 3			
THE COMBINED WEIGHT OF OCCUPANTS AND CARGO SHOULD NEVER EXCEED 392 KG OR 865 LB			
TIRE	FRONT	REAR	SPARE
ORIGINAL TIRE SIZE	P195/65R15	P195/65R15	T125/70D15
COLD TIRE INFLATION PRESSURE	240 kPa, 35 PSI	240 kPa, 35 PSI	420 kPa, 60 PSI
SEE OWNERS MANUAL FOR ADDITIONAL INFORMATION			6T316309

Figure 14.17   **Tire Placard**

Summary

The suspension system absorbs bumps in the road to give you a smooth ride. The steering system allows the operator to control left and right motions of the vehicle. Tires provide the traction (adhesive friction) necessary for maneuvering. Knowing tire specifications can be beneficial when making decisions about new tires. Uniform tire quality grading ratings make it easier for you to compare different tires. Abnormal tire wear patterns show possible problems with the vehicle. Suspension and steering components work in conjunction to provide a safe ride.

 Activities

Suspension, Steering, and Tires

- Suspension and Steering Activity
- Tire Inspection and Rotation Activity
- Chapter 14 Study Questions

Activities can be accessed in the Auto Upkeep workbook or online at www.autoupkeep.com.

 Career Paths

Tire Manufacturing Engineer

Education: Bachelor's Degree
Median Income: $58,000
Job Market: Average Growth
Abilities: Applies material science and technology to design, manufacture, and test tires.

 Servicing

Tire Rotation

- Every 7,500 miles or as recommended by the manufacturer

CHAPTER 15

BRAKING SYSTEM

FUEL FOR THOUGHT

- How are disc and drum brakes different?
- How do antilock brakes work?
- How do you know when brake pads need replacing?

Introduction

The braking system is designed to help the operator control the deceleration of the vehicle. While the suspension and steering systems control the ride and directional movements, the braking system is designed to slow or stop the vehicle. The braking system is crucial to the safe operation of the vehicle. This chapter identifies brake components and the principles that assist in slowing a vehicle.

 ## Web Links

Brake System Related Sites

Bendix Brakes
↳   www.bendixbrakes.com
Federal-Mogul (Wagner Brake Products)
↳   www.federal-mogul.com
Meineke Muffler and Brake
↳   www.meineke.com
Midas International Corporation
↳   www.midas.com
Raybestos Brakes
↳   www.raybestos.com

Objectives

Upon completion of this chapter and activities, you will be able to:
- Define the purpose and principles of the braking system.
- Identify the different types of brakes and their components.
- Identify brake fluid properties.
- Discuss the advantage of antilock brakes.
- Explain how the parking brake works.
- Safely perform basic inspections on the braking system.

Braking System Purpose

The braking system is designed to decrease the speed of a vehicle. In order to slow a vehicle there needs to be friction between parts. Unlike the lubrication system, where minimizing friction is the goal, the braking system is designed to use friction for control. ***Warning: Some brake frictional material contains asbestos. Wear an OSHA approved respirator when inspecting or replacing brake components at the wheels.***

Types of Brakes

Disc and drum are two types of brakes commonly used on automobiles. Some vehicles only have disc brakes, but many vehicles have a combination of both types. On vehicles with discs and drums, disc brakes are the front brakes while drum brakes are the rear brakes. More recently, manufacturers have been installing disc brakes on all four wheels as standard equipment. Hybrid vehicles use regenerative braking in addition to conventional brakes. Regenerative braking turns a motor to recapture energy instead of wasting it as heat from friction.

Braking System Components

Disc and drum brake systems both use a brake pedal, master cylinder, and brake lines. Both disc and drum brake systems use a frictional type material that slowly wears as the brakes are applied. The major difference between the disc and drum brake systems is the hardware at the wheels. This section focuses on:

- Brake Pedal
- Master Cylinder
- Brake Lines
- Disc Brakes
- Drum Brakes

Brake Pedal

The amount of friction created is controlled by the operator exerting force on the brake pedal. Force is defined as the pushing or pulling action of one object upon another. In this example, the operator's foot is one object, while the brake pedal is the other object. Friction increases as the operator pushes harder on the brake pedal.

🚛 Trouble Guide

Pedal Travels to the Floor

- Low brake fluid
- Brake fluid leak
- Air in the brake system
- Incorrect drum brake shoe adjustment

Master Cylinder

The brake pedal is mechanically connected to a hydraulic unit called a master cylinder (*Figure 15.1*). The master cylinder reservoir is where brake fluid is stored.

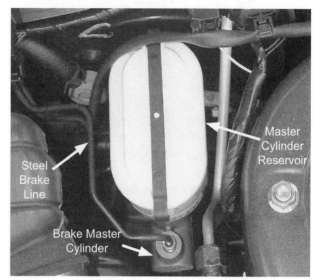

Figure 15.1   Brake Master Cylinder and Reservoir

Brake Lines

As force is exerted on the brake pedal, fluid is sent to all of the wheels from the master cylinder through brake lines (*Figure 15.2*). Once at the wheels, the fluid pressure is converted back to mechanical pressure in the caliper or wheel cylinder. This pressure causes the brake pads or shoes to move against the rotating disc or drum at the wheels creating the needed friction to slow the vehicle.

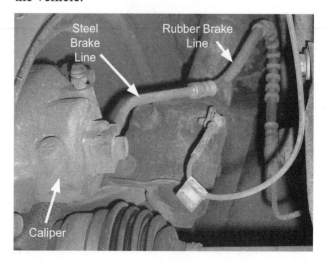

Figure 15.2   **Caliper and Brake Lines**

Disc Brakes

The disc brake hardware at the wheel consists of a rotor, two brake pads, and a caliper (*Figure 15.3*).

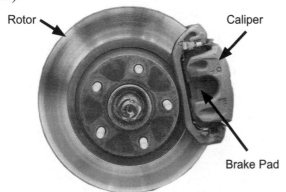

Figure 15.3   *Brake Rotor, Pads, and Caliper*

The disc, also called a rotor, (*Figure 15.4*), connects to the wheel hub. Friction is produced when the brakes are applied. This friction creates a lot of heat, so rotors are often vented to help with cooling. When inspecting rotors check both sides for thickness, cracks, unevenness, warping, and deep scoring. If a rotor measures thick enough, it may be possible to resurface it smooth. It is commonly recommended to replace or resurface rotors in pairs, so their thickness remains balanced and surface finish is consistent.

Figure 15.4   *Brake Disc (Rotor)*

A set of brake pads (*Figure 15.5*) hug the rotor. As force is applied to the brake pedal, the brake pads hug the rotor tighter causing more friction. The friction causes the vehicle to slow down.

Figure 15.5   *Brake Pads*

Some brake pads are engineered with mechanical or electrical wear indicators as a reminder when it is time for replacement. A mechanical indicator (*Figure 15.6*) uses a thin metal strip against the rotor to produce a high-pitched squeal. It is made to squeal once the pad wears down without causing rotor damage. The electrical indicator uses an electrical contact in the pad. When the pad has worn to that electrical ground contact it completes a circuit and a dash indicator lamp (also called a MIL – malfunction indicator light) lights up. The caliper, a type of hydraulic C-clamp with a piston, holds a brake pad on either side of the rotor (*Figure 15.6*). The caliper converts the fluid pressure in the brake lines to the mechanical motion of the pads against each side of the rotor.

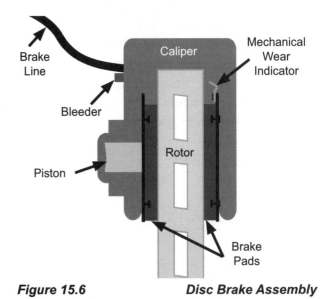

Figure 15.6   *Disc Brake Assembly*

❓ Q & A

Brake Squeal

Q: What is the high-pitched squeal that goes away every time I apply my brakes?

A: The squeal that you hear is most likely coming from a thin metal wear indicator on your brake pad. To stop the squealing you need to install new brake pads. If you don't replace the brake pads you will soon hear a metal on metal grinding noise that will damage the rotors and create a braking hazard.

Drum Brakes

The drum brake hardware at a wheel consists of a drum, two brake shoes, return springs, holddown springs, a wheel cylinder, and other miscellaneous hardware (*Figure 15.7*).

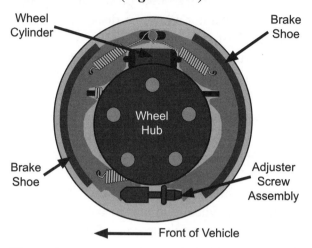

Figure 15.7   ***Drum Brake Assembly***

The brake drum (*Figure 15.8*) connects to the wheel hub. If a newer vehicle has drum brakes, they are on the back wheels. Similar to rotors, it may be possible to resurface the drums if they are thick enough. The drums should be machined equally as a pair.

Figure 15.8   ***Brake Drum***

✓ Tech Tip

Warped Brakes

If a pulsation is noticed when the brakes are applied, the rotors or drums may be warped. Brake rotors or drums can become warped if lug nuts are not tightened to the correct torque. They can also become warped if cold water comes in contact with them immediately after the brakes have been used excessively.

Inside the drum is a set of brake shoes (*Figure 15.9*). When force is applied to the brake pedal or when the parking brake is engaged, the brake shoes are forced out against the brake drum creating friction to slow and stop the wheels.

Figure 15.9   ***Brake Shoes***

A wheel cylinder (*Figure 15.10*) converts the fluid pressure in the brake lines to the mechanical motion of the shoes against the drums.

Figure 15.10   ***Wheel Cylinder***

🕐 Servicing

Brake Pads and Shoes

- Inspect once a year
- Change when worn past specifications

🚛 Trouble Guide

High Pitched Brake Squeal

- Disc brake pads worn out

Grinding Brakes

- Disc brake pads or shoes worn out

Pulsating Brakes

- Disc warped
- Drum warped

Brake Fluid

Brake fluid links the major braking system components. Brake fluid travels through the brake lines to connect the master cylinder to the calipers in a disc brake system and the wheel cylinders in a drum brake system. Brake fluid must remain clear of contaminates (*Figure 15.11*) to flow freely at high and low temperatures. Brake fluid fights corrosion, lubricates moving parts, and protects metal, plastic, and rubber components. Old brake fluid can cause costly brake components to deteriorate and create a hazardous driving condition. It is important to perform recommended brake fluid changes. The most common type of brake fluid is DOT 3, but always refer to the owner's manual for the specific vehicle. A dash light may indicate when brake fluid is low.

Contaminate	Solution
Moisture	Brake fluid is designed to absorb and retain moisture to keep it from corrupting the brake system. Gradually moisture absorbed by brake fluid will reduce the brake fluid's boiling point. To maintain the required temperature properties only use brake fluid from a fresh sealed container and flush the system as recommended.
Dirt	To prevent dirt contamination, always clean the outside of the master cylinder reservoir before removing the cap and adding fluid.
Air	Often when brake components are replaced, air gets into the system. With air in the system the operator will notice a very spongy and soft brake pedal. Air is compressible while fluid is not compressible. Air must be removed by bleeding the system. Bleeding the air out of the system consists of pushing the air out of a "bleeder" at the caliper or wheel cylinder.

Figure 15.11   **Brake Fluid Contaminates**

⏱ Servicing

Brake Fluid

- Change every 4 years, 48,000 miles, or during brake service

Antilock Brakes

Antilock brakes can be used with both disc and drum brake systems. In a conventional braking system, the wheels are likely to lockup if enough force is applied to the brake pedal. During wheel lockup, the operator's braking distance increases and control of steering decreases. An antilock brake system (ABS) minimizes wheel lockup (skidding) by using sensors at each wheel (or in the differential) to monitor wheel speed, a hydraulic control unit (*Figure 15.12*) to regulate hydraulic brake pressure, and a computer/controller to command the system. If a sensor indicates that a wheel is about to lockup, the ABS hydraulic control unit releases hydraulic pressure in the caliper or wheel cylinder at that one wheel. The rapid pressure adjustments of the ABS may make the brake pedal feel like it is pulsating. This is normal. On ABS systems always apply firm constant pressure and do not pump the brakes.

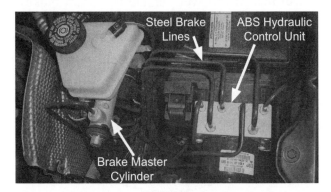

Figure 15.12   **ABS Hydraulic Control Unit**

ABS does not always stop a vehicle faster, but it does help the operator maintain control. Some vehicles have ABS on two wheels and some have it on all four wheels. If a vehicle only has two-wheel antilock brakes, the ABS is usually in the rear of the vehicle. If the ABS light (*Figure 15.13*) comes on have a technician check for diagnostic error codes and inspect the brake system. The conventional part of the brake system will still be operational.

Figure 15.13   **Antilock Brake System Symbol**

Electronic Stability Control

Electronic stability control (ESC) has been added to many vehicles to help drivers maintain control during unstable situations such as attempting to avoid a crash or during unfavorable weather conditions. The ESC system uses information from sensors to improve the lateral stability in a vehicle by applying braking force at any wheel when instability is detected. This technology minimizes oversteer and understeer situations which ultimately helps the vehicle stay on the intended course, lessening the likelihood of skidding and rollovers. Since ESC has proven to be an outstanding safety feature, the National Highway Traffic Safety Administration has proposed that it be required on 2012 model year vehicles sold in the United States.

Parking Brakes

A parking brake usually uses the same hardware at the wheels that is used for stopping a vehicle. However, instead of using fluid as the connection between the pedal and the brakes, a mechanical cable is used. A hand lever (*Figure 15.14*) in the center of the console or small foot pedal on the far left side of the driver's foot controls engages the cable. The mechanical cable allows the systems to work independently of each other. The parking brake usually connects to the two rear brakes. To keep a parking brake cable from seizing, use it whenever parking. Moving the cable helps to keep it from corroding. If you notice that the brake lever or pedal moves further than normal, this may be an indication that your rear brakes or cable are worn.

Figure 15.14   *Parking Brake Hand Lever*

Summary

Brake systems use friction to slow and stop a vehicle. The two types of brake systems used today are disc and drum brakes. Disc brakes use rotors, pads, and calipers. Drum brakes use drums, shoes, and wheel cylinders. Antilock brakes assist in preventing wheel lockup and provide the operator with maximum directional control. The parking brake uses a mechanical linkage (cable) instead of a fluid linkage (brake fluid). Advanced technological systems, such as electronic stability control and antilock braking systems, have been installed on cars to maximize driver control.

🚗 Activities

Braking System

- Brake Inspection Activity
- Chapter 15 Study Questions

Activities can be accessed in the Auto Upkeep workbook or online at www.autoupkeep.com.

🎓 Career Paths

Brake Technician

Education: Technical Training or ASE Cert.
Median Income: $40,000
Job Market: Average Growth
Abilities: Understands principles of electronics and hydraulics. Lathe operation experience.

💰 Price Guide

Brake Fluid
↳ $1.00 to $3.00 a pint
Brake Pads
↳ $30.00 to $50.00 a set (parts)
Brake Shoes
↳   to $30.00 a set (parts)
Brake Rotor or Drum
↳ $50.00 each (parts)

Note:
1 pt = 0.473 L

CHAPTER 16

DRIVETRAIN

FUEL FOR THOUGHT

- What is the purpose of the drivetrain?
- What might be the problem if your vehicle hesitates when shifting gears?
- What types of drivetrain configurations are available?

Introduction

The engine can provide all the power in the world, but if it isn't transferred to the wheels the car will not move. Automobiles need to perform equally well under a variety of loads. The transfer of power needs to accommodate the conditions on the highway, the weight of the vehicle and its passengers, and the performance desired to accelerate. Today's automobile buyers can choose between rear-wheel, front-wheel, four-wheel, or all-wheel drivetrains. This chapter identifies the purpose of the drivetrain, drivetrain components, and types of drivetrains.

Objectives

Upon completion of this chapter and activities, you will be able to:

- Define the purpose of the drivetrain.
- Identify drivetrain components.
- Identify and describe different drivetrain systems.
- Inspect drivetrain systems.

Purpose of the Drivetrain

The purpose of the drivetrain (*Figure 16.1*) is to transfer power from the engine to the wheels in order to propel the vehicle. This transfer needs to be done smoothly and efficiently. Without smooth transitions, the automobile would not be very comfortable or easy to drive. The drivetrain also helps to control the speed and power through gears.

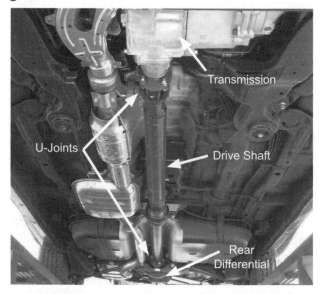

Figure 16.1   **Drivetrain Components on a Rear-Wheel Drive Vehicle**

Transmission Fluid

Transmission fluid plays a vital role in cooling, cleaning, lubricating, and sealing transmission components. When servicing or adding fluid to a transmission, always check the owner's manual for recommendations. This section focuses on:
- Automatic Transmission Fluid
- Manual Transmission Fluid
- Changing Transmission Fluid

Automatic Transmission Fluid

The fluid level on most automatic transmissions is checked with a dipstick under the hood (*Figure 16.2*), similar to an oil dipstick. Keep in mind that an automatic CVT transmission may have a check plug instead of a dipstick. See page 69 for more information on checking automatic transmission fluid. New automatic transmission fluid is typically dyed a pinkish-red color to keep it from being confused with engine oil and to help find leaks. Always check the owner's manual for fluid checking procedures and recommended specifications.

Figure 16.2   *Automatic Transmission Dipstick*

Manual Transmission Fluid

As explained on page 69, manual transmissions have a more complex fluid checking method than automatic transmissions because usually there is not a dipstick under the hood. A plug on the side of the transmission must be removed from under the vehicle. Even though the checking method is not as convenient it is still important to check. Manual transmissions may take automatic transmission fluid, motor oil, or heavyweight gear oil. Always check the owner's manual for fluid specifications.

Changing Transmission Fluid

To maintain any transmission it is necessary to change the fluid as recommended by the manufacturer. Manual transmissions have a drain and fill plug. Automatic transmissions commonly do not have a plug. The pan itself can be removed, but because of various internal transmission components it is not easy to extract all of the old transmission fluid. It is best to take the vehicle to a facility that has a special flushing machine for this purpose. When having the transmission flushed ask for the pan to be cleaned and the filter removed and replaced. This will incur added cost, but will ensure a completely clean system. Another approach would be to alternate service intervals between a transmission flush and a traditional filter and fluid change. Excessive metal shavings are often a sign that the transmission needs further repairs.

✓ Tech Tip

Transmission Filters

Automatic transmissions, more complex than manual transmissions, have filters to clean the fluid. Since automatic transmissions shift by themselves, they have more friction than a manual transmission. Friction increases heat and wear within the transmission. Even though manual transmissions do not have filters, they often require regular service intervals.

Servicing

Automatic Transmission Fluid
- Change every 2 years, 24,000 miles, or as recommended by the manufacturer

Manual Transmission Fluid
- Change according to owner's manual

CVT Transmission Fluid
- Change every 2 years, 30,000 miles or as recommended by the manufacturer

Drivetrain Components

Several components need to work together to transfer an engine's power smoothly and efficiently to a vehicle's wheels. This section focuses on:

- Gears
- Transmissions
- Drive Shafts
- Differentials
- Transaxles
- Clutches

Gears

Gears (*Figure 16.3*) are used in power transfer systems like transmissions and differentials. Gears, always engineered in sets, are used to change speed, torque, and direction of travel.

Figure 16.3   ***Gears***

Transmissions

A transmission can be manual, automatic, or continuously variable. Transmissions adjust the power to the wheels for different applications. Maintaining a steady speed requires less power than accelerating to that speed. In manual transmissions the operator of the vehicle must use a clutch before shifting gears by hand with a gear stick. Manual transmissions commonly come in 3, 4, 5, or 6 speeds. An automatic transmission uses a torque converter with transmission fluid to couple with an engine and provide automatic gear shifting. The operator only has to select a forward or reverse gear. Today there are many computer controlled electronic transmissions that calculate the most efficient time to shift. Continuously variable transmissions (CVTs) have begun to appear more on passenger cars as the advantages of their use have become more apparent (*Figure 16.4*). Instead of using gears, CVTs commonly use two variable speed cone-shaped pulleys in conjunction with a belt for an infinitely variable gear ratio.

CVT Benefits Compared to Automatic Transmission	
Smooth Ride	Acceleration and deceleration seamless. No gear shifting hesitation or jolt.
Improved Fuel Economy	Requires less fuel because engine runs consistently at levels of optimum power.
Increased Acceleration	Less power is lost because it is more efficient at adjusting energy required.
Reduced Emissions	Pollutes less by maintaining needed speed with minimal wasted RPMs.
Less Weight	Design is less complex with fewer parts.

Figure 16.4   ***CVT Benefits***

Drive Shafts

Drive shafts are designed to transfer power from the transmission to the wheels. Constant velocity (CV) shafts are used on front-wheel, four-wheel, and all-wheel drive vehicles. On front-wheel drive vehicles a CV shaft (*Figure 16.5*) on each side connects the transaxle to each front wheel. Rubber boots protect the flexible CV shaft joint areas and hold grease for lubrication.

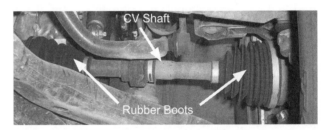

Figure 16.5   ***Constant Velocity Shaft***

❓ Q & A

Clicking Noise

Q: What might cause a clicking noise when I turn sharply on my front-wheel drive car?
A: Worn CV joints can cause a clicking noise. The joints, covered by a boot at the end of the CV shaft, need to be flexible to allow for suspension movement and turning. If the boot gets torn, dirt and moisture may enter and the grease in the joint may come out. Foreign particles, with the absence of a sufficient quantity of grease, corrode and ruin the joint. Eventually if the joint is not replaced it will break and you will need to be towed.

On rear-wheel drive vehicles, the drive shaft connects the transmission to the rear differential, which sends the power to the rear wheels through drive axles. Four-wheel and all-wheel drive vehicles usually have constant velocity (CV) and standard drive shafts (*Figure 16.6*).

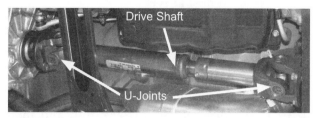

Figure 16.6   *Standard Drive Shaft*

Standard drive shafts are steel or aluminum tubes with welded ends. Their joints, called universal or U-joints (*Figure 16.7*) accept the moving chassis. U-joints can fail if they lose lubrication or eventually wear over time.

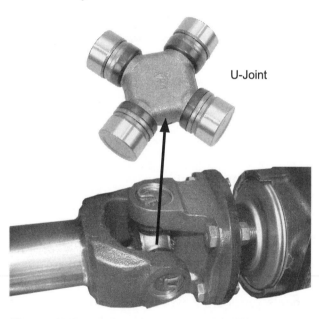

Figure 16.7   *Installed U-Joint*

Differentials

A differential (*Figure 16.8*) is a set of gears inside the axle housing that transfers the torque from the drive shaft to the wheels. The rear differential is located at the end of the drive shaft on a rear-wheel drive vehicle. Four-wheel drive vehicles have front and rear differentials. While turning, a vehicle's outer wheels rotate quicker than the inside wheels. The differential allows wheels to rotate at different speeds.

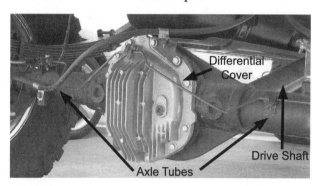

Figure 16.8   *Rear Differential*

Transaxles

Commonly on front-wheel drive vehicles, the function of the transmission and differential is engineered into one component called a transaxle. By combining these functions into one unit, the transaxle can work more efficiently and be compact for transverse engine designs.

🛻 Trouble Guide

Transmission "Clunk" Sound

- Worn universal joints

Automatic Transmission Slips

- Low fluid
- Worn transmission

💰 Price Guide

Automatic Transmission Fluid (ATF)
  ↳ $1.50 to $3.00 a quart
Clutch and Pressure Plate
  ↳ $100.00 to $300.00 (parts)
CV Boot each (parts)
  ↳ $15.00 to $45.00 each (parts)
CV Joint/Shaft
  ↳ $75.00 to $125.00 each (parts)
Manual Transmission Fluid/Differential Fluid
  ↳ $2.00 to $4.00 a quart
U-Joint
  ↳ $15.00 each (parts)

Note:
1 qt = 0.946 L

Clutches

A manual transmission uses a clutch disc in conjunction with a pressure plate (*Figure 16.9*) to allow the operator to shift gears. The clutch is the connection between the transmission and engine. When the clutch is engaged, the engine is driving the transmission. When the clutch is disengaged (when the clutch pedal is pushed down), the transmission is disconnected from the rotational motion of the engine's crankshaft. The pressure plate works with the clutch disc to aid in the engaging and disengaging process, allowing the operator to move a gear stick shifter and change from one gear to the next.

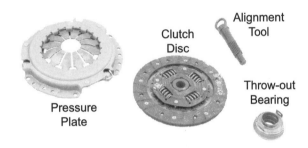

Figure 16.9   ***Clutch Components***

🚛 Trouble Guide

Gears Difficult to Shift

- Worn clutch
- Faulty clutch slave cylinder
- Air in hydraulic clutch system

❓ Q & A

Clutch Slipping

Q: My car struggles to speed up with my foot on the accelerator. When I downshift it doesn't help. There is also a burning smell.

A: Your clutch and/or pressure plate may be worn out. When a clutch is slipping, you can get a burning smell and the car will not accelerate as designed.

Drivetrain Systems

Drivetrain systems can be divided into the following categories:
- Rear-Wheel Drive
- Front-Wheel Drive
- Four-Wheel Drive
- All-Wheel Drive

Rear-Wheel Drive

On a rear-wheel drive (RWD) vehicle the power from the transmission is transferred through the drive shaft, through the differential, and then to the rear wheels (*Figure 16.10*). This was the standard on cars before the 1980s and still is the standard on most pickups.

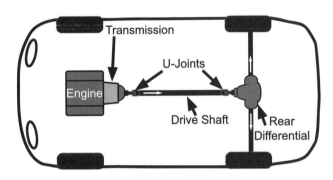

Figure 16.10   ***Rear-Wheel Drive***

Front-Wheel Drive

On a front-wheel drive (FWD) vehicle the power from the transaxle is transferred through the constant velocity shafts to the front wheels (*Figure 16.11*). This is the standard on most cars today. The weight of the engine on the front wheels gives front-wheel drive cars extremely good traction on diverse road conditions.

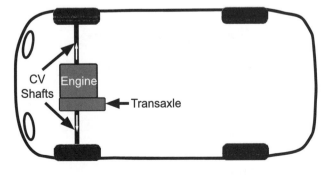

Figure 16.11   ***Front-Wheel Drive***

Four-Wheel Drive

On a four-wheel drive (4WD) vehicle the power from the transmission is transferred to the rear and/or front wheels (***Figure 16.12***). On a four-wheel drive vehicle the operator has the choice of selecting either two-wheel drive or four-wheel drive. Many trucks have this option. Four-wheel drive vehicles have lower fuel economy than two-wheel drive vehicles. This is caused from the addition of friction from the drivetrain turning more components.

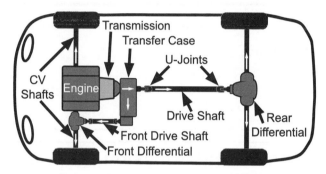

Figure 16.12   ***Four-Wheel Drive***

All-Wheel Drive

On an all-wheel drive (AWD) vehicle the power from the transmission is transferred to the front wheels and rear wheels (***Figure 16.13***). All-wheel drive systems are different from four-wheel drive systems. All-wheel drive vehicles use electronics to control the power transfer to the wheels. Speed sensors are mounted on each wheel to monitor wheel traction. The benefit of an all-wheel drive vehicle is that when traction is lost at any one wheel, the power is automatically transferred to another. The result is superior traction and control. More and more automotive manufacturers are using all-wheel drivetrain systems on a broad range of vehicles.

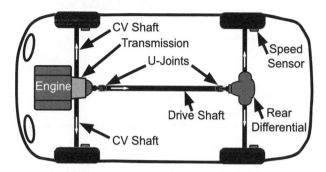

Figure 16.13   ***Symmetrical All-Wheel Drive***

Summary

Drivetrains transfer power from the engine to the wheels. Gears, transmissions, drive shafts, and differentials are used to transmit the power. Vehicles can be front-, rear-, four-, or all-wheel drive. All-wheel drive vehicles have become popular because they have superior traction on all types of road conditions.

Web Links

Drivetrain Related Sites

AutoZone Automotive Parts
↳   www.autozone.com
Brute Power Clutch Kits
↳   www.brutepower.com
Federated Auto Parts
↳   www.federatedautoparts.com
Qualitee International (Clutch Kits)
↳   www.qualitee.com

 ## Activities

Drivetrain

- Drivetrain Activity
- Chapter 16 Study Questions

Activities can be accessed in the Auto Upkeep workbook or online at www.autoupkeep.com.

Career Paths

Transmission Specialist

Education: Technical Training or ASE Cert.
Median Income: $46,000
Job Market: Average Growth
Abilities: Computer knowledge, analytical skills, problem solving, and detail oriented.

CHAPTER 17

EXHAUST AND EMISSION SYSTEM

FUEL FOR THOUGHT

- Why is it critical to move exhaust gases away from the passenger cabin?
- What is the function of the catalytic converter?
- Why is emission testing commonly required?

Introduction

Exhaust and emission systems on newer vehicles have become more complex than in the past. The emission system is used to monitor air-fuel ratios and has many benefits to the operator and the environment. For many years, automotive manufacturers were just concerned about getting the hot and toxic exhaust gases out to the side or rear of the vehicle. Today exhaust and emission systems are complex mechanisms that provide safety, efficiency, and concern for our fragile environment. Periodically, exhaust and emission system components need replacing. This chapter focuses on identifying the components and purposes of the exhaust and emission system.

Objectives

Upon completion of this chapter and activities, you will be able to:

- Define the purpose of the exhaust and emission system.
- Identify and explain the components in an exhaust and emission system.
- Inspect exhaust and emission system components.

Exhaust and Emission Purpose

The exhaust and emission system (*Figure 17.1*) is designed to deal with the inefficient by-products of the internal combustion process. The exhaust components are designed to dampen the sound of the engine. The emission components are designed to lower the pollution of the vehicle. Vehicle pollution is generally categorized into tailpipe, crankcase, and evaporative emissions.

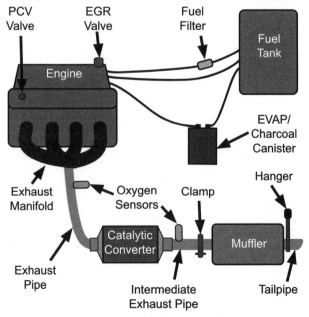

Figure 17.1   *Exhaust and Emission System*

Exhaust Components

The exhaust system consists of the following components:

- Exhaust Manifolds
- Exhaust Pipes
- Muffler
- Hangers and Clamps

Exhaust Manifolds

The exhaust manifolds, usually made out of cast iron, connect directly to the engine. The exhaust manifolds are designed to harness the exhaust gases from combustion in the cylinders into one pipe. Inline engines have one exhaust manifold, while V configured engines have two (one for each bank of cylinders).

Exhaust Pipes

Exhaust pipes are tubes of steel that connect other components such as the exhaust manifolds to the catalytic converter. An exhaust pipe, called the intermediate pipe, connects the catalytic converter to the muffler. Another pipe, a tailpipe (*Figure 17.2*), expels the exhaust from the muffler.

Figure 17.2   ***Tailpipe and Hanger***

Muffler

The muffler (*Figure 17.3*), usually oval or cylindrical in shape, is used to deaden the sound from the engine. It is basically a silencer to aid in the reduction of noise pollution and is located after the catalytic converter, but before the tailpipe.

Figure 17.3   ***Muffler***

✓ Tech Tip

Replacing Exhaust Components

Often the muffler on the exhaust system rusts out before anything else. This is because water vapor has a tendency to collect in the muffler. Most factory exhaust systems are welded assemblies from the catalytic to the tailpipe. It is relatively easy to replace everything from the catalytic on back, even if the muffler is the only worn out part. If you have a shop replace only the muffler, it may cost about as much as if you replaced the system from the catalytic on back. If you just replace the muffler there is usually more labor involved with cutting and fabricating. Replacing all the components from the catalytic back is usually just a matter of bolting and hanging the parts in place.

❓ Q & A

Carbon Monoxide

Q: I was driving yesterday and for no apparent reason I almost fell asleep. Does a car emit carbon monoxide as I drive it?

A: Carbon monoxide (CO), a pollutant, is released from incomplete combustion in internal combustion engines. If there is a leak in the exhaust system you could be getting this odorless, colorless, and poisonous gas in the vehicle. Symptoms include headaches, shortness of breath, dizziness, fatigue, nausea, and confusion. Get the vehicle inspected by a qualified technician right away. Have it towed to a repair facility.

Hangers and Clamps

Exhaust hangers (*Figure 17.4*) suspend the whole exhaust system. The hanger must allow some flexibility. The exhaust system is connected to the engine and to the body. As the engine runs, it vibrates and expands from heat. If the exhaust system was connected solidly to the body, stress cracks would develop. The hangers have flexible rubber components to compensate for this movement.

Figure 17.4   *Exhaust Hanger*

The exhaust clamps (*Figure 17.5*) connect the exhaust pipes to the muffler and catalytic converter. Exhaust clamps are usually a type of U-bolt. On new exhaust systems, welds instead of clamps hold the exhaust pipes to the muffler and the catalytic converter.

Figure 17.5   *Exhaust Clamp*

🕐 Servicing

Exhaust
- Inspect once a year
- Change as needed

🚛 Trouble Guide

Excessively Loud Exhaust
- Hole in muffler
- Hole in exhaust pipes
- Worn exhaust manifold gaskets

Engine Performance Issues
- Emission system malfunctioning

Emission Components

The environment has become a big concern for many people, and rightfully so. Vehicles produce a large amount of by-products that are harmful to our ecosystem. Consumers can minimize pollution by driving more efficient vehicles and by driving less. Planning trips will save petroleum, money, and harmful environmental effects. Emission system components presented are:
- Catalytic Converter
- PCV
- EGR
- EVAP/Charcoal Canister
- Oxygen Sensors
- Powertrain Control Module

Catalytic Converter

The catalytic converter (*Figure 17.6*) is placed under the automobile in the exhaust system between the exhaust manifold(s) and muffler.

Figure 17.6   *Catalytic Converter*

❓ Q & A

Catalytic Converter Clogged

Q: What causes a catalytic converter to fail?
A: A rich fuel mixture can cause the catalytic converter to prematurely fail. If unburned fuel enters the converter, it can overheat. The exhaust gases can be analyzed to determine if the air-fuel mixture is correct. An overuse of some fuel additives can also shorten the converter's life. A loss of power, poor fuel economy, or engine missing can be signs of a clogged converter. A catalytic converter often lasts a vehicle's lifetime. But if you are having a problem, be sure to check your owner's manual for the emission system warranty, which often exceeds the normal warranty.

The catalytic converter contains a catalyst that promotes the chemical change of carbon monoxide (CO), hydrocarbons (HC), and nitrogen oxides (NOx) into water vapor (H_2O), carbon dioxide (CO_2), and nitrogen (N) (*Figure 17.7*). These are tailpipe emissions. Carbon monoxide is a poisonous gas, which reduces the ability of the blood to carry oxygen. Hydrocarbons are toxic and contribute to smog. Nitrogen oxide is the main component that causes smog and acid rain. Carbon dioxide is not immediately harmful, but it does contribute to global climate change (global warming).

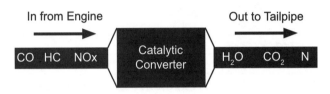

Figure 17.7   *Catalytic Converter Emissions*

PCV

The positive crankcase ventilation (PCV) (*Figure 17.8*) system is designed to remove the effects of blow-by. As the engine runs, some unburned fuel and water vapor get past the cylinders and into the crankcase. Water can turn oil into sludge, while unburned fuel can dilute the oil. If not handled correctly, water and unburned fuel can cause corrosion and increase engine wear. The PCV system recirculates the water vapor and unburned fuel back into the intake. This process will eventually burn the components in the combustion process. In the PCV system is a PCV valve that needs servicing at regular intervals. The PCV valve is commonly found between the cylinder head valve cover and the air cleaner. It is usually in a tube or connected directly into the valve cover.

Figure 17.8   *PCV Valve*

EGR

The exhaust gas recirculation system (*Figure 17.9*) reduces nitrogen oxide emissions by diluting the air-fuel mixture with the exhaust gases. Older EGR systems have an EGR valve that is operated by a vacuum from the engine. Most newer vehicles have EGRs that are electronic. With assistance from the powertrain control module (PCM), the EGR valve regulates the amount of exhaust gases that are redirected to the intake system. The EGR valve is typically mounted on top of the engine.

Figure 17.9   *EGR Valve*

EVAP/Charcoal Canister

An evaporative emissions (EVAP) control canister (*Figure 17.10*), also known as a charcoal or carbon canister, is used in the emission system to lower the release of hydrocarbons (e.g., fuel vapors) into the air. On older vehicles it looks like a coffee can and is located under the hood. On newer vehicles it is located by the fuel tank.

Figure 17.10   *EVAP Canister*

Oxygen Sensors

Oxygen sensors (*Figure 17.11*), also known as O_2 sensors, are usually placed before and/or after the catalytic converter. Some vehicles have four O_2 sensors. The O_2 sensor monitors the oxygen content in the vehicle's exhaust. It sends signals to the PCM (computer) to maintain a 14.7 to 1 (stoichiometric ratio) air to fuel ratio. This ratio of air to fuel makes the engine run smooth, efficient, and in the end, pollute less. The O_2 sensors before the catalytic converter are called upstream O_2 sensors and they monitor the combustion chamber efficiency. Those located after the catalytic converter are called downstream O_2 sensors and they check catalytic converter operation.

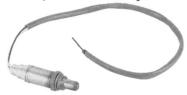

Figure 17.11 *Oxygen Sensor*

Powertrain Control Module

The use of a powertrain control module (PCM) was originally spurred by the government requiring manufacturers to lower vehicle emissions and increase fuel economy. The PCM receives information from sensors and then provides accurate and immediate commands. If the catalytic converter or other emission system component is not working properly or disconnected, the PCM will run the engine either too lean or too rich. Either way, efficiency and engine life will be less.

$ Price Guide

Catalytic Converter
↳ $150.00 to $300.00 each (parts)
Exhaust Pipes
↳ $20.00 to $60.00 each (parts)
Muffler
↳ $20.00 to $80.00 each (parts)
Oxygen Sensor
↳ $30.00 to $100.00 each (parts)

Emission Testing

Many locations require tailpipe emission testing (*Figure 17.12*) in an effort to limit environmental pollution from vehicles. Smog, also known as photochemical smog, is a type of air pollution. The word smog originally came from the two words **sm**oke and **f**o**g**. Photochemical smog forms from hydrocarbons, nitrogen oxides, and sunlight. Automobiles and other fossil fuel burning engines contribute to photochemical smog by emitting hydrocarbons and nitrogen oxides into the air.

Tailpipe Emissions Tested	
Hydrocarbons	(HC)
Carbon Monoxide	(CO)
Nitrogen Oxides	(NOx)

Figure 17.12 *Automotive Emissions Tested*

🖱 Web Links

Exhaust and Emission Sites
Arvin Industries (Exhaust Systems)
↳   www.arvin.com
Bosch
↳   www.boschautoparts.com
Dynomax Exhaust
↳   www.dynomax.com
Gibson Performance Exhaust Systems
↳   www.gibsonperformance.com
J.C. Whitney Inc.
↳   www.jcwhitney.com
Nickson Industries (Exhaust Accessories)
↳   www.nickson.com
Tenneco Automotive
↳   www.tenneco-automotive.com
Walker Exhaust Systems
↳   www.walkerexhaust.com

🕐 Servicing

Oxygen Sensors
• Change every 30,000 miles, or as recommended by the manufacturer

Emission testing determines the amount of pollution a vehicle releases, requiring vehicles that exceed set limits to be repaired, retested, or retired. The testing requirements and standards vary depending on location. Passing specifications and testing methods are also determined by the age and type of vehicle. A vehicle emission control information sticker (*Figure 17.13*) is located under the vehicle's hood.

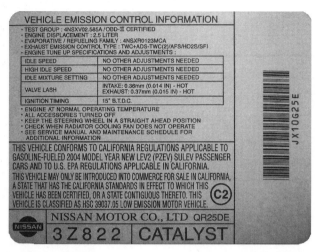

Figure 17.13   **VECI Sticker**

Before having your vehicle tested, plan to perform recommended preventative maintenance. A vehicle with the check engine light on is guaranteed not to pass testing. Never cut off emission components like the catalytic converter - it is illegal and will cause emission test failure. Vehicles are designed to run properly with emission components and will emit large amounts of pollution (*Figure 17.14*) if any of these components are disconnected or removed. If a vehicle does fail testing be sure to review the vehicle's emission performance warranty. Federal law requires the catalytic converter and PCM (computer) to be covered for 8 years/80,000 miles (130,000 km) on 1995 and newer vehicles. Emission repairs may be covered by this warranty, so consult your dealer.

Figure 17.14   **Vehicle Pollution**

✓ Tech Tip

Help for Passing Emission Test

To better control pollution there may be a consumer assistance program to help qualified vehicle owners with emission related repairs. Financial assistance may also be offered for voluntarily retiring a vehicle if it does not pass emission testing and is not worth repairing. Check with your emission testing station to see if a program exists in your area.

Summary

As technology advances, the internal combustion engine will become more efficient and pollute less. Over time, components have been added to vehicles to lower noise and reduce chemical pollution. The exhaust system reduces noise, while the emission control system converts harmful gases into more environmentally friendly by-products. Emission testing helps to keep vehicle emission levels regulated, minimizing the amount of pollution released into the environment.

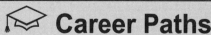

Activities

Exhaust and Emission System

- Exhaust and Emission Activity
- Chapter 17 Study Questions

Activities can be accessed in the Auto Upkeep workbook or online at www.autoupkeep.com.

Career Paths

Emissions Inspection Technician

Education: Technical Training and/or ASE Cert.
Median Income: $40,000
Job Market: Average Growth
Abilities: Understands emission testing equipment and emission regulations.

CHAPTER 18

ALTERNATIVE FUELS AND DESIGNS

FUEL FOR THOUGHT

- Why is it important to learn about alternative fuel vehicles?
- What is the difference between a renewable and a non-renewable resource?
- What issues influence the usability of alternative fuels?

Introduction

Energy is used to propel vehicles. Energy cannot be created or destroyed, but it can be converted from one form to another. In a traditional internal combustion vehicle, gasoline or diesel is used as chemical energy in the combustion process. Gasoline and diesel, both fossil fuels, are non-renewable resources. According to the United States Department of Energy, each day the United States consumes over 800 million gallons (over 3 billion L) of petroleum (crude oil). Over half of all the petroleum is used for gasoline. This chapter will identify a variety of alternative fuel energy sources for propelling vehicles. Some alternative fuels are derived from petroleum (e.g., propane and natural gas), others are non-petroleum based using renewable solar, biomass, hydro, and wind energy (*Figure 18.1*). Some non-petroleum alternatives are not currently practical for automobiles. The most popular alternative fuels and designs are hybrid and flex-fuel vehicles.

Objectives

Upon completion of this chapter and activities, you will be able to:

- Identify differences in automotive design, depending on the fuel source.
- Compare and contrast advantages and disadvantages between vehicles types.
- Compare petrobased and biobased fuels.
- Calculate the payback period on an alternative fueled vehicle.

Solar   Hydro

Biomass (Plant/Waste)   Wind

Figure 18.1   *Non-Petroleum Energy Sources*

Purpose of Alternatives

Automotive manufacturers are researching, developing, and mass producing a wide variety of alternative fuels and designs to increase energy efficiency, lessen petroleum dependency, and reduce or eliminate emissions. Various vehicle fuels and designs are being researched and developed. Examples include biodiesel, flex-fuel, natural gas, propane, bi-fuel, hybrid, electric, solar, and hydrogen fuel cell. The technological considerations of ideal alternative propulsion systems are whether they are environmentally safe, sustainable, practical, renewable, and affordable.

Biodiesel Vehicles

Biodiesel, an alternative to running 100% petroleum-based diesel (petrodiesel), is a renewable resource made from animal fats, vegetable oils, or recycled cooking grease through a refining process called transesterification. Straight vegetable oil (SVO) and waste vegetable oil (WVO) are not considered biodiesel until they have been transesterified. Soybean oil and WVO from restaurants are the most common sources of biodiesel in the United States. Biodiesel requires less energy to produce than ethanol, petrodiesel, or gasoline. Biodiesel can be burned at 100% or it can be blended with traditional petrodiesel. Biodiesel blends are given "B" designations. For example, B20 fuel is blended with 20%

biodiesel/80% petrodiesel. Pure biodiesel (B100) is non-toxic and biodegradable. In older vehicles, modifications commonly have to be made to the rubber components in the fuel delivery system since biodiesel can degrade them. Another disadvantage with 100% biodiesel is that it gels around 32-40°F (0-4°C). Using biodiesel is more environmentally friendly than petrodiesel, reducing pollution emissions and recycling carbon dioxide (*Figure 18.2*). It also has an increased lubricating ability, reducing friction in the engine.

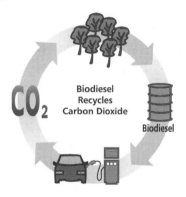

Figure 18.2 Biodiesel Recycles Carbon Dioxide
Source U.S. Department of Energy EERE - www.eere.energy.gov

✓ **Tech Tip**

Switching to Biodiesel

Biodiesel works as a cleaning solvent in a vehicle's fuel system. When switching from petrodiesel it removes sludge and deposits that have collected over the years. As residue is cleaned out it ends up in the fuel filter. A clogged fuel filter will result in a gradual loss of power when stepping on the accelerator. It is a good idea to keep a spare diesel fuel filter handy.

✓ **Tech Tip**

Fuel Energy Content Comparison

The energy content of fuels is rated in British Thermal Units (BTUs). One BTU is equal to the energy of burning one wooden match. Different fuels have different energy contents.

Fuel		Energy Content Per U.S. Gallon (3.785 L)
Gasoline	≈	115,000 BTUs
E10	≈	111,550 BTUs
E85	≈	83,000 BTUs
E100 Ethanol	≈	76,000 BTUs
No. 2 Diesel	≈	129,500 BTUs
B2	≈	129,000 BTUs
B20	≈	127,000 BTUs
B100 Biodiesel	≈	118,000 BTUs
Methanol	≈	56,800 BTUs
Propane	≈	84,500 BTUs
Natural Gas	≈	19,800 BTUs

Flex-fuel E85 Vehicles

E85 vehicles are automobiles that can burn a blended fuel that contains 85% ethanol and 15% gasoline (*Figure 18.3*). Ethanol is a grain alcohol made from renewable resources, commonly corn. Flex-fuel vehicle engines can be run on regular unleaded gasoline or any fuel that is blended with ethanol as long as the ethanol content does not exceed 85%. Millions of vehicles on the road today are flex-fuel compatible. Ethanol has less energy (BTUs) per volume than gasoline. BTU stands for British Thermal Unit, a measure of heat. To illustrate, the amount of energy released by burning one wooden match is approximately one BTU. E85 Fuel (85% ethanol/15% gasoline) contains about 83,000 BTUs per gallon (3.785 L), whereas gasoline has about 115,000 BTUs per gallon (3.785 L). Less energy per volume results in lower fuel economy. Another disadvantage of using E85 is the limited number of refueling stations.

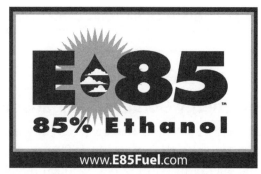

Figure 18.3　　　　　　*Ethanol E85 Logo*
Courtesy of National Ethanol Vehicle Coalition

? Q & A

E85 Compatible Vehicles

Q: How do I find out if my vehicle can run on ethanol?
A: All vehicles manufactured today and sold in the United States can burn at a minimum of 10% ethanol (E10). Many vehicles are also considered flex-fuel vehicles and can burn up to 85% ethanol (E85). Check the owner's manual or go to www.fueleconomy.gov to verify if your vehicle can burn E85.

Natural Gas Vehicles

Natural gas, abundant in North America, is approximately 90 percent methane in pipeline form and is the cleanest fuel currently available for vehicles. An extensive infrastructure of pipelines is already in place. Many of these pipelines supply homes with natural gas for heating and cooking. For natural gas to be used in vehicles, it must be stored as either compressed natural gas (CNG) or liquefied natural gas (LNG). CNG is compressed to around 3,600 psi (24,820 kPa), LNG is cooled to about -263°F (-164°C) in a process called liquefaction to condense it to a more pure liquid form. The liquid form is more dense, containing more energy than CNG, but is more complex to produce and transport. CNG and LNG have found their best fit so far in fleet vehicles, where it is easier to adapt to a reduced driving range and limited access to refilling stations. LNG is generally used in heavy-duty fleet vehicles like trains, transit buses, and semi-trucks. CNG is often found in fleet vehicles like cars, vans, trucks, and school buses. In 2005 Honda started offering the Civic GX to consumers in limited markets, specifically in California, as a CNG vehicle with near-zero emissions. The Civic GX has a range of about 200 miles (322 km). A compact refilling station called Phill by FuelMaker (*Figure 18.4*) can be installed at home to conveniently refill a CNG vehicle overnight. A commercial CNG refilling station must be used for a fast five minute refill.

Figure 18.4　　　　　*CNG Phill Station*
Courtesy of FuelMaker

Propane Vehicles

Currently there are more than a quarter of a million vehicles on the road in the United States and millions worldwide powered by propane. In fact it is the most used alternative vehicle fuel today and has more filling stations accessible than any other alternative fuel. Propane, also known as liquefied petroleum gas (LPG), is colorless and odorless. An odorant is added as a safety measure in the detection of leaks. When used in automobiles, propane is also called Autogas. It is one of the simplest hydrocarbons, making it very clean burning (***Figure 18.5***), even though it is a non-renewable fossil fuel produced from natural gas and oil processing. Similar to natural gas, it is abundant in North America and is commonly used in homes in rural areas for heating and cooking. With minimal emissions, it is also widely used in indoor commercial applications, such as forklifts. It is also a common fuel for barbecues.

Emissions	Reduction of Emissions Propane to Gasoline
Particulate Matter (PM10)	-40%
Nitrogen Oxides (NOx)	-50%
Total Hydrocarbons (THC)	-87%

Figure 18.5   ***Propane Compared to Gasoline***

Propane does not have an extensive pipeline delivery infrastructure like natural gas, but it is efficiently and easily transported and stored under moderate pressure in tanks (***Figure 18.6***). Most propane vehicles are used in fleets, converted from vehicles that were manufactured originally to run on gasoline. One disadvantage of propane is that it contains less energy per volume than gasoline, so a vehicle's driving range is reduced unless additional storage capacity is added.

Figure 18.6   ***Propane Tank***

Bi-fuel Vehicles

Bi-fuel vehicles are different from flex-fuel vehicles. A bi-fuel vehicle has two separate fuel storage and delivery mechanisms. One type of fuel storage may be for gasoline or diesel while the other type may be for compressed natural gas (CNG) or liquefied petroleum gas (LPG). For example, a car that could run on gasoline and propane would be considered a bi-fuel vehicle. Even though compressed natural gas and liquefied propane are fossil fuels, they are much cleaner burning than gasoline or diesel.

🖱 Web Links

Alternative Fuel Vehicles Sites

Ethanol Promotion and Information Council
   ↳   www.drivingethanol.org
Hybridcars.com
   ↳   www.hybridcars.com
Methanol Institute
   ↳   www.methanol.org
National Biodiesel Board
   ↳   www.biodiesel.org
National Ethanol Vehicle Coalition
   ↳   www.e85fuel.com
Propane Education and Research Council
   ↳   www.propanevehicle.org
Schatz Energy Research Center
   ↳   www.humboldt.edu/~serc/
The California Cars Initiative
   ↳   www.calcars.org
The Natural Gas Vehicle Coalition
   ↳   www.ngvc.org
Union of Concerned Scientists
   ↳   www.hybridcenter.org

Hybrid Vehicles

Hybrids have been under development for a long time. Along with manufacturers, students have also participated in hybrid technology exploration by building hybrid vehicles (*Figure 18.7*) for competition. With recent mass production by manufacturers, hybrids have become popular and affordable especially as fuel costs and environmental concerns have risen. This section focuses on:

- How Hybrids Work
- Regenerative Braking
- High Voltage Battery Pack
- Plug-in Hybrids
- Mild Hybrids

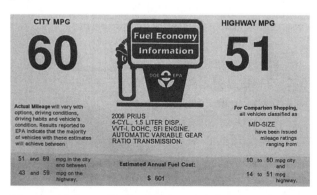

Figure 18.7 *1995 Experimental Hybrid Vehicle*
Student Design Project, University of Redlands, California

How Hybrids Work

A hybrid is any vehicle that has multiple sources of power. Hybrid vehicles have gained increased attention in recent years. They use two power sources, an internal combustion engine and an electric motor. The combined power sources of a hybrid are able to produce a higher than average range between fill-ups (*Figure 18.8*), while greatly reducing emissions and meeting expected performance standards.

Figure 18.8 **Toyota Prius Hybrid MPG Sticker**

The engine is more efficient in hybrids when compared to conventional vehicles because it is sized for average power needs, not peak performance. The electric motor provides the extra power for peak performance requirements, while effectively reusing otherwise wasted braking and surplus engine energy. Surplus energy occurs anytime the engine is running and full power is not needed. This surplus energy can be sent through the generator directly to power the motor or to the high voltage battery pack for storage. The stored energy in the battery pack is used by the electric motor to propel the vehicle when the engine is least efficient and when additional or peak power is needed (*Figure 18.9*). When stopped, the engine commonly shuts down. A conventional starter is not needed because the generator is also used as the starter.

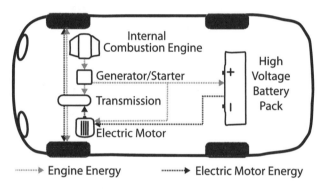

Figure 18.9 *Hybrid Cruising Energy Distribution*

? Q & A

Hybrid Vehicle Upkeep

Q: What maintenance is required on a hybrid?
A: Maintenance is similar to a conventional vehicle. Hybrids need ordinary preventative maintenance like changing oil, replacing filters, adding fluids, and rotating tires. Hybrid specific parts, such as the battery packs and high-voltage electric motors, have been designed to last approximately 150,000 miles (≈240,000 km). Hybrids have a standard 12V DC battery that supplies power for everything except the high-voltage electric motors.

Regenerative Braking

Regenerative braking is when the electric motor acts as a generator capturing kinetic energy that would normally be lost as heat. This energy is used to recharge the batteries while slowing the vehicle (*Figure 18.10*). Hybrids also have conventional brakes to assist when needed.

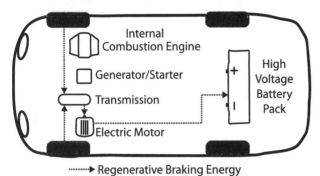

Figure 18.10   *Regenerative Braking Energy*

High Voltage Battery Pack

Hybrid vehicles have a standard 12V DC battery and a separate high voltage battery pack for storing energy. The hybrid battery pack is usually found under the back seat, behind the back seat, or in the trunk. These batteries, commonly nickel metal hydride (NiMH) or lithium-ion, can hold a great deal more energy than a standard lead acid battery. High voltage battery cables can be identified by their bright orange color. *Warning: To avoid injury, shock, burn, or death the high voltage battery pack is equipped with a service disconnect. You should always follow manufacturer recommended precautions in the service manual and on warning labels when servicing a hybrid vehicle (Figure 18.11).*

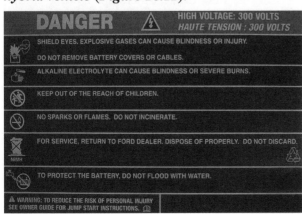

Figure 18.11 High Voltage Battery Warning Label

Plug-in Hybrids

Because the gasoline engine and regenerative braking process recharge the hybrid battery system, the need to plug a hybrid into an electrical outlet can be eliminated. However plug-in hybrids are gaining attention in the research field. Originally car manufacturers did not want to confuse buyers between all-electric vehicles and gas-electric hybrids, so "grid" chargers were not added. Currently companies are researching aftermarket products to give gas-electric hybrids the added flexibility of being plugged in. Installing a larger battery capacity allows the hybrid to go further on the electric motor before the gas engine starts up, minimizing fossil fuel consumption. Whenever plugging into the grid for environmental benefits, the source of electricity should be considered. For example, electricity from a solar or wind power plant is cleaner than from a coal fired power plant.

Mild Hybrids

An integrated starter/generator (ISG), also known as a belt-alternator-starter (BAS) system, is a type of mild hybrid. In an ISG system, the alternator and starter are combined into one unit. The ISG connects to the engine via a serpentine belt and is mounted like a traditional alternator. The ISG has the ability to crank over the engine, provide additional power during acceleration, and incorporate regenerative braking. In addition to being able to reclaim some previously lost energy through regenerative braking, vehicles with ISG systems can shut down at stops and restart upon acceleration which further increases fuel economy.

> ### ✓ Tech Tip
> **Regenerative Braking**
>
> Apply even pressure gradually when braking. If you brake too hard or brake and release repeatedly the regenerative braking will not be able to recapture the energy as efficiently.

Electric Vehicles

Pure all-electric vehicles need to be plugged into an electrical outlet to recharge their high voltage batteries. When driving, the chemical energy stored in batteries is converted to electricity to run electric motors that propel the vehicle. The main issue continues to be obtaining enough storage capacity in the batteries to make full-size all-electric vehicles suitable for normal driving habits with adequate range. Compact GEM all-electric vehicles (***Figure 18.12***) have a range limit of 30 miles (48 km) and speeds of up to 25 mph (40 km/h). When used on short neighborhood trips or in-town they are extremely practical and environmentally friendly. All-electric cars were actually extremely popular with city dwellers in the early 1900s until low cost, reliable internal combustion engines were developed.

Figure 18.12   ***GEM e2 All-electric Vehicle***

❓ Q & A

The Quiet Electric Vehicle

Q: I was startled by a car that drove by because it was really quiet. How can a car be so quiet?

A: Electric vehicles are quiet, because there is not an internal combustion engine to make noise. This also means that there is no need for an exhaust system to muffle engine noise. Drivers of electric vehicles need to be more careful around pedestrians because it is not as easy to hear the car approaching.

Solar Vehicles

Solar powered vehicles are basically all-electric vehicles that are powered by the sun's energy collected with hundreds of photovoltaic (solar) cells. The energy collected must be shared between running the motor and recharging the high voltage batteries. In addition to battery storage capacity issues, incorporating costly photovoltaic cells onto a vehicle's body makes it currently impractical for common use. Solar race challenges, such as the North American Solar Challenge (***Figure 18.13***) and World Solar Challenge, are held to promote the fields of science and engineering and the development of renewable energy efficient technologies.

Figure 18.13   ***Solar Vehicle***
Photo by Stefano Paltera/North American Solar Challenge

🖱 Web Links

Alternative Fuel Vehicles Sites

American Solar Energy Society
↳   www.ases.org
California Fuel Cell Partnership
↳   www.fuelcellpartnership.org
Fuel Cells 2000
↳   www.fuelcells.org
International Solar Energy Society
↳   www.ises.org
National Fuel Cell Research Center
↳   www.nfcrc.uci.edu
National Hydrogen Association
↳   www.hydrogenassociation.org
North American Solar Challenge
↳   www.americansolarchallenge.org

Hydrogen Powered Vehicles

Hydrogen is NASA's fuel choice for space shuttles. As an element, hydrogen is the simplest and the most plentiful, but it must be derived from other substances like water, coal, biomass, and natural gas. It is not found as a gas in nature. Currently 95% of hydrogen is obtained from natural gas (a fossil fuel) through a steam reformation process. However, this process also releases carbon dioxide (a greenhouse gas) into the atmosphere. The use of dirty fossil fuels to produce hydrogen, a clean energy, only redistributes pollution concerns. There are two ways to power vehicles with hydrogen:

*   Burn Hydrogen in an ICE
*   Hydrogen Fuel Cell

Burn Hydrogen in an ICE

Hydrogen can be burned in a modified internal combustion engine (ICE). An engine burning hydrogen instead of gasoline is 25% more efficient. Only a limited number of hydrogen ICE vehicles have been built, but manufacturers are still weighing the options. The challenges relating to hydrogen storage, processing, and distribution are major influential factors.

Hydrogen Fuel Cell

One hydrogen gas molecule (H_2) contains two hydrogen atoms. Each hydrogen atom contains one negatively charged electron (e^-) and one positively charged hydrogen proton (H^+) (*Figure 18.14*).

$$ H = e^- + H^+ $$
(Atom)   (Electron)   (Proton)

Figure 18.14   *Hydrogen Atom*

A hydrogen fuel cell vehicle is an electric vehicle that gets its energy from hydrogen gas. A catalyst is used in a fuel cell to trigger a reaction that strips the electrons from hydrogen. After separation, the electrons are conducted on an anode (negative electrode). The electrons are attracted to the cathode (positive electrode), but they cannot flow through the membrane with the hydrogen ions (protons). The membrane only accepts protons. The electrons are routed through an external circuit, which includes an electric motor. Electricity is the flow of electrons, so the motor is powered as the electrons move toward the cathode (positive electrode). Upon returning to the fuel cell they reconnect with the hydrogen ions and join with oxygen to form water (H_2O) and heat, the only exhaust by-products of a fuel cell (*Figure 18.15*). Various types of fuel cell membranes perform the function of extracting the electrons somewhat differently. However, the end result is the movement of electrons which is electricity. Fuel cells are used in stacks to increase voltage. Currently several fuel cell types are under development for different applications from cars to power plants: polymer electrolyte membrane (also known as proton exchange membrane), direct methanol, alkaline, phosphoric acid, molten carbonate, solid oxide, and regenerative. Proton exchange membrane technology appears to be promising for automobiles. The technology involved is currently cost prohibitive for mass produced vehicles. An efficient way to produce, store, and distribute hydrogen is needed to make it more practical.

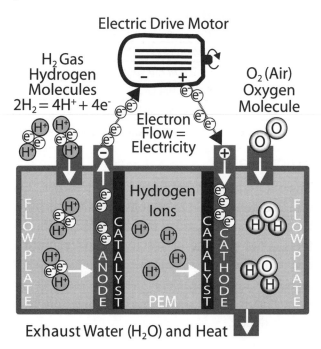

Figure 18.15 Hydrogen PEM Fuel Cell Operation

Technological Issues

With so many different energy sources and technologies all of the advantages and disadvantages should be weighed. Factors are constantly changing as inventions and innovations occur. Ideally we are striving to use fuels and develop vehicles that are:

- Environmentally Friendly
- Sustainable
- Renewable
- Affordable
- Practical

Environmentally Friendly

Gasoline and diesel engines are major contributors to smog, acid rain, and greenhouse gases. Most of the alternative fuels and designs described in this chapter reduce harmful emissions, but still do not eliminate them when the life cycle analysis is completed. Classifications help identify the varying levels of emissions, with ZEV having no emissions (*Figure 18.16*). The two alternative energy technologies that show the most promise for protecting the environment are solar and hydrogen fuel cells, however they are very cost prohibitive to mass produce at this time.

Emission Classifications	
TLEV	Transitional Low Emission Vehicles
LEV	Low Emission Vehicles
ULEV	Ultra Low Emission Vehicles
SULEV	Super Ultra Low Emission Vehicles
ZEV	Zero Emission Vehicles

Figure 18.16   *Emission Classifications*

Sustainable

The fuel source supply needs to meet the fuel source demand for it to be considered sustainable. Research indicates today that the supply of fossil fuels is not going to be sustainable at the current demand. The only sustainable alternative energy resources known that may work in vehicles are solar and hydrogen, unless demand is dramatically reduced.

Renewable

Fossil fuels are non-renewable. However, there are several alternative fuels that are renewable, but not necessarily sustainable. Biodiesel (refined from animal fats and vegetable oil) and ethanol (made from corn) are renewable. Solar energy from the sun, electrical energy from wind and water, and hydrogen produced from the electrolysis of water are also renewable.

✓ Tech Tip

Non-renewable Resource

Gasoline is considered a non-renewable energy resource because it cannot be formed again in a short time period. The fossil fuels that we use today started to form from the remains of sea plants and animals that lived hundreds of millions of years ago.

Web Links

Alternative Fuel Vehicles Sites

Alternative Fuel Vehicle Institute
↳   www.afvi.org
California Energy Commission
↳   www.energyquest.ca.gov
Clean Energy Portal (Canada)
↳   www.cleanenergy.gc.ca
Consumer Energy Center
↳   www.consumerenergycenter.org
Energy and Environmental Research Center
↳   www.undeerc.org
National Renewable Energy Laboratory
↳   www.nrel.gov
Northeast Sustainable Energy Association
↳   www.nesea.org
Office of Energy Efficiency (Canada)
↳   www.oee.nrcan.gc.ca
US DOE - Efficiency and Renewable Energy
↳   www.eere.energy.gov
US DOE - Fuel Economy Website
↳   www.fueleconomy.gov

Affordable

The cost of a technology influences its development and popular acceptance. As the price of gasoline and diesel continues to rise, more money is given to research alternatives. As the purchase price comes down on alternative vehicles like hybrids, people are more willing to consider the new technology.

🖩 Calculations

Fuel Economy Payback Period

If your primary reason for purchasing an alternative vehicle is to increase fuel economy (spend less at the gas pump) and not just protect the environment, then you should determine the payback period. To illustrate this, let's compare vehicles with similar options. In the following example, one is a conventional vehicle and the other is a hybrid achieving 50% more mpg.

Vehicle	MPG	MSRP
Hybrid	60	$24,000
Conventional	30	$20,000
Difference	30	$ 4,000

How many miles do you have to drive before the new technology begins to save money?

Vehicle	Cost Per Mile	Cost 100,000 Miles
Hybrid	$2.40 Gal. / 60 MPG = $0.04	100,000 x $0.04 = $4,000
Conventional	$2.40 Gal. / 30 MPG = $0.08	100,000 x $0.08 = $8,000

Considering only fuel costs (with gas at $2.40 a gallon), the break even point would be at 100,000 miles (≈160,000 km) for the example above. If the price of gas increased the payback period would shorten. The payback period would also fluctuate depending on actual fuel economy, fuel cost, purchase price, and upkeep.

Practical

Being practical is where many of the alternative fuels have the most difficulty competing with gasoline and diesel. The infrastructure for supply is not readily available for many of the alternatives. The technology available for solar vehicles does not suitably meet our expectation of speed and range. The cost for hydrogen fuel cell vehicles is currently too expensive for consumers.

Summary

The exponential growth of technology, fossil fuel prices, and consumer acceptance of new technology will drive the marketplace. Consumers have a wide variety of vehicle types to consider. The alternative fueled and designed vehicles available to consumers are attracting attention. From E85 ethanol burning to hybrids to hydrogen fuel cells, changes are being made to make personal transportation more efficient and environmentally friendly. Continued technological advancements will help us work towards implementing better alternatives in the future.

 Activities

Alternative Fuels and Designs

- Payback Period Activity
- Chapter 18 Study Questions

Activities can be accessed in the Auto Upkeep workbook or online at www.autoupkeep.com.

Career Paths

Research and Design Engineer

Education: Bachelor's Degree in Engineering
Median Income: $62,000
Job Market: Average Growth
Abilities: Strong science, math, analytical, and problem solving skills in research and design.

Automotive Accessories

FUEL FOR THOUGHT

- What types of accessories are available for your vehicle?
- How can accessories enhance the look of a vehicle?
- What accessories improve a vehicle's safety or make driving more enjoyable?

Introduction

Automotive accessories are an integral part of enhancing aesthetics, personalizing a vehicle, and often serve a practical purpose. They may also add comfort, convenience, protection, and safety. This chapter will identify some of the most common accessories and their functions.

Objectives

Upon completion of this chapter and activities, you will be able to:

- Identify automotive accessories.
- Explain different accessory functions.
- Estimate the cost of selected accessories for your vehicle.

Interior Accessories

Basic interior accessories include:

- Floor Mats
- Cargo Organizers
- Seat Covers
- Sun Shades
- Traveling with Pets
- Window Tint

Floor Mats

Floor mats help protect a vehicle's carpet from dirt, mud, snow, salt, and other debris tracked in on feet. They can be easily removed and cleaned. If the floor mats begin to show wear, it is much less expensive to replace them than your vehicle's carpet. High quality floor mats (*Figure 19.1*) are molded to fit the contour of the floor so they don't interfere with brake or gas pedal operation.

Figure 19.1   **Floor Mats**

💰 Price Guide

Cargo Organizers
↳ $10.00 to $100.00
Floor Mats
↳ $20.00 to $80.00
Seat Covers
↳ $25.00 to $100.00
Window Tint
↳ $20.00 to $100.00 (parts)

Cargo Organizers

A wide variety of handy cargo organizers are on the market. Specialized net, truck cab, seat, console (*Figure 19.2*), clothing, and visor organizers help to keep items in place. Make sure you find one that fits properly and does not interfere with your ability to see and drive.

Figure 19.2   *Console Organizer*

Seat Covers

Seat covers are used to protect the original seat fabric or to provide a custom look inside the vehicle. Seat covers come in a rainbow of colors, designs, and material types. Specialty pet seat covers can also add safety and comfort for traveling pets.

Sun Shades

Sun shades (*Figure 19.3*) are often used inside the windshield to block out the harmful ultraviolet rays that cause interiors to fade. They also reduce the inside temperature when a vehicle is parked in the sun. Mesh style shades can be used in the side windows to protect young children from the sun while driving.

Figure 19.3   *Windshield Sun Shade*

Traveling with Pets

Pet car seats, travel kennels, vehicle barriers, and seatbelts (*Figure 19.4*) can all make transporting your pet safer. Keeping pets in a designated space minimizes distractions to the driver.

Figure 19.4   *Pet Seatbelt*
Courtesy of HandicappedPets.com

Window Tint

Window tint (*Figure 19.5*) is used to customize a vehicle, prevent interior fading, and keep you cooler in direct sun. Tint can be purchased in various shades. Dark tint makes it harder to see at night. Check your local laws to determine what shade and placement of tint is legal in your area. During installation be careful to not trap any air, dust, lint, or other contaminants between the tint and the glass. Tinting requires patience, especially if your windows are curved. For quality results, consult a professional, research techniques, and follow directions.

Figure 19.5   *Window Tint*

🖱 Web Links

General Accessories Sites

AutoAnything
↳   www.autoanything.com
CarAccessories.com
↳   www.autoaccessories.com
Gila Film Products (Window Tint)
↳   www.gilafilms.com
LLumar Window Film (Window Tint)
↳   www.llumar.com
PetSmart (Pet Travel Accessories)
↳   www.petsmart.com

Electronic Accessories

Basic electronic accessories include:
- AC/DC Converter
- Audio Systems
- Cell Phone Car Kits - Hands Free
- DVD and Entertainment Systems
- Engine Heaters
- Gauges
- Keyless Entry
- Lights
- Navigation Systems
- OnStar
- Remote Starter
- Security and Alarms

AC/DC Converter

Some vehicles come from the factory equipped with a 120V AC power outlet for running accessories. However, many do not. By using a plug in power converter (*Figure 19.6*) you can easily convert the DC power from your 12V DC accessory plug to 120V AC power. This is a convenient way to use your vehicle as a power source for laptops, cell phones, and other portable electronic devices.

Figure 19.6   *AC/DC Power Converter*

Audio Systems

Audio systems include basic AM/FM radios, cassette players, HD radio (high definition digital), single CD players, multi-disk CD changers, MP3 players, WMA (Windows Media Audio), and satellite radio. Quality speakers can enhance the audio system in your automobile. Automotive speakers are generally grouped into two categories: component and multi-range speakers. Multi-range speakers include woofers and tweeters into one unit. Component speakers are single unit woofers or tweeters, strategically mounted into the passenger cabin using a crossover unit for maximum clarity.

Cell Phone Car Kits - Hands Free

Hands free cell phone kits are safer to use than hand held cell phones. However, both can be dangerous. A driver concentrating on a phone conversation is not as attentive to road situations as someone that is not engaged in a conversation. Cell phone car kits may include wireless Bluetooth technology, a volume amplifying receiver, speakerphone, voice recognition, earpiece (*Figure 19.7*), automatic stereo mute, and a way to attach the device to the dash, visor, or headrest.

Figure 19.7   *Cell Phone Earpiece*

DVD and Entertainment Systems

DVD and entertainment gaming systems are available as portable units or can be incorporated into a vehicle's passenger cabin. Common locations are a vehicle's dash, ceiling, (*Figure 19.8*) or the back of headrests. A special input may be required to listen through your vehicle's existing audio system.

Figure 19.8   *Ceiling Mount DVD Player*

> ✓ **Tech Tip**
>
> **Watching While Driving**
>
> Laws exist against operating a DVD or entertainment screen where the driver can watch while driving. If a screen is visible to the driver it must be installed so it can only be turned on when the parking brake is engaged, ensuring that the vehicle is not in motion.

Engine Heaters

Engine heaters are a necessity in cold climates. Without one, an engine may not start. Several types of engine heaters exist: dipstick, oil pan, hose heater, and block heater. All of them plug into 120V AC electrical outlets. Dipstick heaters are electric dipsticks that warm engine oil. They should not be used on vehicles with plastic dipstick tubes. Magnetic oil pan heaters stick to steel oil pans, but not aluminum oil pans. Some oil pan heaters have a sticky pad that can be installed on all clean surfaces. A hose heater is installed in a radiator hose or heater hose, heating and circulating the coolant. A block heater (*Figure 19.9*) is installed into one of the engine's soft plugs (also known as freeze plugs). This type of heater consists of a heating element that heats the coolant. Block heaters are commonly installed in new cars as standard equipment in cold climates. Look under the hood or at the front of your vehicle for a 120V AC plug. Be sure to unplug the engine heater before driving away.

Figure 19.9   **Block Engine Heater**

Gauges

A vehicle may come with a variety of gauges already mounted as part of the instrument cluster. Aftermarket gauges can be added. Tachometer, oil pressure, water temperature, voltmeter, and ammeter gauges are the most popular types that are added to vehicles.

✓ Tech Tip

Engine Heater and Emissions

Warming engine coolant conducts heat to other components. In addition to enhancing the ability to start an engine, engine heaters can also reduce tailpipe emissions. A cold engine releases more pollution than a warm one.

Keyless Entry

Keyless entry systems, also known as remote entry systems, are popular on vehicles. Like any communication device, this system depends on a transmitter and a receiver. The receiver is mounted inside the vehicle and the transmitter is on the key or key chain (this device is also known as an electronic key fob) (*Figure 19.10*). To aid in security, keyless entry systems use a rolling code (also know as code-hopping) that can randomly generate millions of encrypted codes. The transmitter and receiver stay synchronized so they can communicate to one another.

Figure 19.10   **Keyless Entry Remote**

? Q & A

Keyless Entry Not Working

Q: What could be causing my keyless entry system not to work?
A: Periodically you will need to change the battery in the keyless remote. As the remote battery's life is near the end, it may work intermittently. You can purchase a new battery at most department and automotive parts stores.

💰 Price Guide

AC/DC Converter
↳ $10.00 to $40.00
DVD and Entertainment System
↳ $250.00 to $1,000.00 (parts)
Engine Heater
↳ $30.00 to $60.00 (parts)
Hands Free - Cell Phone Car Kits
↳ $50.00 to $200.00
Keyless Entry System
↳ $35.00 to $100.00 (parts)

Lights

Fog, daytime running, and off-road lights (***Figure 19.11***) can enhance driver visibility in a variety of conditions. Fog forms when water vapor condenses; it is basically a cloud that is near the ground. Fog makes visibility difficult. Fog lights are mounted low to the ground to get underneath the fog. Many vehicles today come with automatic daytime running lights. The theory is that daytime running lights reduce vehicular accidents. Vehicles that are used for off-road purposes often use lights on a brush guard or specialized light bar to aid visibility. If you use specialty lights on the highway make sure they are aimed correctly so they don't blind oncoming traffic.

Figure 19.11   *Off-Road Specialized Light Bar*

💰 Price Guide

Fog Lights
↳ $40.00 to $150.00 (parts)
Navigation System
↳ $200.00 to $1,000.00
OnStar
↳ $200.00 (annual fee "Safe & Sound")
Remote Starter
↳ $40.00 to $100.00 (parts)
Security and Alarms
↳ $40.00 to $200.00 (parts)

Navigation Systems

Global positioning systems (GPS) are navigational tools that are becoming common on new vehicles. A GPS receiver (***Figure 19.12***) mounted in a vehicle communicates with satellites orbiting the earth to calculate the exact vehicle location. The satellites send the signals and the GPS receiver receives the signals. Three satellites are required to obtain latitude and longitude on the earth, while four satellites are required to obtain latitude, longitude, and precise altitude. This process is called trilateration. Standard GPS systems are accurate within 50 feet (about 15 meters). Advanced GPS systems that also use ground relay stations can improve accuracy by pinpointing the location within 3 to 10 feet (about 1 to 3 meters). Used with electronic maps, the receiver constantly sends signals to update a display for the driver to point out upcoming roads, intersections, landmarks, airports, hospitals, and businesses.

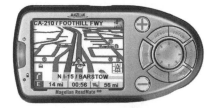

Figure 19.12   *Portable Magellan® RoadMate™*
Courtesy of Thales Navigation, Inc.

🚛 Trouble Guide

GPS Inaccurate

- Outdated maps
- Satellites' signals interrupted
- Satellites' signals not available

✓ Tech Tip

Navigate Safely

Do not input a new destination into a navigation system while driving. Factory installed systems on new vehicles are now made so that they cannot be adjusted unless the vehicle is in park with the parking brake engaged.

OnStar

OnStar (*Figure 19.13*), installed as standard equipment on 2007 General Motors vehicles sold in the US and Canada, is a security and safety system. The three buttons allow for the driver to complete hands free calling, talk to an OnStar advisor, or request emergency assistance. OnStar can also provide vehicle diagnostic information and maintenance intervals on some vehicles.

Figure 19.13   **Rearview Mirror with OnStar**
Courtesy of OnStar by GM

Web Links

Electronic Accessories Sites

Auto Meter (Gauges)
↳   www.autometer.com
Cyberdyne (Digital Gauges)
↳   www.cyberdynegauges.net
Crutchfield (Audio)
↳   www.crutchfield.com
Garmin International (GPS)
↳   www.garmin.com
Gorilla Automotive Products (Security)
↳   www.gorilla-auto.com
Hella Inc. (Lights)
↳   www.hella.com
KC HiLiTES (Lights)
↳   www.kchilites.com
LoJack Corporation (Security)
↳   www.lojack.com
Magellan (GPS)
↳   www.magellangps.com
ProHeat Products Inc. (Engine Heaters)
↳   www.engineheaters.com
Sirius Satellite Radio (Audio)
↳   www.sirius.com
Webasto (Sunroof and More)
↳   www.webastoshowroom.com
XM Satellite Radio (Audio)
↳   www.xmradio.com

Remote Starter

Remote starters (*Figure 19.14*) are often used to start a vehicle on an extremely cold or hot day. Remote starters can be used in the comfort of a home to start a vehicle and defrost a windshield or air condition a hot interior. *Warning: Never start your vehicle and leave it running in a garage without sufficient ventilation to remove the carbon monoxide.*

Figure 19.14   **Starter Remote**

✓ Tech Tip

Pollution from Remote Starters

Negative impacts relating to remote starters do exist. Idling an engine increases air pollution. Many municipalities have anti-idling laws to reduce pollution.

Security and Alarms

As vehicle theft has increased, so has the technology to deter thieves. Alarms and security features can provide peace of mind. A wide range of alarm and security systems are available. The simplest of security devices can be used to lock your steering wheel. This visual deterrent may help a thief bypass your vehicle and pick an easier target. More sophisticated security systems disable the engine (*Figure 19.15*), track the vehicle, and notify the police.

Figure 19.15   **Security System Window Decal**

Exterior Accessories

Basic exterior accessories include:

- Bug Deflector
- Brush Guard/Push Bar
- Car Cover
- Grill Insert
- Running Boards and Steps
- Sunroof Deflector
- Splash Guards and Mud Flaps
- Spoiler
- Undercoating and Rustproofing
- Wheel Customizing
- Wheel Lock Lug Nuts

Bug Deflector

A bug deflector (also known as a hood shield) (*Figure 19.16*) can be installed to protect the hood of the vehicle, provide a cleaner windshield during bug season, or for aesthetics. Bug shields come in a variety of colors, clear, or tinted (smoked gray). Most bug shields are made from rugged acrylic.

Figure 19.16   *Tinted Bug Deflector*

Brush Guard/Push Bar

A brush guard is a push bar with mounted headlight protectors (*Figure 19.17*). Some brush guards (also called grill guards) are one piece units. These chrome or colored bars are usually added for aesthetics or to mount additional driving lights. Brush guards often give trucks and SUVs a more rugged off-road look.

Figure 19.17   *Brush Guard*

Car Cover

Car covers are most frequently used when people are storing classic or collector vehicles (*Figure 19.18*). High quality fitted car covers can help protect a vehicle's exterior finish from rain, snow, dust, sunlight, and airborne pollution. To properly install a car cover make sure the vehicle's finish is clean, dry, and not hot. Never drag the cover across the finish, unfold it from the roof center down. Dirt under the cover can scratch the finish if the cover moves. It is best to not leave a cover on when it is windy. If the cover becomes wet, take it off to dry to avoid marking the finish.

Figure 19.18   *Custom Car Cover*
Courtesy of Coverking.com

Grill Insert

A grill insert can be installed on some vehicles to warm up the engine quicker in cold climates. Most styles snap easily into the grill. Be sure to remove the air restricting grill inserts when the outside temperature warms up. You can also change to a mesh insert in the summer to prevent bugs from clogging up the radiator fins.

 Price Guide

Bug Deflector
↳ $45.00 to $100.00 (parts)
Car Cover
↳ $50.00 to $250.00
Mud Flaps
↳ $10.00 to $40.00 (set of 2)
Running Boards
↳ $50.00 to $350.00 (parts)
Sunroof Deflector
↳ $35.00 to $100.00 (parts)

Running Boards and Steps

Running boards, nerf bars (*Figure 19.19*), and steps are commonly added to trucks and SUVs to give the driver and passengers an added step in entering a high-sitting vehicle. They also provide a custom look often desired by car enthusiasts. They are made from stainless steel, aluminum, fiberglass, and ABS plastic. Some vehicles even have automatically extending running boards that retract in when the door is closed.

Figure 19.19   *Nerf Bar*

Web Links

Exterior Accessories Sites

AZTrucks, Inc. (Truck Accessories)
↳   www.aztrucks.com
Century Fiberglass, Inc. (Bed Covers)
↳   www.centurycaps.com
Covercraft (Car Covers and More)
↳   www.covercraft.com
Coverking (Custom Covers)
↳   www.coverking.com
Dee Zee, Inc. (Truck Accessories)
↳   www.deezee.com
JC Whitney
↳   www.jcwhitney.com
Leer (Bed Covers)
↳   www.leer.com
Lund International (Shields and More)
↳   www.lundinternational.com
WeatherTech (Automotive Accessories)
↳   www.weathertech.com
Westin (Truck Accessories)
↳   www.westinautomotive.com
Ziebart International (Rustproofing and More)
↳   www.ziebart.com

Sunroof Deflector

Sunroof deflectors, made out of acrylic plastic, are designed to reduce dust, noise, and wind in the vehicle when the sunroof is open. The deflector redirects the air over the top of the vehicle. They also provide some shade when the sunroof is open.

Splash Guards and Mud Flaps

Mud flaps and splash guards (*Figure 19.20*) help protect a vehicle's finish from rocks and other debris that are thrown up from the tires. Commonly made from plastic, rubber, or metal, mud flaps and splash guards are used on all types of vehicles. Once only common on large trucks, they are now specially molded to fit all types of cars and luxury vehicles.

Figure 19.20   *Splash Guards*

Spoiler

Rear spoilers (*Figure 19.21*) are added to give a custom look to vehicles. In the past they were common on sports cars, but are gaining attention on a variety of two door coupes and four door sedans.

Figure 19.21   *Spoiler*

✓ Tech Tip

Custom Spoilers

If you are planning on installing a spoiler keep in mind that it may drastically limit your view from your rearview mirror. Also if the spoiler was not designed for your vehicle it may increase drag, lowering fuel economy.

Undercoating and Rustproofing

Undercoating can be added to the underside of the vehicle to deaden road noise and lessen the chance of rust forming. Rust (iron oxide) is formed when oxygen and water come in contact with iron. Since iron is used to make steel, rust can form on unprotected steel automotive components. To rustproof a vehicle more thoroughly, rust-inhibitors can also be sprayed inside body panels. Automotive manufacturers go to great lengths to rustproof vehicles during manufacturing. Most automobiles have corrosion perforation warranties for a designated period of time. Since perforation means hole formation, before the warranty applies, the steel would have to completely rust through.

✓ Tech Tip

Undercoating a New Vehicle

Many new vehicles come from the manufacturer with a good rustproof coating, making it unnecessary to pay for this additional dealer applied option.

Wheel Customizing

Adding custom wheels is one way to personalize a vehicle. In the past, most vehicles came with standard steel wheels covered by hubcaps. Common sizes were 13″, 14″, 15″, and 16″. Today, the most common custom wheels are painted, chrome (*Figure 19.22*), and polished aluminum. Custom wheel sizes come in a variety of sizes: 17″, 18″, 19″, 20″, 22″, 24″, 26″, and 28″. Costs for a set of custom wheels can range from a couple hundred dollars to over ten thousand dollars.

Figure 19.22   *Custom Chrome Wheel*

Wheel Lock Lug Nuts

Wheel lock lug nuts are commonly put on vehicles with expensive alloy wheels. Lock lug nuts come in packs of four, one for each wheel. A special coded key tool (*Figure 19.23*) is used to remove the lug nuts. It is a good idea to keep this tool locked in the glove box or center console.

Figure 19.23   *Locking Lug Nut Key Tool*

✓ Tech Tip

Locking Lug Nut Key Tool

If you take your vehicle to a repair facility to have the tires rotated or serviced, switch the lock lug nuts with standard lug nuts prior to having service completed or make sure the technician returns the lug nut key after the service is performed. Sometimes when technicians get busy they forget about returning the key. Also, if a technician uses an impact wrench on your lug nut key it may become damaged. You will need this key to put on the spare if you have a flat.

🖱 Web Links

Performance Accessories Sites

American Eagle Wheel
↪ www.americaneaglewheel.com
American Racing (Performance)
↪ ww.americanracing.com
Center Line Forged Wheels
↪ www.centerlinewheels.com
JEG's High Performance
↪ www.jegs.com
Summit Racing Equipment (Performance)
↪ www.summitracing.com
Weld Wheel Industries
↪ www.weldracing.com

Hauling and Towing Accessories

Basic hauling and towing accessories include:
- Bike Rack
- Luggage Rack
- Ratchet Tie Down Straps
- Tow Rope/Strap
- Towing Mirrors
- Trailer Brake Controller
- Trailer Brake Wiring and Plugs
- Trailer Hitches
- Trailer Hitch Balls
- Trailer Safety Chains
- Truck Bed Accessories
- Winch

Bike Rack

If you are an outdoor enthusiast, you may like to have a bike rack for your vehicle. Bike racks can be mounted on the roof, trunk, trailer hitch, or in the bed of a pickup. They allow you to safely and easily transport your bike to a park or bike trail.

Luggage Rack

Luggage racks and roof cargo containers are used to transport items outside of the vehicle. The transported items (e.g., luggage, coolers, kayaks, and surfboards) may be too large for the inside of the vehicle, so a mounting system is needed on the outside of the vehicle to safely carry them. Another reason to put the items outside is because the room inside the cabin may be needed for passengers.

Ratchet Tie Down Straps

Ratchet tie down straps (*Figure 19.24*) are used to securely hold cargo in place. They come in different sizes, lengths, ratings, and styles.

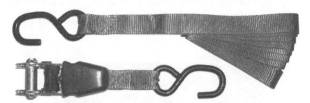

Figure 19.24   *Ratchet Tie Down Straps*

Tow Rope/Strap

Tow ropes or straps can be used for emergency towing and moving vehicles short distances at a slow speed. Tow bars or dollies should be used for any long distance towing.

> ### ✓ Tech Tip
> **Tow Rope/Strap Rating**
>
> Never use just anything to tow a vehicle. Tow ropes and straps are rated for a reason. Never stand where a tow rope can snap back at you. Use the tow rope to get the vehicle to the side of the road. Call a tow truck for transporting the vehicle to an automotive repair shop.

Towing Mirror

Towing mirrors can completely replace the original equipment manufacturer's (OEM) style mirror or can be installed as extensions on the existing mirrors (*Figure 19.25*). Both styles help the driver see around large trailers. They often extend out from the doors much further than standard mirrors.

Figure 19.25   *Towing Mirrors - Extension Style*

> ### Price Guide
>
> Bike Rack
> ↳ $30.00 to $200.00
> Ratchet Tie Downs
> ↳ $10.00 to $40.00
> Rustproofing
> ↳ $200.00 to $400.00
> Towing Mirrors - Extension Style
> ↳ $20.00 to $50.00 (pair)
> Wheel Lock Lug Nuts
> ↳ $15.00 to $50.00

Trailer Brake Controller

When towing a trailer with independent brakes, a brake controller (*Figure 19.26*) is necessary. The brake controller adjusts the power to the electrically operated trailer brakes during deceleration. Some trucks have brake controllers as standard equipment.

Figure 19.26   *Trailer Brake Controller*

Trailer Brake Wiring and Plugs

Electricity is necessary to power the running and brake lights on a trailer. Several types of trailer wiring plugs are available: 4, 5, 6, or 7 pole (*Figure 19.27*). On vehicles that tow lightweight trailers, the four pole flat plug is the most common. On vehicles that tow larger heavyweight trailers, a seven pole round plug is commonly used.

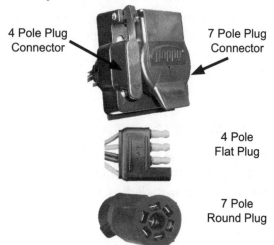

4 Pole Plug Connector

7 Pole Plug Connector

4 Pole Flat Plug

7 Pole Round Plug

Figure 19.27   *Trailer Wiring Plugs*

✓ Tech Tip

Trailer Light Check

Trailer wiring can easily become corroded or damaged. To be on the safe side, the brake lights and turn signals should be visually inspected every time before you tow.

Trailer Hitches

Trailer hitches are used to pull boat, snowmobile, motorcycle, utility, and recreational trailers. Some hitches have ball mount receivers (*Figure 19.28*).

Figure 19.28   *Ball Mount Receiver*

Trailer hitches are commonly classified into five classes (*Figure 19.29*). The style that you install depends on the vehicle. Specialty bed mount hitches are used on heavy-duty trucks to pull fifth wheel and gooseneck trailers. Refer to your owner's manual to identify the maximum towing capacity and the correct trailer hitch.

Class	Tongue Weight (TW)		Gross Trailer Weight (GTW)		Vehicle Type
	lbs	kg	lbs	kg	
I	200	91	2000	907	Mid-sized Cars Compact Trucks
II	300	136	3500	1588	Mid-sized Cars Compact Trucks
III	600	272	6000	2722	Full-sized Cars Mid-sized Trucks Mid-sized SUVs
IV	1000	454	10000	4536	Full-sized Trucks Full-sized SUVs
V	1200	544	12000	5443	Full-sized Trucks Full-sized SUVs

Figure 19.29   *Trailer Hitch Classifications*

Trailer Hitch Balls

Trailer hitch balls (*Figure 19.30*) come in three basic sizes: $1^7/_8''$, $2''$, and $2^5/_{16}''$. These sizes relate to the ball diameter. The trailer tongue size determines the ball size needed.

Diameter →   ←

Figure 19.30   *Trailer Hitch Ball*

Trailer Safety Chains

Safety chains (*Figure 19.31*) attach to a trailer tongue to prevent runaway trailers. Safety chains hook onto the vehicle's hitch or frame to keep the trailer connected to the vehicle if the trailer tongue slips off or breaks away from the trailer ball. A runaway trailer could cause serious injury and damage. Safety chains need to be attached loose enough so they do not bind when turning, but tight enough so they do not drag on the road. ***Warning: Never tow anything without properly attaching approved safety chains.***

Figure 19.31   Trailer Tongue with Safety Chains

Truck Bed Accessories

A wide range of truck bed accessories are available. Tonneau covers, tie down systems, tool storage devices, bedliners, cargo mats, bed rails, and truck bed caps are just some of the widely popular bed accessories.

Winch

A winch (*Figure 19.32*) can be added to a vehicle that is used for off-road conditions. The size of winch (pulling power and line strength) depends on the vehicle's weight and what it intends to pull. Add-on winch systems are electrically or hydraulically driven.

Figure 19.32   **Winch**

Summary

Vehicle accessories can be for function or aesthetics. Be sure the accessories you add are designed specifically for your vehicle.

🖱 Web Links

Hauling and Towing Accessories Sites

Derovations Corporation (Bike Racks)
↳   www.dero.com
Draw-Tite Hitches
↳   www.draw-tite.com
Hopkins Mfg. Corp. (Towing and More)
↳   www.hopkinsmfg.com
Ramsey Winch Company
↳   www.ramsey.com
Reese Hitches
↳   www.reeseprod.com
Tekonsha Brake Controllers
↳   www.tekonsha.com
Warn Industries, Inc. (Winches and More)
↳   www.warn.com

🚗 Activities

Automotive Accessories

- Automotive Accessories Activity
- Chapter 19 Study Questions

Activities can be accessed in the Auto Upkeep workbook or online at www.autoupkeep.com.

🎓 Career Paths

Alarm Installation Technician

Education: Technical Training
Median Income: $28,000
Job Market: Average Growth
Abilities: Mechanical, electrical, and programing aptitude. Fast learner and detail oriented.

CHAPTER 20

COMMON PROBLEMS AND ROADSIDE EMERGENCIES

FUEL FOR THOUGHT

- What are common automotive problems?
- What should you do during a roadside emergency?
- What can be done to avoid an accident?

Introduction

This chapter will cover some of the most common problems that automobile owners encounter. Sometimes the solution is so simple it is often overlooked. It will also cover what to do during roadside emergencies.

Objectives

Upon completion of this chapter and activities, you will be able to:

- Identify common automobile problems.
- Analyze basic automotive problems and make a decision about a solution.
- Replace a headlight.
- Prepare for roadside emergencies.
- Jump-start a vehicle safely.

✓ Tech Tip

Check Engine Light

If your check engine light is on, some automotive parts stores and repair facilities will hook up a scan tool to retrieve trouble codes for free. By helping to identify parts or services needed, they hope to attract your business.

Diagnosing Problems

Being familiar with the various systems that keep a vehicle operating properly will better prepare you to diagnose problems. Use your senses and pay attention to your vehicle. At times it may be difficult to get a problem to duplicate for a technician, so keeping a record of possible symptoms and any maintenance performed will help. Malfunction indicator lights and gauges act as problem or potential problem indicators. They communicate important information from your vehicle's electronic computer system. The warning of a gauge or light should never be ignored. You can often see, hear, smell, or feel a problem arising before it leaves you stranded on the side of the road. This section focuses on:

- On-Board Diagnostics
- Check Engine Light
- Low Fuel Indicator
- Oil Pressure Indicator
- Charging System Indicator
- Coolant Temperature Indicator
- Fluid Leaks
- Smoke from Tailpipe
- Unusual Sounds
- Unusual Smells

On-Board Diagnostics

On-board diagnostics (OBD) have been in many vehicles since the 1980s. However, in 1996 a new OBD system was mandated – OBD II, which standardized some aspects. A scan tool plugs into the OBD II compliant 16 pin Data Link Connector (DLC) (*Figure 20.1*). The DLC is usually located under the dash on the driver side near the steering column. The OBD II requirement is that the DLC is accessible from the driver's seat. The scan tool retrieves any information and diagnostic codes that have been stored on the powertrain control module (PCM) to help diagnose the problem.

Figure 20.1   *Data Link Connector for OBD II*

Check Engine Light

The check engine light (*Figure 20.2*) lets the driver know if the PCM detects an emission system or engine performance problem, triggered by sensors. The problem could be anything from a loose gas cap to a failing catalytic converter to an engine misfire. The rule of thumb is to check the gas cap first. Some vehicles even have a special check fuel cap light. A check engine light that stays on steady is a sign that a technician's service is needed soon. Under most conditions you can still drive your vehicle. However, the longer you drive it the more damage you could cause, along with emitting additional pollution. A blinking light is a sign of a serious problem. Check your owner's manual because your manufacturer may suggest having the vehicle towed in for repair. In the future, new types of OBD systems may actually transmit a signal to a highway monitor to enforce emissions compliance.

Figure 20.2   *Check Engine Light*

Low Fuel Indicator

When the light by the fuel gauge (*Figure 20.3*) comes on you are almost out of fuel. The vehicle may still have some fuel, but it is best to refill your fuel tank before this light comes on.

 LOW FUEL

Figure 20.3   *Low Fuel Light*

Oil Pressure Indicator

Do not drive your vehicle if the oil pressure light (*Figure 20.4*) is illuminated. Low oil pressure can cause immediate engine damage. Check your oil level and add if low. If the light still does not go off, have the vehicle towed to a service facility.

Figure 20.4   *Oil Pressure Light*

Charging System Indicator

The charging system light (*Figure 20.5*) indicates that the battery is not being recharged. This does not necessarily mean that the battery is malfunctioning. The problem may be another part of the charging system, such as the alternator.

Figure 20.5   *Charging System Light*

Coolant Temperature Indicator

When the coolant temperature (*Figure 20.6*) exceeds the normal operating range a warning light or gauge will indicate that the engine is overheating. On a gauge the red area indicates overheating. Pull your vehicle over and allow the engine to cool. Serious engine damage could result from driving an overheated engine.

Figure 20.6   *Coolant Temperature Light*

Fluid Leaks

A drip on the garage floor or driveway can give you insight into an occurring problem. Don't ignore a leak just because it starts out small. Note the fluid's color (*Figure 20.7*), approximate amount, location, and texture to help determine if a component is failing, needs to be retightened, or serviced.

Fluid Leak	Black	Golden Brown	Red	Orange	Green
Oil	●	●			
Automatic Transmission			●		
Manual Transmission	●	●	●		
Power Steering		●	●		
Coolant			●	●	●

Figure 20.7   *Fluid Leak Color Indicators*

Smoke from Tailpipe

Tailpipe smoke (*Figure 20.8*) can be an indicator of faulty components or engine performance problems.

Smoke	Problem
Black	Black smoke is usually an indication of the engine getting too much fuel (running rich). Excess fuel may be entering the combustion chamber. A faulty fuel injector, fuel pressure regulator, PCV valve, clogged catalytic converter, vacuum leak, overdue tune-up, or various engine control sensors could cause the engine to run rich.
Blue	Blue smoke indicates oil burning. This usually signifies that the piston rings are worn. When the piston rings are worn, oil can bypass the piston and enter the combustion chamber. The oil is then burned with the air-fuel mixture. Your engine may need rebuilding.
White	White smoke indicates that the engine is burning coolant. This means that coolant is getting into the cylinders and burning with the air-fuel mixture.

Figure 20.8   *Tailpipe Smoke Color Indicators*

✓ Tech Tip

Check Vehicle Warranty

If you are having trouble with your vehicle, check the warranty. You may have complete bumper-to-bumper coverage. If so, take it back to the dealer and let them address the issue. Also, keep in mind that emission related warranties are often longer than powertrain and bumper-to-bumper warranties. Read the warranty that covers your vehicle. Commonly it is divided into the following categories: bumper-to-bumper, emissions, powertrain, corrosion-perforation, and roadside assistance.

❓ Q & A

Oil Dripping After Oil Change

Q: I had my oil changed. It looks like my drain plug is leaking oil. Why?

A: Some oil plugs have rubber or plastic gaskets. Over time this gasket can become cracked. If the plug is tight, this gasket may need to be replaced.

✓ Tech Tip

Clear Fluid Drip

If you see clear fluid dripping from your car after you have run the air conditioner, don't worry. This is just water condensation.

❓ Q & A

Technical Service Bulletins

Q: What is a technical service bulletin (TSB)?

A: A TSB is a written advisory statement by a vehicle manufacturer to assist dealerships in diagnosing reoccurring problems. TSBs, are separate from safety or emissions recall notices and can address anything from suspension vibrations to engine misfires. To access TSBs and safety recalls visit the National Highway Traffic Safety Administration website, www.nhtsa.dot.gov, and search the "Office of Defects Investigation" division.

Unusual Sounds

Do not ignore sounds (*Figure 20.9*) coming from your vehicle. If you heed a warning sound you may be able to avoid your vehicle leaving you stranded or needing expensive repairs.

Sound	Problem
Squeal From Engine When Accelerating	A squeal from the engine when accelerating generally indicates a loose or glazed belt. When accelerating the belt is forced to rotate faster and may be slipping. Some belts can be tightened manually, while others have a tensioner that keeps them tight. Look for cracks, pieces missing, or fraying. Replace the serpentine belt and accompanying tensioner on scheduled maintenance intervals.
Knocking	Internal engine problems may have occurred. Take the vehicle to a qualified technician for diagnosis.
Pinging While Accelerating	A pinging sound while accelerating is a sign of low octane rating in the fuel. At the next fill up, put in a mid-grade or premium fuel to see if the pinging sound goes away.
Rattling	Loose or worn belt or belt tensioner. Replace components as necessary.
Screech From Wheel Area	If you hear a screech from the wheel area, the brake pads on the vehicle may be worn. Take the vehicle to a service center as soon as possible when brake problems occur. Brakes are vital to the vehicle's safe operation.
Loud or Rumbling Muffler	A rumbling sound coming from underneath the car could indicate a hole in the exhaust system. Inspect and replace components as necessary because a hole in the exhaust can pose a carbon monoxide hazard. Inside most mufflers are baffles to help reduce noise. You may not see any visible holes as a muffler rusts from the inside out, but it can become increasingly louder.
Engine Clicking	Clicking valvetrain noise is caused by low oil pressure or too thick of oil viscosity in cold temperatures. Check oil level and pressure. Use a lower viscosity oil in cold temperatures as recommended by the manufacturer.
Clicking When Turning	A clicking sound when turning a front-wheel, four-wheel, or all-wheel drive vehicle signifies worn constant velocity (CV) joints.
Clunk In Trunk	The annoying clunk noise coming from the trunk area during rapid braking may be as simple as a loose spare tire or jack rolling around as the vehicle changes speeds.

Figure 20.9   *Unusual Sound Indicators*

Unusual Smells

If you smell (*Figure 20.10*) something abnormal, check it out.

Smell	Problem
Rich Fuel	A rich fuel smell when attempting to start is a sign of a flooded engine. If you continue to crank over the engine, more fuel will be sprayed into the cylinders fouling out the spark plugs and contaminating the oil. Let the vehicle sit for a period of time so the gasoline can evaporate off the spark plugs.
Rotten Egg	A rotten egg/sulfur smell is usually linked to a faulty catalytic converter or other component in the emission system.
Sweet	Smells that have a sweet odor to them may indicate a coolant leak. Take the vehicle to a service center to have the cooling system pressure tested.
Burning	A burning smell can signify an electrical problem. Your automobile could have an electrical short or a failing electrical component.

Figure 20.10   *Unusual Smell Indicators*

 # Web Links

Automotive Parts Sites

AC Delco Replacement Parts
↪ www.acdelco.com

Advance Auto Parts and Service
↪ www.advanceautoparts.com

Auto Value and Bumper to Bumper
↪ www.autovalue.com

AutoZone Auto Parts
↪ www.autozone.com

CarQuest Auto Parts
↪ www.carquest.com

CSK Auto Inc. Parts and Service
↪ www.cskauto.com

J.C. Whitney Inc. Automotive Parts
↪ www.jcwhitney.com

NAPA Online Automotive Parts and Service
↪ www.napaonline.com

O'Reilly Automotive Inc. Parts and Service
↪ www.oreillyauto.com

Pep Boys Automotive Parts and Service
↪ www.pepboys.com

Common Problems

Common automotive problems can range from your car not starting to the wipers not cleaning the windshield. It is important to know when it is safe to drive your vehicle and when you should have it towed to a repair facility.

- Light Bulb
- No-Start
- Battery Cables and Terminals
- Wipers
- Shaking
- Steering
- Overheating
- Leaking Tire

Light Bulb

Vehicles have several lights that will burn out over time. The most common ones that cause inconvenience and a safety hazard are headlights, turn signal lights, and brake lights (*Figure 20.11*).

Figure 20.11   *Taillight Unit*

Light bulbs are generally not too expensive and take few or no tools to replace. Most involve disconnecting a bulb's socket and electrical connector, removing the burned out bulb, and replacing it with the new bulb. Your owner's manual should describe the specific procedure for your vehicle. The following is a general procedure for replacing a headlight bulb (*Figure 20.12*).

🚛 Trouble Guide

Light Not Working

- Blown fuse
- Burned out bulb
- Loose wire
- Corroded socket or connector

Headlight Bulb Replacement

STEP 1	Open the hood and look behind the headlight assembly. You should only have to turn the bulb socket or a retainer clip that holds the bulb in place a quarter turn.

Figure 20.12a   *Back of Headlight Assembly*

STEP 2	After the retainer clip is removed or bulb assembly is turned, carefully pull on the bulb. It may seem a little snug. It has a rubber O-ring gasket that keeps it tight.

Figure 20.12b   *Remove the Bulb*

STEP 3	Once the bulb is removed, lift up on the clips that hold the electrical wiring harness to release the bulb.

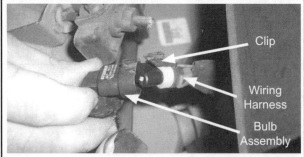

Figure 20.12c   Release Bulb from Harness Clip

STEP 4	Remove and replace the bulb. Do not touch the glass part of the new bulb. It will shorten the life.
STEP 5	Reverse the procedure to install the new bulb and reconnect the wiring harness assembly.
STEP 6	Once the new bulb is installed be sure to test the headlights.

Figure 20.12   *Replacing a Headlight Bulb*

No-Start

One thing you may encounter is a no-start situation (*Figure 20.13*). During one type of no-start situation the engine will not crank. In the other, the engine will crank but will not start.

Condition	Problem
Will Not Crank	If the engine will not crank over, you may have a dead battery. Turn on the headlights to see if you have electrical power. If you don't have any electricity, the headlights or interior light may have been left on and drained the battery over time. If that is the case all you need to do is follow jump-start procedures, restart the car, and drive the car for 15 to 20 minutes to recharge the battery. Also check the battery cables to make sure they are tight.
Cranks, But No Start	If your engine cranks over but will not start, then the engine may not be getting fuel or spark. This type of situation usually warrants a call to a repair shop.
Key Will Not Turn	The key will not turn in the ignition if there is pressure on the steering wheel, the gear shifter is not in park, or you are not applying the brake.

Figure 20.13   ***Vehicle No-Start Conditions***

? Q & A

Alternator or Battery

Q: My car will not start. When I turn the key there is a clicking sound. With a jump-start it starts right up. After jump-starting, I ran it for 20 minutes and then shut it off. When I tried to start it again, it just clicked. I jump-started it again, but let the cables stay attached for 10 minutes. Now the car starts several times with no problem. What is happening here?

A: Sounds like an alternator problem. When you left the cables on for 10 minutes the other car's charging system may have recharged your battery. The best way to tell is to use a multimeter set to DC volts to measure the voltage at the battery while your car is running. With the car running you should get a reading between 13.5 to 14.5V DC at the battery. If you are only receiving a reading of 12.0 to 12.6V DC while the car is running, then the alternator is probably faulty.

Battery Cables and Terminals

One of the most common problems in vehicles over three years old is battery failure. Battery failure is often caused by poor connections, corrosion, improper maintenance, and age. Although many batteries are considered maintenance-free, you still need to keep the battery terminals and cables free of corrosion. Always make sure the clamps and battery mounts are securely connected. The following is a general procedure for cleaning a battery (*Figure 20.14*). See the Battery Activity for more detailed information.

Battery Cleaning	
STEP 1	Make sure the key switch is in the off position. Visually inspect the battery for loose battery cables, corroded terminals, deposits on connections, cracks or leaks in the case, and frayed or broken cables. Remove your rings and watch. ***Warning: Battery electrolyte irritates skin and will eat through clothing. Always wear gloves, a dust mask, and safety goggles.***
STEP 2	Prepare a baking soda solution. Mix about one tablespoon of baking soda per pint (≈0.5 L) of water.
STEP 3	If you need to remove the cables to get at all of the corrosion, remove the negative cable first and then the positive.
STEP 4	On top post batteries, use a battery post cleaner tool to remove corrosion from the posts after the cables have been removed.

Battery Post Cleaner Tool

Battery Cable Clamp

Battery

Figure 20.14a   ***Battery Post Cleaner Tool***

STEP 5	Scrub the cables, terminals, and surface of the battery with the baking soda solution and a parts brush.
STEP 6	Rinse away all of the baking soda solution with clean water and dry the battery and cables.
STEP 7	If you have removed the cables, reattach them by installing the positive cable first and then the negative cable.
STEP 8	Use an anti-corrosive spray over the cable ends to minimize corrosion coming back.

Figure 20.14   ***Cleaning a Battery***

Wipers

Worn wipers can cause a dangerous driving condition and if you don't check your wipers you may not know they need replacing until you need them (*Figure 20.15*). Over time the rubber on wipers dries out, making them stiff. Without being flexible, the wipers have a tendency to chatter, smear, streak, or skip across the windshield.

Figure 20.15 Windshield Wipers on a Rainy Day

Wipers are relatively inexpensive and in most cases simple to replace. To size wiper blades measure the length in inches or millimeters. Wipers may come with several adapters to fit multiple automotive models. To determine the proper method of installation look in the owner's manual or the example that matches your wipers on the new wiper instruction sheet. It is best to replace wipers in pairs and the whole blade, not just the rubber "refill" component. If the metal pivoting points have worn out, the blade will apply uneven pressure across the windshield. Many vehicles have back window wipers that also need replacement. The following is a general procedure for replacing wiper blades on a hook style wiper arm (*Figure 20.16*).

 Servicing

Windshield Wipers

- Check at oil change intervals
- Change once a year or as needed

Wiper Blade Replacement	
STEP 1	Raise the wiper blade assembly up from the windshield and locate the lock assembly.

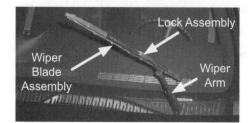

Figure 20.16a **Wiper Blade Assembly Raised**

STEP 2	A wiper blade may have a little cover over the blade lock assembly. If yours has a cover, push the cover tabs to release the cover.
STEP 3	The hook style blade assembly has a lock tab that needs to be pressed and held down.

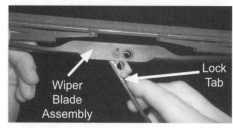

Figure 20.16b **Press Lock Tab Down**

STEP 4	Move the blade assembly toward the wiper arm to release the wiper arm hook.

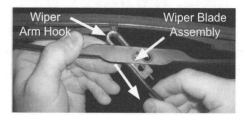

Figure 20.16c **Move Blade Assembly**

STEP 5	Remove the old blade assembly once it is free from the wiper arm hook.

Figure 20.16d **Release Blade Assembly**

STEP 6	Reverse the procedure to install the new wiper blade assembly and repeat the above steps for other wipers on the vehicle.
STEP 7	Check the windshield washer fluid reservoir, add fluid as needed, and test the wipers.

Figure 20.16 **Replacing Wiper Blades**

Shaking

A shaking or vibrating automobile can cause a potentially dangerous driving situation. Tires out of balance, belts broken in tires, worn suspension and steering components, transmission problems, worn CV joints or U-joints, broken motor or transmission mounts, and engine misfires can cause shaking and vibrations while driving. Try to determine if it is engine, drivetrain, brake, or suspension components that are the culprit.

Steering

If your vehicle is pulling in one direction, you may have a steering system or tire problem. One of the simplest things to check is the tire pressure. Check the tire placard inside the driver's side door and inflate the tires to the correct pressure. If the vehicle still pulls after you have inflated the tires properly, you may have a defective tire, worn steering component, or incorrect wheel alignment. If the tire pressure was the culprit, you need to determine why that tire lost pressure. You may have a nail puncture or faulty valve stem that is leaking air. See page 172 for finding a tire leak.

Overheating

Overheating can be caused by, among other things, a burst radiator hose, a faulty water pump, blown head gasket, or a leaky radiator. The key here is that if the engine begins to get hot you should shut it down. Severely overheating an engine can lead to more costly repairs. ***Warning: Never open a hot radiator cap.*** Once the engine is cool, check the radiator and heater hoses. If a hose is leaking, that is an easy fix. If your radiator is spewing out coolant through the radiator fins, you will probably need a new radiator. One of the more complex scenarios is an internal engine leak. If your engine is leaking coolant internally the probable cause is a blown head gasket or cracked cylinder head.

🖱 Web Links

Transportation Safety Sites

Bureau of Transportation Statistics
↳ www.bts.gov
Insurance Information Institute
↳ www.iii.org
Insurance Institute for Highway Safety
↳ www.iihs.org
U.S. Department of Transportation
↳ www.dot.gov

❓ Q & A

Frozen Wipers

Q: During cold winter mornings my husband turns on the wipers to push the snow off the windshield. Is this bad for the wipers?

A: Turning the wipers on before clearing snow could burn out the wiper motor, strip the wiper arms, or blow the wiper fuse. Anytime it is below freezing outside make sure the wipers are not frozen down before turning them on. Lift them up carefully so you don't rip the rubber blade or bend the wiper arm. If the wiper is really frozen down hard and you are unable to break it free, you should turn on the defrost to melt the ice on the windshield first. It is also a good practice to always allow the wipers to go to the "park position" before shutting off the ignition.

💰 Price Guide

Change Flat Tire
↳ $25.00 (labor)
Jump-start
↳ $25.00 (labor)
Roadside Emergency Kit
↳ $40.00 to $80.00
Snow Traction Cables or Chains
↳ $25.00 to $70.00 pair
Tow
↳ $50.00 to $75.00 (local tow)
Unlock
↳ $25.00 to $50.00 (labor)
Wiper Blades
↳ $10.00 to $15.00 each

Leaking Tire

If a tire is low you should locate the leak. Look for any obvious sidewall, tread, or wheel damage. Make sure there are no foreign objects embedded in the tread. If you can't see the leak source, the following easy steps may help (*Figure 20.17*).

Finding a Tire Leak	
STEP 1	Put about a teaspoon of dish washing soap in a spray bottle with water. Slowly squirt the tire, working all the way around the tire tread.

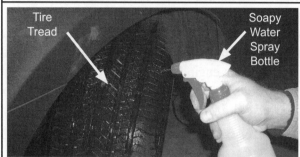

Figure 20.17a   ***Spray Tire with Soapy Water***

STEP 2	Don't forget to spray the valve stem and bead (the connection between the rubber tire and the rim) which are common culprits for slow leaks.

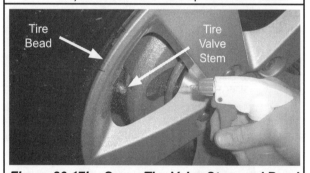

Figure 20.17b   ***Spray Tire Valve Stem and Bead***

STEP 3	As you spray the tire you will see many bubbles from the soap, but look carefully. Eventually the leak will start to blow a pile of bubbles.

Figure 20.17c   ***Air Leak Pile of Bubbles***

STEP 4	Note the location of the leak in reference to the wheel and distance from the valve stem. Take the tire to a service facility for repair.

Figure 20.17   ***Finding a Tire Leak***

Roadside Emergencies

It is important to learn what to do in an emergency. This section focuses on:
- Accidents
- Car-Deer Collisions
- Running Out of Fuel
- Being Prepared
- Dead Battery
- Jump-Starting
- Lockout
- Burst Radiator Hose
- Broken Belt
- Flat Tire
- Tire Traction in Snow

Accidents

If you are in an accident, try to remain calm. Turn on your hazard lights (*Figure 20.18*). Do not leave the scene of the accident. Use a cell phone to call for assistance. If nobody is hurt and the accident was minor, move the cars (if possible) to the side of the road out of traffic. If you have safety cones, reflective triangles, or flares in an emergency kit, set them out to warn oncoming traffic. After human safety considerations have been taken, wait for police to arrive, take pictures of the accident or sketch the accident scene, and exchange information with the other party (i.e., names, addresses, phone numbers, insurance policies, driver's license numbers, car information, and license plate numbers). Discuss the specifics of the accident only with the police. Do not accept blame or accuse the other party. Request a copy of the police report. If you believe you may have been injured, visit a doctor and contact a lawyer for advice. Finally, call your insurance company and re-read your policy.

Figure 20.18   ***Hazard Lights Button***

Car-Deer Collisions

Vehicle collisions with deer can cause significant damage and personal injury. Hundreds of thousands of accidents happen each year involving animals. Drivers need to be particularly attentive during the evening hours and around sunrise. October through December are very active months for car-deer collisions due to the deer rutting (mating) season. If you see one deer on the side of the road or running, be cautious. Deer commonly run in groups. Follow all posted speed limits, use high beams when possible, always wear your seatbelt, and be especially cautious in designated deer crossing areas (*Figure 20.19*). Do not swerve into oncoming traffic or off the road to miss a deer. Brake firmly and honk your horn. If you do collide with a deer, don't touch it. It may be injured and could cause you personal harm. Call law enforcement. After the accident, contact your insurance agent to see if the damage to your car is covered by your policy. Comprehensive policies cover damage caused by vehicle-animal collisions. Also check your policy deductible to see if it makes sense to have the insurance company pay for the damage.

Figure 20.19 **Deer Crossing Sign**

Running Out of Fuel

It is pretty common for every driver to run out of fuel at least once in their driving career, but making a habit of it might eventually cause some damage and shorten the life of an in-tank fuel pump. Fuel acts as a cooling system for the fuel pump and when the fuel is low the pump doesn't cool as effectively. Running a tank low repeatedly can accelerate electric fuel pump wear. When the low fuel light turns on or the gauge drops to E you may still have some fuel left, but it depends on your vehicle. If you do run out, never put gas in an unapproved container. Some gas stations will let you borrow an approved gas can if you leave a deposit.

Being Prepared

Leave your vehicle only as a last resort. If you cannot call for help with your cell phone and someone else offers you assistance, ask them to contact the police or a tow company for you. Do not get into a stranger's vehicle. An emergency roadside kit (*Figure 20.20*) should be in every vehicle. You may find yourself stranded late at night in a parking lot, alongside a desolate road, or in a ditch. Certain items can help you get through an unexpected situation until help arrives. Winter driving can be hazardous. Before it gets cold outside and the snow is blowing put together a winter safety kit. When you leave for a trip don't forget your cell phone and a couple bottles of water. Always let someone know your travel route and when you are expected to arrive.

Emergency Roadside Kit Checklist	
☐	Heavy Duty Jumper Cables
☐	Road Flares and Reflective Triangles
☐	Distress Flag and Sign
☐	Disposable Gloves and Work Gloves
☐	Fire Extinguisher
☐	Safety Vest
☐	First Aid Kit
☐	Flashlight with Spare Batteries
☐	Hand Wipes
☐	Shop Towels
☐	Basic Tool Kit (Screwdrivers and Pliers)
☐	Electrical Tape and Duct Tape
Winter Safety Kit Checklist	
☐	Blanket
☐	Warm Gloves and Extra Winter Clothing
☐	Hand/Feet Warmers
☐	Protein/Energy Bars and Water
☐	Pocket Knife
☐	Candles and Matches
☐	Windshield Ice Scraper
☐	Coffee Can Full of Sand and Portable Shovel

Figure 20.20 **Emergency and Winter Safety Kits**

Dead Battery

A dead battery is usually caused when the driver forgets to turn off the headlights or interior cabin light. It can also be caused by leaving a door ajar or if there is something draining the battery. If you have a dead battery and you know it was caused by leaving a light on, you should only need a jump-start. Follow the correct steps to jump-start a battery. If you are unsure, call a tow truck for assistance.

Jump-Starting

Complete each step of the jump-start procedure carefully and check your owner's manual for any specific suggestions. Some vehicles have remote jumper blocks (*Figure 20.21*) if the battery is not easily accessible. Use the jumper block for your jumper cable connection.

Remote Jumper Block

Figure 20.21   *Remote Jumper Block*

Vehicles' computers can be damaged if the cables are not connected with the correct polarity. The red jumper cable clamps should always go to the positive battery terminals (+) and the black jumper cable clamps should always go to the negative battery terminal (−) and bare metal (ground). Some vehicles have a labeled and designated negative jump-start attachment for the ground (*Figure 20.22*). The following are the steps for connecting jumper cables (*Figure 20.23*). *Warning: Never try to jump-start a battery that is low on electrolyte or that is frozen.*

NEGATIVE JUMP START ATTACHMENT

Figure 20.22   *Negative Jump-Start Attachment*

Jump-Start Pre-inspection and Setup	
•	Put on eye protection and visually inspect the discharged/weak battery for damage, cracks, loose connections, or bad cables. Correct any problems.
•	Make sure the batteries are the same voltage.
•	Maneuver the vehicle with the good battery so the jumper cables reach both batteries. The vehicles should not be touching.
•	Turn off the ignition switch, lights, and accessories on both vehicles, place them in park or neutral, and engage the parking brakes.

Steps for Connecting the Cables	
STEP 1	Connect one positive jumper cable (red) to the positive terminal (+) on the discharged/weak battery.
STEP 2	Connect the other positive jumper cable (red) to the positive terminal (+) of the booster/good battery.
STEP 3	Connect the negative jumper cable (black) to the negative terminal (−) of the booster/good battery.
STEP 4	Connect the other negative jumper cable (black) to a clean/bare metal part of the discharged/weak vehicle's engine block or frame for a good ground connection.

BE SURE VEHICLES DO NOT TOUCH

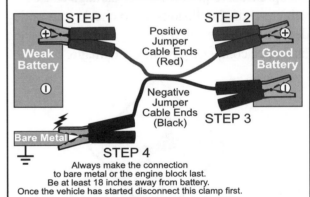

Figure 20.23a   *Jump-Start Cable Connections*

Starting	
•	Start the engine of the booster vehicle and rev it slightly. Let it charge for a few minutes.
•	Start the engine of the vehicle with the discharged battery. Do not crank the engine for more than 20 seconds at a time. Starter damage could result.

Steps for Disconnecting the Cables	
•	Disconnect the jumper cables in reverse step order (4-3-2-1). Hold the clamps away from the cars' parts and other cable clamps.

Finishing Up	
•	Let the engine of the discharged/weak vehicle run.
•	Put away the jumper cables.
•	Determine why the battery failed.

Figure 20.23   *Jump-Starting Procedure*

Lockout

Locking keys inside a vehicle is common. Use a magnetic key-holder to store a spare someplace on the vehicle body or frame. If you don't have an extra set, many towing companies have tools to unlock your door without damaging the window or paint. Some locksmiths also specialize in this service. If you have a service like OnStar, you can call the toll free number and a representative will send a cellular signal to your vehicle's computer module to unlock the doors. If your vehicle's battery is dead and the keys are locked inside, the car doors will not unlock with the remote signal from OnStar. Do not break a window to get inside the vehicle. Commonly it only takes minutes for an experienced tow driver or locksmith to enter a vehicle.

Burst Radiator Hose

Cooling system failure is a common cause of roadside emergencies. If a hose bursts, pull off to the side of the road. Shut off the engine so you don't risk overheating it. Do not open the radiator cap and be careful while under the hood of the car. Antifreeze/coolant can be extremely hot. You will need to call a tow truck or get the replacement part and fix it on the side of the road. If you do replace the hose, do so when the engine is cool. Also, refill the radiator and coolant recovery tank with the proper coolant mixture (usually 50% water to 50% antifreeze).

Broken Belt

On most vehicles today, only one belt (called a serpentine belt) runs all of the engine's vital systems and accessories. The serpentine belt often turns the water pump, air conditioning compressor, alternator, and power steering pump. If this belt breaks, you should not drive the vehicle. You will need a tow to a local repair facility or you will need to replace the belt on the side of the road. If you drive the vehicle, you risk overheating the engine. The vehicle will also not turn effectively if the power steering pump is not operational. The following is a general procedure for replacing a belt (*Figure 20.24*).

Belt Replacement	
STEP 1	Apply the parking brake. Remove the key from the ignition. Disconnect the negative battery cable.
STEP 2	Review the belt routing diagram which is commonly on an engine compartment label.

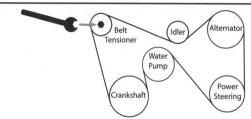

Figure 20.24a   ***Belt Routing Diagram***

STEP 3	Find the belt tensioner. Be careful when using a wrench or ratchet to release the tensioner, it uses a spring mechanism to keep the belt tight.
STEP 4	Once tension is released, slip the belt off. Check the tensioner bearing and spring for wear. Make sure all of the accessory pulleys rotate freely.

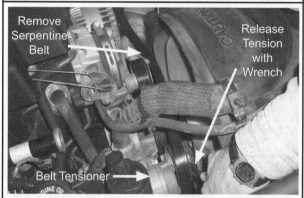

Figure 20.24b   ***Relieving Tension***

STEP 5	Route the new belt, lining up the ribs in the grooves, use a wrench to relieve tension, position belt, and then carefully release the belt tensioner.

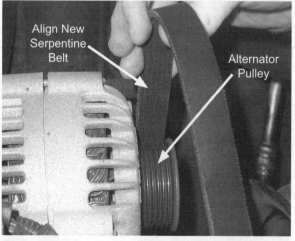

Figure 20.24c   Lining Up the Ribs and Grooves

STEP 6	Double check to make sure the belt is positioned correctly. Reconnect negative battery cable.

Figure 20.24   ***Replacing a Belt***

Flat Tire

Encountering a flat tire is a common roadside emergency. If you anticipate that a tire is going flat, firmly grasp the steering wheel and pull onto the road's shoulder or as far off the road as possible. If there is a nearby driveway or side street, turn to get to the least traveled road. Be prepared by checking your vehicle's spare tire pressure and condition periodically. Depending on the location, whether you are on a busy freeway or desolate rural road, may impact your decision to use a liquid spray, change the tire, or to call a tow truck. Changing a driver's side tire on a busy highway can be dangerous. If your vehicle is in a safe spot, use the following general procedure (*Figure 20.25*) along with the specific procedure in your owner's manual to change the tire. If you do not feel comfortable or safe, call a tow truck for assistance.

Changing a Flat Tire	
STEP 1	Park where the ground is flat, solid, and level. Set the parking brake and turn on the hazard lights.
STEP 2	Review owner's manual tire change steps. Get out your spare tire, jack, and lug wrench.

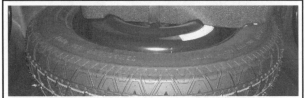

Figure 20.25a　　　　*Spare Tire in Trunk*

STEP 3	If your wheel has a wheel cover, read the owner's manual if you cannot tell how it comes off.
STEP 4	Break the lug nuts loose about a 1/2 turn each counterclockwise. A 4-way lug wrench makes it easier if they are tight.

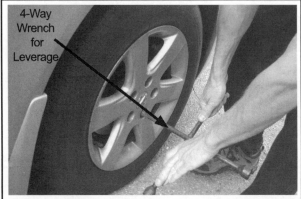

Figure 20.25b　　*4-Way Breaking Lug Nuts Free*

STEP 5	Align the notch in the top of the jack with the designated jacking location. Turn the handle to lift the vehicle until the flat tire is off the ground.

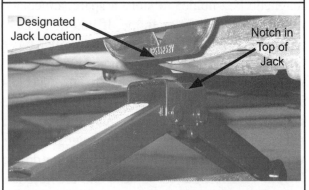

Figure 20.25c　　　　*Align Jack with Jacking Point*

STEP 6	Remove lug nuts and keep them in a safe location. Put on gloves.
STEP 7	Lift off the flat tire and lay it on the ground under the vehicle. If the jack failed, it could help to keep the vehicle from crushing you.

Figure 20.25d　　*Flat Tire Used for Added Safety*

STEP 8	Carefully lift the spare tire onto the wheel studs and thread the lug nuts (cone end towards wheel) on clockwise with your fingers until tight. Move the flat tire out from under the vehicle.
STEP 9	Slowly lower the vehicle just until the spare tire touches the ground. With the lug wrench, securely tighten the lug nuts using a star pattern.
STEP 10	Lower the vehicle completely and remove the jack. Double check to make sure you tightened all the lug nuts. Put away the jack, tools, and flat tire.
STEP 11	Remember to have the lug nuts torqued once you reach a service facility.

Figure 20.25　　　　*Changing a Flat Tire*

✓ Tech Tip

Driving on a Flat Tire

Driving on a flat tire can ruin the tire and wheel. It is much less expensive to fix a flat or replace a tire than to also replace the wheel.

Liquid sprays (*Figure 20.26*) that are inserted into the tire valve are only recommended for temporary emergency fixes. The liquid can corrode the inside of the wheel and throw the tire off balance. After use, the tire should be taken off the wheel so the inside can be dried, patched, and rebalanced. Prior to service, inform the tire technician if you used a liquid tire spray. Special precautions need to be taken to avoid injury. *Warning: Do not use liquid tire sprays on vehicles with tire pressure monitoring systems (TPMS).*

Figure 20.26 *Liquid Tire Spray*

Tire Traction in Snow

When driving in cold climates it is best to be prepared for unexpected snowy weather conditions. Tire traction devices (*Figure 20.27*) can keep you on the road when you would otherwise not be able to get traction. Before buying tire traction devices for your tires, check the owner's manual for the recommended style. There are different classes of traction devices and they must be sized to your vehicle's tires. Some are made with cables and others with metal chains.

Install the snow traction devices according to the instructions that come with them and make sure they are tight. If they loosen up while going down the road they can be a hazard and damage your vehicle.

Figure 20.27 *Tire Traction Cables*

Summary

Common problems and roadside emergencies can range from minor mechanical issues to serious accidents. The key to getting through these often difficult and stressful situations is to be prepared and stay calm. Analyze the situation and find an appropriate solution. Keep in mind that vehicles can be replaced. Human safety needs to be the number one priority.

? Q & A

Temporary Spare Tire Speed

Q: How fast can you drive on a spare tire?
A: Most temporary spare tires are designed for a maximum speed of 50 mph (80 km/h). Only use it to reach a facility that can repair or replace your original tire. Before putting your spare away, check the air pressure. It is common that the air pressure in a temporary spare is higher than in your regular tires. Always read the tire placard for specific pressure.

🚗 Activities

Common Problems and Roadside Emergencies

- Changing a Flat Tire Activity
- Jump-Starting Activity
- Lighting Activity
- Chapter 20 Study Questions

Activities can be accessed in the Auto Upkeep workbook or online at www.autoupkeep.com.

🎓 Career Paths

Tow Truck Driver

Education: Technical Training
Median Income: $32,000
Job Market: Average Growth
Abilities: Excellent driver, customer service skills, safety conscious, and ingenuity.

ONLINE/WORKBOOK ACTIVITIES

CHAPTER 1
CAR IDENTIFICATION ACTIVITY
Identify an automobile by make, model, year, and type.

CHAPTER 2
BUYING AN AUTOMOBILE ACTIVITY
Differentiate between MSRP, dealer invoice, and dealer cost.

CHAPTER 3
AUTOMOTIVE EXPENSES ACTIVITY
Calculate automotive expenses.

CHAPTER 4
REPAIR FACILITIES ACTIVITY
Choose a quality repair facility. Interpret a repair invoice.

CHAPTER 5
AUTOMOTIVE SAFETY ACTIVITY
Identify the location of emergency and safety equipment.

CHAPTER 6
BASIC TOOLS ACTIVITY
Identify basic tools that are used in automotive shops.

CHAPTER 7
INTERIOR CLEANING ACTIVITY
Clean the inside of a vehicle.

EXTERIOR CLEANING ACTIVITY
Clean the outside of a vehicle.

WAXING ACTIVITY
Wax the finish on a vehicle.

CHAPTER 8
FLUID LEVEL CHECK ACTIVITY
Safely check the fluid level in various vehicle components.

CHAPTER 9
BATTERY ACTIVITY
Safely clean and test the battery.

CHARGING ACTIVITY
Safely test the alternator.

STARTING ACTIVITY
Safely test the starter.

CHAPTER 10
OIL AND FILTER CHANGE ACTIVITY
Safely change the oil and filter on a vehicle.

CHAPTER 11
FUEL SYSTEM ACTIVITY
Identify the components of the fuel system. Change the air filter, CCV filter, PCV valve, and fuel filter.

CHAPTER 12
AIR CONDITIONING ACTIVITY
Inspect and identify the components within the air conditioning system.

CABIN AIR FILTER ACTIVITY
Replace the cabin air filter on a vehicle.

COOLING SYSTEM ACTIVITY
Safely test, inspect, and service the cooling system. Observe thermostat operation.

CHAPTER 13
IGNITION SYSTEM ACTIVITY
Install spark plugs. Inspect, test, and install spark plug wires. Inspect and install distributor cap and rotor on conventional or distributor systems.

CHAPTER 14
SUSPENSION AND STEERING ACTIVITY
Safely inspect and perform basic service procedures on suspension and steering components.

TIRE INSPECTION AND ROTATION ACTIVITY
Safely inspect tires for wear and rotate tires.

CHAPTER 15
BRAKE INSPECTION ACTIVITY
Safely inspect disc brakes.

CHAPTER 16
DRIVETRAIN ACTIVITY
Safely inspect drivetrain components.

CHAPTER 17
EXHAUST AND EMISSIONS ACTIVITY
Safely inspect exhaust and emission components.

CHAPTER 18
PAYBACK PERIOD ACTIVITY
Calculate payback period.

CHAPTER 19
AUTO ACCESSORIES ACTIVITY
Estimate the cost of accessories for a vehicle.

CHAPTER 20
CHANGING A FLAT TIRE ACTIVITY
Safely change a spare tire.

JUMP-STARTING ACTIVITY
Safely jump-start a vehicle.

LIGHTING ACTIVITY
Replace various lights on a vehicle.

REPLACING WIPERS ACTIVITY
Replace wipers on a vehicle.

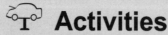 **Activities**

Activity Access
- Activities are available in the *Auto Upkeep* workbook
  OR
- Go to *www.autoupkeep.com*
- Click on the Activities tab

Contact us at: info@autoupkeep.com if you need assistance accessing the online activities.

ACRONYMS/ABBREVIATIONS

'	Foot
"	Inch
4WD	Four-Wheel Drive
A/C	Air Conditioning
AAA	American Automobile Association
ABS	Antilock Braking System
AC	Alternating Current
ACEA	European Automobile Manufacturer's Association
ANSI	American National Standards Institute
API	American Petroleum Institute
ASE	Automotive Service Excellence
ASTM	American Society for Testing and Materials
ATF	Automatic Transmission Fluid
AWD	All-Wheel Drive
B	Biodiesel
BAS	Belt-Alternator-Starter
BBB	Better Business Bureau
BTS	Bureau of Transportation Statistics
BTU	British Thermal Unit
C	Celsius
CA	Cranking Amps
CCA	Cold Cranking Amps
CCV	Crankcase Ventilation
CNG	Compressed Natural Gas
CO	Carbon Monoxide
CO_2	Carbon Dioxide
COP	Coil-On-Plug
CV	Constant Velocity
CVT	Continuously Variable Transmission
dB	Decibels
DC	Direct Current
DI	Distributor Ignition
DLC	Data Link Connector
DOHC	Dual Overhead Cam
DOT	Department of Transportation
DRL	Daytime Running Lights
E	Ethanol
e.g.	For example
ECU	Engine Control Unit
EEC	Electronic Engine Control
EEM	Electronic Control Module
EGR	Exhaust Gas Recirculation
EI	Electronic Ignition
EPA	Environmental Protection Agency
EPS	Electric Power Steering
ESC	Electronic Stability Control
ETBE	Ethyl Tertiary Butyl Ether
EVAP	Evaporative Emissions
F	Fahrenheit
ft	Foot
FWD	Front-Wheel Drive
GPS	Global Positioning Systems
H	Hydrogen
H_2O	Water
HC	Hydrocarbons
HVAC	Heating, Ventilation, and Air Conditioning
i.e.	That is
ICE	Internal Combustion Engine
IIHS	Insurance Institute for Highway Safety
ILSAC	International Lubricant Standardization and Approval Committee
ISG	Integrated Starter/Generator
kg	Kilogram
km	Kilometer
km/h	Kilometers Per Hour
kPA	Kilopascal
lb	Pound
Li-ion	Lithium Ion
LNG	Liquefied Natural Gas
LPG	Liquefied Petroleum Gas
LT	Light Truck
m	Meter
M+S	Mud and Snow
MAF	Mass Airflow Sensor
MIL	Malfunction Indicator Light
mm	Millimeter
mpg	Miles Per Gallon
MSDS	Material Safety Data Sheet
MSRP	Manufacturer's Suggested Retail Price
MTBE	Methyl Tertiary Butyl Ether
N	Nitrogen
NADA	National Automotive Dealers Association
NHTSA	National Highway Traffic Safety Administration
NiMH	Nickel Metal Hydride
No.	Number
NOx	Nitrogen Oxides
NSC	National Safety Council
O_2	Oxygen
OBD	On-Board Diagnostics
OEM	Original Equipment Manufacturer
OSHA	Occupational Safety and Health Administration
P	Passenger
PCM	Powertrain Control Module
PCV	Positive Crankcase Ventilation
R	Radial
R	Resistance
RPM	Revolutions Per Minute
RWD	Rear-Wheel Drive
SAE	Society of Automotive Engineers
SI	International System of Units
SRS	Supplemental Restraint System
ST	Special Trailer
SUT	Sport Utility Truck
SUV	Sport Utility Vehicle
SVO	Straight Vegetable Oil
T	Temporary
TAME	Tertiary Amyl Methyl Ether
TPMS	Tire Pressure Monitoring System
U-Joint	Universal Joint
ULSD	Ultra-Low Sulfur Diesel
UTQG	Uniform Tire Quality Grading
V	Volt
VECI	Vehicle Emission Control Information
VIN	Vehicle Identification Number
WVO	Waste Vegetable Oil

Procedures

Q & As

Tech Tips

Calculations

TROUBLE GUIDES

SERVICING

WEB LINKS

CAREER PATHS

GLOSSARY

A

ABS – an acronym for Antilock Braking System, a system used to minimize wheel lockup when braking to maximize driver control.

AC – an acronym for Alternating Current, a type of electrical current where electron (electricity) flow changes direction (alternates) back and forth.

Aftermarket part – a term used to identify a replacement part made by a company that did not originally make the part for the vehicle when the vehicle was assembled.

Alternator – a device that converts mechanical energy to electrical energy to recharge the battery.

Amperage – measured in amperes (or amps), is the strength (quantity of electrons) in the electrical circuit.

Antifreeze – a substance with its main ingredient glycol, which has a high boiling point and a low freezing point when mixed with water, used to create engine coolant.

API – an acronym for American Petroleum Institute, a trade organization that represents oil and natural gas stakeholders that, among other things, develops consensus standards within the oil and gas industry (e.g., engine oil service ratings).

Automatic transmission – a transmission that shifts automatically from one gear ratio to another without the assistance of the driver.

B

Battery – a device that stores chemical energy.

Blow-by – combustion gases that leak past the piston rings and into the crankcase.

Brake fluid – a hydraulic fluid used in automotive brake systems that withstands high temperatures and freezing.

BTU – an acronym for British Thermal Unit, a measurement of energy.

C

Carnauba – a wax, commonly found in automotive waxes, made from the carnauba wax palm (Copernicia prunifera) plant.

Catalytic converter – a device used to convert carbon monoxide, hydrocarbons, and nitrogen oxides into water vapor, carbon dioxide, and nitrogen.

Camber – a term used during wheel alignments to identify the tilt of the top of a wheel/tire assembly. When the top of a wheel/tire assembly tilts away from the car, it has positive camber. When the top of a wheel/tire assembly tilts toward the vehicle, it has negative camber.

Chamois – a leather towel, commonly made from sheepskin, used to dry a vehicle after washing.

Conductor – a material that easily allows electrons movement (electricity) from one point to another.

Crude oil – a fossil fuel that is also known as petroleum, a substance mainly containing carbon and hydrogen (hydrocarbons) found naturally in the earth that is used to make gasoline, diesel, kerosene, and a wide range of products.

CV shaft – an acronym for Constant Velocity shaft, a drive shaft commonly used on front-wheel and all-wheel drive vehicles that allows for power transfer to the wheels while also allowing for suspension movement.

CVT – an acronym for Continuously Variable Transmission, a type of automatic transmission commonly utilizing a chain or belt system that does not have a limited number of gear ratios like traditional automatic transmissions.

D

dB – decibel, a measurement of the loudness of sound.

DC – an acronym for Direct Current, a type of electrical current where electrons (electricity) flow in one direction.

Diesel – a fuel (chemical energy) made from crude oil that has an energy content of approximately 129,000 BTUs per gallon.

Diesel, Rudolf – invented the diesel engine that eliminated a spark plug by instead using high compression to ignite the fuel.

Diodes – an electronic device that allows electricity to flow in only one direction.

Distillation – the process of using heat to refine crude oil to make a variety of products.

E

Electricity – the movement of electrons through a conductor.

Electrolyte – a water and sulfuric acid solution in an automotive lead acid battery.

Engine (internal combustion) – a machine where fuel (chemical energy) is burned inside a combustion chamber within the engine to produce motion (mechanical energy).

Engine configuration – the design of the engine block, most commonly inline or V shaped.

Engine (motor) oil – a substance, made from crude oil and/or synthetic compounds, that lubricates, cools, cleans, and seals moving parts inside an engine.

Engine size – the size of the engine calculated from the combined volume of all the cylinders.

F

Firewall – the divider, commonly made of steel with insulating material, between the engine compartment and the passenger compartment.

Ford, Henry – entrepreneur and founder of Ford Motor Company that successfully mass-produced cars on a moving assembly line in the early 1900s.

Fuse – an overcurrent protection device that safeguards electrical components.

G

Gasoline – a fuel (chemical energy) made from crude oil that has an energy content of approximately 115,000 BTUs per gallon.

H

Hybrid – a vehicle that uses more than one method for propulsion or power.

I

Ignition coil – a step up transformer used to convert a low voltage of the battery into a high voltage at the spark plugs to ignite the air-fuel mixture.

Independent suspension – a type of suspension that allows the wheel/tire assembly to move up and down without relying on movements from another wheel/tire assembly.

Insulator – a material that resists the flow of electrons (electricity).

Insurance – a policy that provides protection against financial loss when accidents occur.

M

Manual transmission – a transmission that requires the driver to manually shift gear ratios with a gear stick shift and a clutch.

Master cylinder – a component in the braking system that converts movement from the brake pedal to hydraulic pressure.

MIL – an acronym for Malfunction Indicator Light, illuminates when a problem or potential problem exists within one of the vehicle's systems.

O

Octane rating – a number visible on a gasoline pump, the higher the number the more the fuel resists igniting (an antiknock quality that resists premature combustion).

OEM part – an acronym for Original Equipment Manufacturer used to identify a replacement part that is made by the same company as the original part when the vehicle was assembled.

Oil – see engine oil.

OSHA – an acronym for the Occupational Safety and Health Administration, a governmental organization that was created to help prevent work related deaths, illnesses, and injuries.

Otto cycle – named after Nikolaus Otto, the most common internal combustion engine design for automobiles which consists of four piston strokes (intake, compression, power, exhaust).

P

PCM – an acronym for Powertrain Control Module, the main computer on an automobile that processes data from sensors and sends commands to engine controls.

Photovoltaic cells – solar arrays that convert sunlight directly to electrical energy.

Polish – a product used to remove minor scratches and oxidation on painted surfaces.

R

Rebuilt part – a replacement part that has been fixed by removing and replacing the defective component(s), but has not necessarily been completely reworked.

Recall – a notice informing the owner that a service needs to be completed to remedy a defective or unsafe component or design.

Refrigerant – a compound used in the A/C system of an automobile that changes from a liquid to a gas, absorbing heat when evaporated and dissipates heat during condensation.

Regenerative braking – a type of braking where a generator is used to recapture energy that would be normally lost when the driver is attempting to slow down the vehicle.

Remanufactured part – a replacement part that has been completely disassembled, inspected, and wearable parts replaced.

Resistance – usually measured in ohms (Ω), a measure used to identify the degree of an opposing electron flow (electricity).

S

SAE – an acronym for Society of Automotive Engineers, a professional organization that establishes standards (e.g., engine oil classifications).

Serpentine belt – the most common type of drive belt (flat belt with grooves on one side and smooth on the other) used on today's automobiles to turn the alternator, power steering, A/C compressor, and other components.

Starter – a device that converts electrical energy to mechanical energy to turn over (crank) an engine.

Stoichiometric mixture – the mass ratio of 14.7 parts of air to 1 part of fuel, the ideal mixture for combustion.

Synthetic oil – oil made from chemically derived base stock (molecular engineered) with additives that create an oil with exceptional lubricating abilities.

T

Technical service bulletin – also called a TSB, a written advisory statement by a vehicle manufacturer to assist dealerships in diagnosing reoccurring problems.

Toe – a term used during wheel alignments to identify the outward (toe out) or inward (toe in) position of the front edge of a wheel/tire assembly.

Torque – rotational force.

U

UTQG – an acronym for Uniform Tire Quality Grading ratings, used to compare treadwear, traction, and temperature capabilities between different tires.

V

Viscosity – the measure of resistance of a fluid to flow (e.g., low viscosity oils flow easier than high viscosity oils).

Voltage – the electrical potential measured in volts.

W

Wax – a product used to protect the exterior finish on an automobile.

Wheel chock – a device used to block a wheel to help keep a vehicle from rolling.

Windshield washer fluid – specially formulated fluid which resists freezing that is added to the windshield washer reservoir, assisting in cleaning the windshield.

Z

Zerk fitting – a fitting that can be greased using a grease gun commonly found on a steering or drivetrain component.

INDEX

A

B

C

Explore Auto Upkeep Online

Check out the following at www.AutoUpkeep.com:

↪ Ask a car care question and get an answer.

↪ Learn more about the book *Auto Upkeep*.

↪ Find links to helpful websites.

↪ Read what automotive instructors think.

↪ Discover why schools adopt *Auto Upkeep*.

↪ Learn more about the authors.

↪ Send comments. We are listening!

↪ Order your own copy of *Auto Upkeep*.

↪ Access DIY activities.

List of Activities

BUYING AN AUTOMOBILE
CAR IDENTIFICATION
AUTOMOTIVE EXPENSES
REPAIR FACILITIES
AUTOMOTIVE SAFETY
BASIC TOOLS
WAXING
INTERIOR CLEANING
EXTERIOR CLEANING
FLUID LEVEL CHECK
BATTERY
CHARGING
STARTING
OIL AND FILTER CHANGE
FUEL SYSTEM

JUMP-STARTING
TIRE INSPECTION AND ROTATION
EXHAUST AND EMISSIONS
AIR CONDITIONING
CABIN AIR FILTER
COOLING SYSTEM
IGNITION SYSTEM
BRAKE INSPECTION
DRIVETRAIN
SUSPENSION AND STEERING
PAYBACK PERIOD
AUTO ACCESSORIES
CHANGING A FLAT TIRE
LIGHTING
REPLACING WIPERS

AUTO UPKEEP ZONE

Activities Online at WWW.AutoUpkeep.com

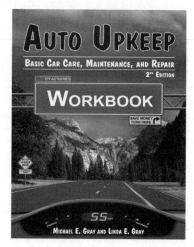

ISBN (13-digit): 978-0-9740792-2-6
Trade Paperback

AUTO UPKEEP

BASIC CAR CARE, MAINTENANCE, AND REPAIR

WORKBOOK

To order the workbook or download
the activities, visit us at

www.AutoUpkeep.com

A Teacher Resource CD is also available.
Email: info@autoupkeep.com

Auto Upkeep Reviews

2nd Edition

Just Right

"I'm going to recommend that we use your book in at least 3 of our intro classes. My experience is that it is almost impossible to find a good textbook for intro classes, they either have too little or too much information in them. I feel yours is just right!!!!!"

John Sweet, Automotive Department Chair
Victor Valley College, Victorville, CA

Easy Book for Students

"*Auto Upkeep* is an easy book for students to follow along in and understand what the text is communicating. I recommend this book to anyone that wants a basic knowledge of automobile functions, repair, and maintenance."

Adam Burlett, Automotive Instructor
Turner USD 202, Kansas City, KS

Simple and Easy to Read

"This book provides the information needed to own, drive, and maintain a vehicle. For people who don't consider themselves very technical, it is perfect. It is simple and easy to read, but covers a lot of important material."

Justin Miller, Automotive Instructor
Brigham Young University, Rexburg, ID

Maximum Student Benefit

"I find this book to be a valuable asset to the consumer classes I teach. It is well organized and written to the point. Subjects are written in plain English for maximum student benefit and the information is complete."

J. Bruce Osburn, Assoc. Prof. Auto. Technology
Chaffey College, Rancho Cucamonga, CA

Well Thought Out

"This text is a considerable improvement from the first edition. It is well thought out, suitably illustrated, filled with appropriate web links, and has just the right amount of information for a beginning or 'Consumer Auto' type class. I am looking forward to using it upon publication."

John Stokes, Automotive Instructor
Cuesta College, San Luis Obispo, CA

Covers the Basics

"This is an easy to read book that covers the basics for students just interested in their own cars, but has enough information that it can serve as introduction to other auto technology courses offered at our school."

Jim Sainsbury, Automotive Instructor
Madison Memorial H.S., Madison, WI

Great for Students

"This textbook will be great for students entering the field of automotive repair as well as for students who would like general knowledge."

Tim Isaac, Automotive Instructor
Foothills Composite H.S., Okotoks, Alberta, Canada

Activities are Phenomenal

"The book *Auto Upkeep* is the single greatest textbook for the classroom teacher with an auto care class offering. The chapters are short, but complete, with many illustrations. This text is obviously geared toward the visual learner. The chapters do not intimidate students with reading difficulties. ... Since I started using this book as my classroom text, my students seem to love reading the chapters and enjoy discussing them. The lab activities are phenomenal, they all can be done in a single period with limited tools. They are very easy to understand and complete. Since I began using this text three years ago, my job has become more enjoyable. Thanks Mike, the new release is awesome, and I look forward to incorporating it into the curriculum as soon as it is published."

Michael Farren, Technology Education Instructor
Valley Forge H.S., Parma Heights, OH

A Great Place to Start

"This latest edition is an expansion on the original version which covered many automotive topics in an easy to understand format. Now with even more subjects, illustrations, and resources, this book is a great place to start when studying automotive technology or just owning a car."

Eric Zebe, Automotive Instructor
Cuesta College, San Luis Obispo, CA

Just What I Needed

"Wow, this is just what I needed for my intro class - good foundation for those who want to move on and great reference book for others who want to learn a little for the future car of their dreams."

Rick Andruchuk, CTS Teacher
James Fowler H.S., Calgary, Alberta, Canada

Learn the Bare Basics

"It is a book that can help a student learn the bare basics of the automotive industry. This will teach a student how far he or she can go in repairs of their vehicles. Also this allows the student some knowledge if he or she has the vehicle repaired at a automotive repair/service shop."

Ray Quon, Dept. Chair and Coord. of Auto. Tech.
San Diego Miramar College, San Diego, CA

Great Fit

"I have been using the first edition for two years and find it a great fit for my General Auto Care class. The addition of more graphics and illustrations as well as the new chapters will vastly improve this text as a resource for my students. I'm looking forward to receiving the new publication."

Melvin Higgs, Automotive Instructor
J.M. Tawes Tech. & Career Center, Westover, MD

Very Useful

"I thought the text was easy to read and very useful to my transportation systems course."

David Farrell, Technology Education Instructor
Carmel H.S., Carmel, NY

See Page 190 for Ordering Information